There is a thread of Truth in all things
But Truth is only whole in the present

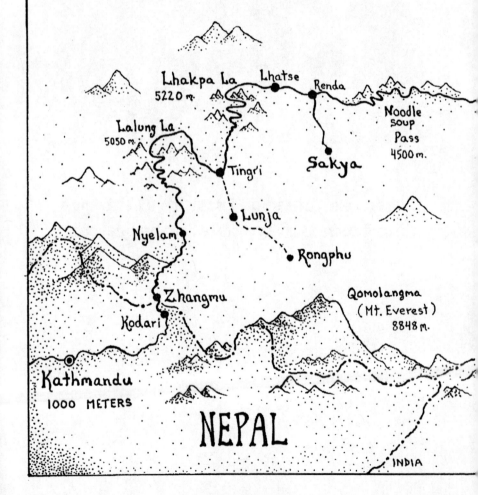

TIBET

Lhakpa La
5220 m

Lhatse

Renda

Noodle
Soup
Pass
4500 m.

Lalung La
5050 m.

Tingri

Sakya

Nyelam

Lunja

Rongphu

Zhangmu

Kodari

Qomolangma
(Mt. Everest)
8848 m.

Kathmandu
1000 METERS

NEPAL

INDIA

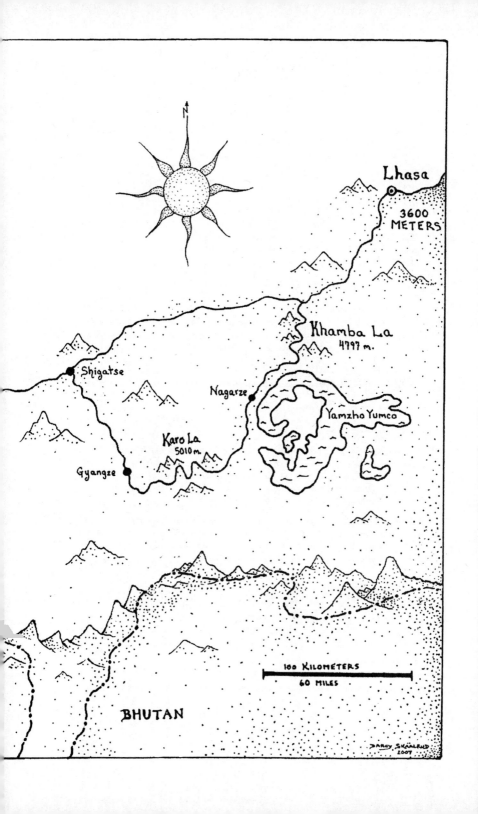

Lhasa

3600
METERS

Khamba La
4797 m.

Shigatse

Nagarze

Yamzho Yumco

Karo La
5010 m.

Gyangze

BHUTAN

100 KILOMETERS
60 MILES

DARCY SKARLUD
2007

Order this book online at www.trafford.com/07-0920
or email orders@trafford.com

Most Trafford titles are also available at major online book retailers.

Note for Librarians: A cataloguing record for this book is available from Library
and Archives Canada at www.collectionscanada.ca/amicus/index-e.html

Printed in Victoria, BC, Canada.

ISBN: 978-1-4251-2688-9

*We at Trafford believe that it is the responsibility of us all, as both individuals
and corporations, to make choices that are environmentally and socially sound.
You, in turn, are supporting this responsible conduct each time you purchase a
Trafford book, or make use of our publishing services. To find out how you are
helping, please visit www.trafford.com/responsiblepublishing.html*

*Our mission is to efficiently provide the world's finest, most comprehensive
book publishing service, enabling every author to experience success.
To find out how to publish your book, your way, and have it available
worldwide, visit us online at www.trafford.com/10510*

 Trafford PUBLISHING™ www.trafford.com

North America & international
toll-free: 1 888 232 4444 (USA & Canada)
phone: 250 383 6864 ♦ fax: 250 383 6804 ♦ email: info@trafford.com

The United Kingdom & Europe
phone: +44 (0)1865 722 113 ♦ local rate: 0845 230 9601
facsimile: +44 (0)1865 722 868 ♦ email: info.uk@trafford.com

10 9 8 7 6 5 4 3

SPOKES and DUST

ERIC HEIDE

Before
Tibet

LEATHERFOOT

He looked at the bikes. They were covered in a layer of light brown dirt. It was the same dirt that covered the hills to the sides, and the vast Tibetan plateau that stretched to the horizon and ended at the incredible blue sky. His two companions were covered in a layer of the dirt too, as was Dogi himself. It was a physical blending with the earth. Then came the rumbling noise, and as the truck passed, it kicked up so much dust that his nose couldn't filter it anymore, and the grit seeped into the back of his mouth. Dogi chuckled, thinking it didn't mix too badly with the residual oil that still coated the inside of his cheeks after drinking the Yak Butter Tea. And, as the rumble faded, the deep silence returned, only to be broken a few moments later by the next wave of wind. It gusted strongly enough that Dogi stumbled. It always seemed to be blowing in their faces. Dogi's mind drifted back with the wind. Back past Lhasa, Kathmandu, India and Thailand. It drifted all the way back to Japan, and the time he first met Leatherfoot.

It was a lovely autumn day when a small group of friends, and friends of friends were meandering along a beaten path under a canopy of trees along the east side of a small river. The forest trail was on the way to a waterfall somewhere in rural Japan in a prefecture known as Gunma. It is a side of Japan that most who have never been there are unaware of. Perhaps it is a side that a great many of the Japanese urbanites from the huge cities are unaware of themselves. Situated near one of the many small villages that dot the valleys carved through the mountainous areas of Japan, it is a natural environment, and the air is fresh and clean. For Dogi, his girlfriend Kat, and the rest of the lot, it represented a welcome respite from breathing the smog and exhale of the millions of people from the concrete jungle of Tokyo.

Nicknamed Dogi by his girlfriend, they had been living together in Yokohama, an extension of the huge city of Tokyo, for over a year. It had been an enjoyable year. Dogi was enthusiastic about teaching English at a small private school, and about exploring the vastly different Japanese language and culture. He would spend a lot of his free time wandering the neighborhoods, chatting with locals, playing with kids and observing diverse life go by. He couldn't help but find human nature fascinating, comparing and contrasting thoughts that he previously held with behaviours he witnessed. Yet, as someone who grew up with a lot of exposure to the outdoors in his homeland of Canada, the lack of fresh air and solitude wore on him heavily at times. The one grassy forested park near their home would satiate some of his cravings for greener space, but there were times when the need became greater, and that's why he always got so excited when he and Kat got a chance to get out of the city, and into the mountains and the woods.

The area of Gunma lies about three hundred kilometers to the north-west of Tokyo right in the middle of the main Japanese island of Honshu. Like most places in Japan, it is accessible by rail or road and most of the group arrived the previous day by way of the train. Dogi and Kat, however, came in on their motorbike, thrilled by the narrow winding mountain roads that cut their way along the steep valley walls, following the flow of big rivers, past farm fields and through small towns right to the door of the guesthouse, which was surrounded by old trees, both deciduous and evergreen.

Though a late night led to a sluggish morning start, there was a hike planned, and Dogi was giddy with anticipation. It took much of his patience in waiting for the group to assemble and make their way to the trailhead. By the time they did, his exuberance was no longer able to be stifled. He set off out in front sniffing and almost slobbering at the sight of every big tree, side creek, mushroom, and bird. As much as human nature intrigued him, Mother Nature captivated him even more. The colours and patterns on boulders or bark, the rotting of big old logs, the sounds the ground would make with each footstep, the wind rustling the branches, the gurgle of the stream and the song of the bird. The forest was alive and fascinating. Having escaped the big city, Dogi reveled in the fresh air and good energy.

Many of the rest of the group were also English teachers, and conversation amongst them was lively as the latest amusing anecdotes where told. There is never a shortage of funny stories to come out of time spent teaching people a foreign language. With some in the group still being new to each other, the hike gave them a chance to continue getting to know one another. Yet, as the time passed, the upward nature of the trail began to take its toll on some of those less used to the physical exercise. Conversation began to wane and the first few murmurings of discontent were surfacing. This, however, went unnoticed by Dogi, who had a feeling of boundless energy. He was hyper. So much so in fact, that the regular path no longer wanted to contain him. He was having one of his undeniable cravings for a foray off the main path and into the bush.

"Hey can you hear that? It sounds like there's a little waterfall down there. See? See? You can see the drainage out the top!"

"I hear Dogi. Nice sound. We keep going?"

Though her English skills were not yet fluent, Kat could sense the implications in Dogi's voice. She already knew him quite well by then, having been together for well over a year. Hers also is an apt nickname, as she walks with stealth and has a particularly keen sense of vision in the present. Though she enjoys a lot of rest time, she also has a strong deeper sense of curiosity, which can be peaked when the right circumstances are around to entice her. This, however, was not an enticing situation for Kat. She'd padded enough suspect adventures with Dogi in the preceding months and wasn't in the mood for it. She just wanted to keep it simple and hang out with their other friends. Most others in the group, who had arrived with Kat, sensed her caution, and saw no point in making the hike more challenging than it already was. They were already on their way to a waterfall after all.

"Dogi, are you gonna go that way?" asks one of their friends.

"Sure. I don't think I can get too lost. I'll just meet you guys up there."

"How're ya gonna get across that pool and up the hill?"

"I don't know right now. I guess I'll deal with that reality when it happens."

"Can I come?" asks the friend of a friend.

Dogi turns to see that the question comes from one of the guys in the group whom he had met only the day before. They hadn't chatted much yet, and Dogi had been wondering about him for a while. Unlike most of the rest of the gang, he was showing no signs of strain at all from the hike. He had been walking along quite happily, not talking too much, but obviously enjoying the forest environment a great deal.

"Of course you can come Rutherford. I don't know how far we'll make it, but in the very least we can have a closer look at the waterfall that sounds like it's down there, and then catch up to the others later."

"Sure, that sounds great."

"Ki-o-tsukete ne Leatherfoot. Be careful."

"Leatherfoot! That's cute Kat. I like it. Can we call you Leatherfoot?"

"Sure why not."

Kat is confused at first by the conversation and the ensuing laughter by the group, who, being English teachers, were quite familiar with the difficulties Japanese people have in pronouncing the letters "R" and "L." The Japanese version of the sound is somewhere in between the two making it all sound the same to them. Rutherford is kind enough to forward a short explanation to Kat about the spelling of his name, and assures her that he would be quite happy to be called Leatherfoot. Kat sees the humour in the situation and is happy that she needn't struggle with his name. And as the rest of the group disappears up the pathway, Dogi looks around with a smile beaming across his face.

"I'm happy to have the company Leatherfoot. Welcome to Randomland!"

"Randomland?"

Randomland. Unplanned. Life with a little spice. It's nowhere in particular, just somewhere you've never been before, and somewhere that might hold some kind of adventure. Going to Randomland, by it's very nature, is unpredictable. You can just as easily come away from it with scrapes, bruises, and critter bites as you can with smiles, and stories to last a lifetime. Most often it's both.

Ambling down the forested side bank of the small river, through a few bushes and over a fallen tree, Leatherfoot and Dogi are immediately rewarded with a pristine little waterfall whose view was obscured from the path a mere twenty paces away. They soak in the peaceful new environment, sharing the energy received from the nature and solitude around them. Dogi bends down to cup some water in his hands which he splashes on his face. Leatherfoot grabs a stick, drops it in the stream and watches it float gently away. They begin to chat in a little more depth for the first time, learning a few things beyond the usual trivialities from one another. Along the conversation, they suddenly discover that they were born on the same day of the same year! A long pause settles between the two as they stare at one another, and begin to regard each other as though through a distorted mirror.

More conversation leads them to discover that they are both great lovers of hiking and most other sporting and outdoor activities. Sharing further details, they are amazed at how much they have in common. Even a physical resemblance is there, both being relatively tall with lean frames, though the details of their faces are not overly similar. It wouldn't be shocking for someone who didn't know them to mistake them for brothers.

Ready to continue, they look around and go through the options for trying to get above and beyond the little waterfall they have been appreciating. They could head downstream a bit and then skirt along higher up on the opposing ridge, but it looks rather full of tangled underbrush, making it unappealing. Returning to the path to get around the mini waterfall would be the most secure option, but that would not be in the vein of the random adventure Dogi had in mind.

"What do you think of climbing the little cliff right beside the waterfall Dogi? It's not too high, and there appear to be enough good holds."

Dogi grins, thinking he likes Leatherfoot more and more by the minute. He so desperately loves to do these spontaneous things, but the company willing to participate in them is few and far between. Doing so solitarily is always a greatly increased risk and the level of fun is often far better with the right kind of friend.

"You know Leatherfoot, if I were on my own, I think I'd have to shy away from it, but with two of us, I figure it won't be a big deal. Why don't you go ahead and I'll spot."

Leatherfoot analyzes the patch of rock more thoroughly deciding on his route and proceeds to climb it with little difficulty. Dogi follows smoothly, and confidence in one another grows stronger swiftly. They are looking up at a dry, rocky river gully, with only the occasional appearance of water, and they begin scrambling up it. At first, the ravine is easily negotiated, but in due time the pitch of it increases rapidly. Leatherfoot, who is trailing, must leave ample space and be aware to avoid the tumbling rocks. After stepping on a head sized rock that gives way and rolls and bounces past him, Dogi stops.

"Hey man, this is getting steep and somewhat sketchy. If we keep going it's gonna be tough, and I can't tell what'll happen at the top. But heading back down this could be dicey too if an impasse exists up there."

Leatherfoot looks up past Dogi and sees that the crest of the gully is only about twenty meters above him. Then he looks down to where they came from, and back up once more. He knows it wouldn't be easy, and hopes it won't be necessary, but he figures he can make it back down this slope if he has to.

"I'm okay Dogi. If you're into it, let's keep going. I'm going to stay to the side until you get up there though, then I'll come."

Knowing Leatherfoot is in a safe spot below gives Dogi the confidence to be more aggressive, scrambling up the final section to reach the small ledge at the top. Pulling out his water, he enjoys watching Leatherfoot's skilled moves as he makes his way up the final steep pitch. Arriving dirty and sweaty, Leatherfoot gratefully accepts a sip of water and sits until he catches his breath. In the distance in front of them is a deciduous forest in the infancy of the turning of autumn. There are some birds riding the currents of the breeze above, and others in the forest beyond who have greeted their arrival with a song. It all feels wonderful, until they move along the ledge a little further to discover that the gully which they just ascended happens to have a sister fork which is even steeper and more raw looking, and it ends with a long sheer drop of unknown height. Both stare at it for a time before either of them speak.

"Well Leatherfoot, I can see that your knees are in full agreement with my heart rate! We're in a bit of a spot. The safest thing to do at this point would be a retreat, but even that looks a bit hectic."

Male instinct tells Dogi to hide his fear, but he's not much for that kind of bravado. He prefers to get it out in the open, which makes it easier to deal with. He takes a good long look at the concave upper portion of this new gully. It's not too far across, perhaps fifteen steps, but the consequences of going for a slide are dire, causing the adrenaline induced heart thump and the quiver in the knees. He takes several more deep breaths in order to settle the system.

"Well, what do you say?"

"I just don't know," says Leatherfoot, as he begins to sweat even more, and his eyes shift from option to option uncomfortably. "What do YOU think?"

"I think I can deal with it. The footholds look decent and there are a few little bushes and that one small tree to hang onto out in the middle. I just don't fancy scraping myself up trying to descend the gully we just came up. Once we're across this new chute, we're home free through that forest."

The air is suddenly thick and hazy, and Leatherfoot's mind is visibly grinding. The situation has the kind of certainty that could seal the bond of a great new friendship, or snap it like a dry branch broken for kindling.

BANGKOK

SATURDAY APRIL 18, 1998, BANGKOK, THAILAND. HOT, STINKY, noisy, chaotic... and wonderful. After a lifetime for Kat, and roughly two years for Dogi of living in Japan, this is where they would begin their new adventure together. Perhaps a lifetime adventure, but that is something no one ever knows for sure. Thailand suited the two of them. It's a place they'd both travelled before, but this was their first visit together. They both had a love affair with the food and the people alike. A diverse country north to south, the landscape and people of Thailand have many different faces. The north has a few more cities, though much of it is rolling hills occupied by tribes of various ethnicity. The narrow southern portion of the country becomes quite tropical, with scenic coastlines fringed by picturesque islands. Though not as large as Tokyo, Bangkok is still a huge city, and the heart of the country. Thicker with both noise and pollution than most other big cities, Bangkok still did have its appeal.

The Kao San Road area in Bangkok, once a travellers hangout, increasingly a tourist destination in its own right, has its ugliness but also its beauty, which comes mostly in the form of convenience. As a tourist or traveller, it is a safe haven where you can get almost anything you could ever want or need. In this case, it also provided a very easy place for Kat and Dogi to arrange a meeting with Leatherfoot who was flying in a couple of days later. Being his first time to Thailand, Leatherfoot wasn't so sure about Dogi's meeting place, but Dogi assured him it would be obvious enough.

"Meet us at 11:00 am on Tuesday the 22nd at the end of Kao San Road near the police station."

Those were the only directions communicated, and sure enough they easily found one another. It hadn't been too long since they'd last seen each other. A farewell party before leaving Japan at Kat and Dogi's place ten days earlier, where they discovered the coincidence of their flights to Bangkok at such a similar time. Having had such an enjoyable time months earlier during their Gunma hiking adventure and foray into Randomland, they all agreed that it would be fun to meet in Bangkok and see what happens.

"Kat! Dogi! How are you guys?"

"Good Leatherfoot, good. How was your flight?"

"Well, the food wasn't great, but otherwise okay."

"Well then, let's get something good to eat now and get out of this hot sun."

"Sure. So what have you guys been up to?"

"Wandering and eating mostly, and talking about Tibet."

"Oh yea, you mentioned wanting to go to Tibet at your party. Tell me more."

The seed of going to Tibet had been planted in Dogi's mind a few years earlier, when he first went to Nepal in 1993. He'd barely even heard of the place back then, but was inundated with the multitude of FREE TIBET propaganda going on in the capital city of Kathmandu. Having grown up in such a peaceful place and times in Canada, it was Dogi's first real life exposure to this kind of political opposition. Delving slightly further into the topic, he discovered that Tibet was a huge plateau sitting several thousand meters above sea level on the northern side of the great Himalayan mountains. Once an autonomous region, it was now occupied by the Peoples Republic of China. In late 1950, shortly after communism began to take over the rest of China, Central Tibet was attacked by Chinese troops. A combination of armed force and political trickery continued in the years following, leading to much destruction and oppression.

By 1959, the situation had become bad enough that the Dalai Lama was forced to flee his homeland, never yet to return. It was during this time period that many Tibetan monasteries were bombed and destroyed, numerous cultural artifacts plundered and stolen, Buddhist scriptures defaced and burned, and monks and other notables were forcefully re-educated in a process known as struggle sessions, or thamzing. Tibetan farming practices were altered, substituting wheat for rice, which didn't grow successfully on the high altitude Tibetan plateau.

This general trend of destruction and forced communist education continued under the pretext of Mao Zedong's Cultural Revolution for many years to follow. By the time of Mao's death in 1976, it had been estimated that over one million Tibetan people had died, not to mention those who were forced to flee the country or work in labour camps. Over six thousand monasteries and nunneries were partially or wholly destroyed, and much of the land had been deforested.

Since this time, there has been a lessening of violence, and a loosening of the guarded nature of the region to the outside world, but Tibet remains the property of the Chinese government, and there has been ongoing encouragement for Chinese people of Han decent to immigrate to, and populate the plateau. And though the Dalai Lama has tried, in perhaps the most peaceful resistance known since Gandhi, the rest of the world has done little to help restore Tibet to its own rule.

Dogi, however, was little educated about the history of Tibet before his first trip to Nepal, and even then he only skimmed the surface, but the signs in Kathmandu were everywhere and this had peaked his curiosity enough for the idea to stick over the next number of years.

"When are you thinking of going to Tibet, Dogi?"

"Maybe May. It gives us a little time, and I think the weather should be ideal for cycling by then."

"CYCLING?"

Undertaking a bicycle trip across the great plateau was something Dogi had dreamed of only years after that seed had been planted during his 1993 visit to Nepal. When back in Canada, he had purchased the Tibet guidebook, and was flipping through it while in the comfort of his mother's home. There was only one short paragraph in it about riding bicycles. It was not necessarily encouraged as a light hearted or convenient option, but Dogi never really paid attention to that part. He just noticed that it could be done, and to him, that sounded like fun. And of all the "idea" seeds that get planted, many die, some grow and flourish at the hands of Mother Nature alone, and others still need help, even to be given a chance of life.

"Cycling Leatherfoot. Didn't I mention that part of the idea at the party last week? I kinda wanna ride a bicycle from Lhasa to Kathmandu."

"Sounds interesting. Where would we get the bikes?"

"According to the guidebook, we can buy some reasonably cheap ones in Lhasa and even sell them again in Kathmandu. I'm not so sure I wanna do it if it's just Kat and me though. That's why it'd be awesome to have you along."

Tibet. Bicycles. Dogi sensed it was a seed that would need a lot of help to come to fruition, and as he continued to sell Leatherfoot on the idea, it grew beyond simple possibility in his own mind. Dogi was going to ride a bike across Tibet. He was suddenly quite sure. Kat was going to Tibet with Dogi, but she wasn't so sure of this biking idea. In her mind, it was very much wait and see. Dogi was prone to outlandish ideas, she knew, but she also knew that as often as not, he followed through on them. Rather than think about it too much, for the time being, she just put it out of her mind. In any case, she was happy that Leatherfoot was showing some interest in coming along. Any adventure with Dogi felt safer with company, and Leatherfoot seemed to her like a nice guy.

Leatherfoot didn't have any concrete plans beyond getting out of Japan and doing some travelling in other parts of Asia for a few months. The Tibet idea had floated through him without registering much at that party in Japan. It had been a busy and emotional time of preparations and farewells. But ever since his plane was touching down in Bangkok, his thoughts began to leap forward. "Japan is gone, work is finished, what now?" He knew he was going to meet Kat and Dogi, which was a comforting thought. It gave him something tangible to look forward to. Now, as he chewed a delicious mouthful of Pad Thai, he tried to envision riding a bike across Tibet and hanging out with these two people sitting at the table with him. They were nice. He'd thoroughly enjoyed that hiking adventure back in Japan, nerve racking though it was, and he'd enjoyed their company on subsequent occasions when he'd seen them. They seemed happy individually and together. That was an issue though, travelling with a couple, but these two didn't seem to bicker or be too cutesy with each other. He didn't know Kat that well yet, but sensed an inner strength. Dogi was unpredictable. Outwardly he was upbeat and fun, but there was an edge there. Leatherfoot had never seen it cut anybody, but he liked to study people, and this is what his intuition suggested. He decided, as he swallowed his last mouthful, that he would do it. He would go to Tibet with them. Tibet. There was something mysterious about that place. He didn't know much other than what Dogi told him, but it had allure. Maybe, he thought as he inhaled the exhaust from a passing tuk tuk, it was simply a yearning for the antithesis of the urban chaos that he'd been living in. Tibet with Kat and Dogi. Cool. It sounded like one of Dogi's hairball Randomland adventures. If worse comes to worst, he could always bail out. They after all, had each other.

With the decision made, it was time to work out some of the logistics. Kat and Dogi had a special festival in northern India that they wanted to attend and Leatherfoot wanted to explore Northern Thailand before flying to Nepal. This meant sorting out plane tickets and a Chinese visa. The flights were easily enough purchased from a travel agency on Kao San Road, and the latter they decided would be more easily and conveniently obtained at the Chinese embassy in Bangkok than later in Nepal. Thus it was, a day later inside the Chinese embassy, that Dogi found himself wondering. He does that a lot. Wondering. Sometimes he wonders so much that his brain starts to feel like the inside of a golf ball which is usually when he wonders why his brain can't be more like the inside of a tennis ball. So, as he filled out an application form for a Chinese visa, he was wondering why the credit card company should share its name with such a troublesome and bureaucratic, though arguably necessary, stamp in the book that one carries to pass ports.

"Who are you? Where do you live? What do you do?"

These can be challenging questions when you are on the road with no fixed address and no job. The name part Dogi could deal with, and the parent's address has always been welcome, but the last one he always figured he could have some fun with. Over the years, he has left various bits of paper around the world suggesting that he is a brain surgeon, a semi-retired goat breeder, a professional traveller, a swimming pool floor inspector, a star gazer, eyebrow raiser, a reality hazer and… a writer. He was to discover some time later, as he went to pick up his passport at the embassy, that this last one was a bad idea. Particularly when applying for a rather particular document from a particularly protective place like China.

Having spent an enjoyable time exploring a National Park a few hours north of Bangkok for the past week, Leatherfoot, Kat and Dogi return to the big city to pick up their passports at the Chinese embassy. They are in a jovial mood as they enter the bureaucratic domain. Ladies first, Kat is handed her passport, stamped with a Chinese visa without question. Leatherfoot also walks away without incident. Dogi, however, is asked to go over to the interview desk. "Why always me?", he thinks. "Airport security, customs inspections, I always get pulled over!"

"What kind of writing you do?"

"Ahhh, umm, well, you know, umm, poems and stuff, umm, nothing published yet. Uhh, actually, I'm an English teacher in Japan! Well I was an English teacher, but…"

The Chinese official waited patiently for Dogi to finish stuttering, challenged him with a few more questions, and then told him to sit and wait. Somewhat in stunned disbelief, Dogi plopped down on a hard wooden bench and sweated it out. Finally his name was called again, and without a word, the official slid his passport across the desk. Walking out the door, he slowly thumbed his way through the pages. Old Japanese visa, Thailand visitors stamp, Chinese visa! In the end, the interviewer probably figured he was too foolish and inarticulate to write anything politically detrimental to his country.

"What happened in there Dogi?"

"I think it's just the curse of being a long hair man!"

"Did you get your visa?"

15

HARI

FOOD IS GOOD. GOOD FOOD IS EVEN BETTER. HARI HAS HIS travel agency on Freak Street. Freak Street is in Kathmandu. Kathmandu is in Nepal, and Nepal is a beautiful country. Huge mountains, fertile valleys, friendly people, and very good food. Especially around Freak Street. Freak Street is home to Trippy the bowlegged dog, Crazy Happy Lady and The Drug Dealer. The Drug Dealer offers *something*. "*Something?*" Sometimes he offers *hash ganja opium mushrooms acid*, but usually it's just *something*. He's pretty whacked out on *something* himself, but after politely declining *anything* for the past couple of days and getting tired of evasive maneuvers, Dogi decides to confront The Drug Dealer. He stops face to face with him in the middle of Freak Street, grasps him firmly by the shoulders and stares into his rather distant, crooked, spindling eyes and says "HEY MAN, you have asked me about twenty times in the last three days if I want *something*, but I don't need *anything* because I have *everything* I want, which is *nothing*. So please try to remember my face and don't offer me *something* anymore."

Hari has a jubilant and enigmatic personality. He has the kind of smile that could brighten up the dullest of days, and he is also a very astute businessman. Hari's prices are affected to a large degree by current market conditions and whether or not he likes you. Fortunately, Hari liked the gaggle of Leatherfoot, Kat, and Dogi. And, fortunately, they finally found Hari, as he was the only one that would sell them an "officially semi-unpackaged package tour" to Tibet.

Tibet is still an area of political sensitivity, and the Chinese government, particularly coming from the direction of Nepal, is trying to inhibit travellers from entering as individuals. Foreigners are allowed, but only in the form of group tours. Such is the story, at least throughout Kathmandu. Though China has laid claim to it, simply having a valid Chinese visa is supposedly not good enough to go into Tibet.

Dogi, of course, either didn't inform himself of this little wrinkle in the first place, or simply chose to ignore it and proceed on blind faith as usual. He had found this pattern emerging in his life. He felt that even if you were warned otherwise, or there were big obstacles in the way, that if you just **believed**, and **tried**, most things were possible. Not all things, but most. He knew that some warnings should be heeded, some obstacles not messed with, but in so many instances, this was not the case. There was usually no harm in trying.

Almost a month had passed since those days in Bangkok. After visiting the National Park together in Thailand and sorting out their Chinese visas, Kat and Dogi took leave of Leatherfoot and flew into India. Landing in the city of Delhi, they acquainted themselves with the chaos. Fortunately, they had a dose of Thailand in between Japan and India, though arriving in the subcontinent is almost sure to provide a heavy dose of culture shock. India is a barrage on the senses. It is simultaneously evocative and appalling. Even the simplest of things, like trying to arrange transportation, can turn into hours of confusion and stress. Yet somehow, someway, though it doesn't always seem that way at the time, it's fun. And having finally managed to work their way onto the right bus, Kat and Dogi made their way north, up into the foothills of the Himalayan Mountains, and then down along the upper reaches of the holly river Ganges to the city of Rishikesh, and eventually the town of Haridwar. There they caught the tail end of a huge festival that happens only once every seven years. The location of the festival changes each time, and pilgrims come from far and wide to attend. The festival was colourful and fascinating. People were camped out in tight quarters all along both sides of the river throughout the town. Kat and Dogi were fortunate to find an empty room in a nearby hotel, and enjoyed several days of wandering amongst the masses. Though the festival was splendid, the weather had been excruciatingly hot, often up into the mid-forties on the Celsius scale. Truly unbearable, particularly through the middle of the day. Even the temperatures in the high thirties which followed were a welcome respite.

From this area of northern India, they worked their way by bus towards the border at the western end of Nepal. Things had gone smoothly until they reached the town of Haldwani. From here it was not much further to the town nearest the border, but catching a bus was a classic case of Indian chaos. Though there are exceptions, particularly in the southern end of the country, a typical bus station in India is a big open parking area with buses, taxis and rickshaws leaving, arriving and parked in no semblance of order whatsoever. Or if there is any order, it certainly isn't apparent to the Western eye. At times there is an information area, though these are often dubious at best, and don't always get you the bus you really want. At other times, when there is no information area, or no one attending the one that is there, the best approach is to find someone who looks helpful and, if at all possible, somewhat educated. This person may or may not be able to help. If all else fails, just start yelling the name of the place where you want to go and eventually, if you're lucky, you'll be funneled in the right direction. It was just such a case in the town of Haldwani. It was plenty early in the day when Kat and Dogi arrived, and with the town holding nothing of great appeal to them, they thought they'd continue on to the border town of Banbassa. Dogi, using his loud voice, was finally directed to a typically decrepit looking bus that was already packed, though there was no driver on board. Before it got completely stuffed, Kat and Dogi managed to still squeeze themselves on, and stand in the aisle with their packs jammed between their legs. There they waited. With little air circulation and still a stinking hot day, it was like being in a sauna. Half an hour later, still there was no driver, and people began to file off, eventually joined by Kat and Dogi. Twenty minutes after that, the rumour must have started that the bus would soon leave, and on everyone piled once again. Fifteen minutes later, everyone back off. Again the loading frenzy happened, this time Kat running in to secure a seat while Dogi kept tabs on the packs. Still no driver. After three hours had passed and four loadings and unloadings of the bus, and there was still no driver in sight or no one that could give them a definitive answer as to what in the heck was going on, Dogi and Kat decided to abort the attempt for the day. They went to check out the nearest few hotels and settled on the cheapest one. Tomorrow would be another day.

The following morning, there was someone working the information area, and the bus, which they fortunately boarded early, departed Haldwani ten minutes early. When they arrived in Banbassa they were surprised to learn that the actual border was a way outside town and would need to be accessed by taxi or rickshaw, of which they chose the latter. Finally they were ready to leave India and make their way into Nepal, and what they discovered was one of the more interesting borders either of them had crossed to date. Beginning, not surprisingly, with the Indian officials monitoring their posts in no great hurry whatsoever to process the small volume of people. Kat and Dogi, being the only non-Indian or Nepalese there at the time, were instructed to wait until last. When they finally were deposited on the other side, they found themselves on a dusty little network of roads with no idea which way to go.

"Umm, excuse me, ahh, which way is Nepal?" asked Dogi of the Indian official.

A vague wave of the hand given in response at least gave them a rough idea of which direction to start, and they soon found themselves fascinated by the fact that they were walking through fields of hemp. It seemed the oddest of sights in a neutral zone between countries. Just the fact that there was such a huge neutral zone in the first place felt peculiar. So many borders in the world are being fought over, and here's one that no one seems too fussed to own. Besides all the hemp, the fields had goats, sheep and cows wandering about. Who owned these? The Indians or the Nepalese? Not really certain of where they were going, they finally saw another small building in the distance that was flying the Nepalese flag. They must have walked a good kilometer between country exit and entrance. Far more friendly than their Indian counterparts, the Nepalese officials were not above keeping a little "present" for themselves in addition to the regular fees. Unfortunately, there is little to be done in those circumstances but appease them.

The tiny place they first found themselves in Nepal was not a ghost town, but for all the activity, it might as well have been. One main road stretched a few hundred meters, lined with old weathered buildings. Not more than one or two souls could be seen, the midday heat likely keeping everyone inside at the time of their arrival. Seeing a crooked old bus parked at the far end of town, Kat and Dogi went to inquire and eventually found someone who told them it was leaving for Kathmandu in a few hours.

"How long will it take to Kathmandu?"

"Thirty hour."

"Thirty hours? Woa."

"Road not good. Much construction. Go many detour. Thirty hour."

"Okay. Two tickets please."

A thirty-hour ride from the western border of Nepal all the way to Kathmandu along a pitted gravel road, when they were even on the road. There was so much construction going on that the bus was often crawling over the raw dirt, rock and shrubs. Thirty hours in a most non-luxurious vehicle pounding potholes. Where to sit became a tough decision. The middle section of the bus, which would be the most stable, was stuffed with locals. The front, mostly filled with locals was noisy from the engine and music, which left the back as the only real option for Kat and Dogi. They placed themselves at the tail end of the bus, which received the most violent of thrusts from the endless supply of bumps, such that flying up off the seat was not uncommon. Though the bench seats were somewhat padded, this did little to keep their back ends from some serious bruising. Even lying horizontally, trying to get some sleep, Dogi would literally take air. At one point, using his bum bag, which contained all his valuables, as a pillow, he flew so high that he almost lost it out the window, catching it by the end of the strap at the last second. After that, he just gave up on the idea of sleep. Suddenly, a country that looks so small on a world map felt endless. Just to punctuate the agony, the home stretch that took them hours through the sprawl of the Kathmandu valley, offered no bathroom breaks. For the last hour or so, Dogi was literally meditating on his sphincter so that his innards wouldn't spill all over the bus. Upon arrival in the Kathmandu bus terminal, Kat was left with two packs to deal with as Dogi speed waddled to the outhouse a hundred meters across the parking lot.

Ahh, relativity. How fine even a basic bed can feel after such a long and grueling journey on a bus. The beginning of what would become a week of good sleep and good food. Welcome to Kathmandu.

Dogi and Kat met up with Leatherfoot in much the same way as they had in Bangkok. Try Monday, and if not, then Tuesday, May 5th at 2:00 p.m. on the steps of the main temple in Durbar square. As it turned out, Leatherfoot had already been in Kathmandu for a couple of days, but he missed their Monday meeting as he was off on a little day trip. That was okay, however, as Durbar Square must surely be one of the best places on earth to watch life go by. It is a place of constant bustle, with people, and animals and vehicles of all sorts plying the surroundings. Far superior to the entertainment of any movie or TV show, Dogi and Kat happily sat there for a couple of hours and met up with him on the Tuesday.

O O O

There was an abundance of travel agents throughout the Thamel and Freak Street areas of Kathmandu, at any one of which they assumed they would be able to purchase a simple one way flight from Kathmandu to Lhasa. This was all they desired. Yet at each where they made their request, they got the same old story over and over again. "The Chinese visa you have in your passport is not valid for Tibet. You are not allowed to travel there as an individual. You must have it cancelled and purchase a *tour* which will include a Tibet only *tour* visa, a flight to Lhasa, and a 4X4 *tour* that will take you from Lhasa back here to Kathmandu in four or five days."

This did not sound appealing to any of them in any way. First of all, the tours were grossly expensive, and secondly, the speed of them was way too fast to be able to appreciate the country or the culture. Four or five days stuffed in a 4X4 hurtling across Tibet?

21

No thanks. Being seemingly thwarted from flight, they started to consider doing a round trip overland, but began to hear too many stories of individual travellers approaching the land border into Tibet at Kodari and being turned back. What was truth, and what was rumour? Could you get over the land border from Nepal into Tibet? Were their current visas really not valid or were the agencies in Kathmandu in on a racket trying to make a bigger buck? They didn't really want to go overland anyway. Dogi wanted to cycle from Lhasa to Kathmandu. The other way would comprise far too much uphill for their riding desires or capabilities, and going that way by bus or truck or 4X4 would spoil the mystery of riding back again. No, Dogi wanted to go *from* Lhasa *to* Kathmandu. They all did. They believed, they tried, they persisted.

"All we want is a one way flight to Lhasa. That's all. No tours, just the flight. These Chinese visas ARE valid!" This would be what Dogi or Kat or Leatherfoot would plead as they walked into travel agent after travel agent. "Not possible," would be the inevitable reply. Not possible, at least, until Leatherfoot talked to Hari. It was near the end of their second day of trying, when hope was beginning to fade, that Leatherfoot found Hari. He was the first and only one that had suggested it might be possible to get a one way flight ticket from Kathmandu to Lhasa. To be done, he said, it had to include a two day "Lhasa tour" to get through the red tape, but that would at least get them from the airport into the city and two nights accommodation if nothing else. From there, said Hari, they were on their own and at the mercy of the current and, apparently, unpredictable political rules in Tibet. He went on to tell them stories of how some individual travellers had been deported either by plane or overland, and other stories of minor bribes required to be left alone. "It comes and goes," said Hari, "but recently seems to be fairly settled."

Hari knew the right people. Hari bought them the sweet milky tea known as chai and repeatedly ushered Trippy the bowlegged dog out of his office. And as they sat for a chat in his office on several occasions, they watched his credit card rates ebb and flow from two percent to five percent depending on how arrogant the attitude was that came through his door. And buses that were full to jerks, miraculously had space for nice people. Hari got nice people what they wanted. He got Kat, Dogi, and Leatherfoot their one way plane tickets.

The flight was booked for the following week, and in the days of preparation leading up to their departure, the three of them spent many hours hanging out in Hari's office. Hari was full of great stories. Many of which were uplifting, some of which were sad. Crazy Happy Lady was one that was in many ways both. She was still young, perhaps in her twenties, and had the kind of smile that was infectious. Involved in an accident during her childhood, she lost her family and incurred a head injury which altered her mind. Since then she talks out loud to herself continuously, and aimlessly wanders the streets of the city. Everyone in the community helps out a little to care for her. They learned that Hari worked seven days a week, but that he loved his job. Every morning someone would come and go through a small Hindu ritual with water and paint and leave him with a red dot or line on his forehead between his eyebrows. If it wasn't Kat, Dogi, and Leatherfoot hanging out in his office, it was other travellers. Without fail, the first thing he would do when he got a visitor was offer chai. The drinks would then be brought to his office by one of his young helpers who would go out and run errands for him whenever needed.

"We're going to buy bicycles in Lhasa Hari, and ride them from there all the way back to here," told Dogi the day before they were going to leave.

Hari then looked them over one at a time with his big grin. First at Dogi, towards whom he just shook his head and laughed. Then Leatherfoot with much the same reaction. Finally, his gaze rested on Kat with a slightly more serious and earnest look on his face. Kat can be deceiving to many people, particularly outside of her own culture of Japan. She has the appearance of being shy, but this is mostly induced by the barrier imposed by language. Also, she is often assumed to be petite and perhaps even frail having neither great height nor physical stature. What is not apparent to many, particularly at first, is the strength of her muscularity, her natural athletic abilities, and her quiet mental fortitude. "You're going to do this too?" inquired Hari.

23

STUFF

ANY TIME PEOPLE UNDERTAKE AN ADVENTURE IN TRAVEL, WHAT TO bring is a major decision. There is usually only one backpack to work with, and what gets carried in it is subject to change based on environment and style of travel. All the contents increase greatly in value, particularly as fellow humanity is left behind, as it is bound to be up on the Tibetan plateau. What is it like up there? What kind of things are available? What will they need, and what can they do without? In the end, it comes down to food and shelter. As humans, we need enough to eat, clean water to drink, and a way to stay warm enough or cool enough as well as protected from the elements. Out of one backpack in a foreign land away from the conveniences of cities or towns these are the basics. Food and shelter.

Now that they were equipped with visas and their desired plane tickets, the group began preparations for their cycling journey. The bikes themselves they would buy in Lhasa, that was agreed, but what other items of need they would find in Lhasa and beyond was open to some speculation. With the abundance of things available in Kathmandu however, wisdom suggested that they equip themselves as well as possible before leaving. Things of all description were available here. The city of Kathmandu must be one of the outdoor mecas of the world. Climbers, trekkers, river enthusiasts all have an abundance of wonderful options from which to choose. Signs posted here and there advertise used goods for sale, and the city is full of small shops selling new and used outdoor gear, authentic and unauthentic brand names alike. Quality being variable, goods always require thorough scrutinizing, and prices, always inflated, are subject to intense bargaining.

Already equipped with their own sleeping bags, they set out to buy a tent, a stove and some fuel canisters, some basic cooking gear, a water filter, and some extra warm and protective clothing. Most of this they found in the small shops, but some they were able to get from other travellers. One traveller in particular who they met had quite an assortment of items mostly suited to mountaineering. Among them was a neck warmer made of a stretchy fabric that was long enough to be pulled right up over the head. Though it was not with him, he said that this particular garment had been to the top of Mount Everest. True or not, Kat decided that it looked and felt warm, so they bought it along with a pair of striped footless stockings that shared the same story. As a bonus, the traveller gave them a small bottle of tea tree oil, which he said might be useful for what they were undertaking. Finally, they stocked up on some food, including oatmeal, nuts, and a variety of dried fruit.

The balance of their possessions that they would not need in Tibet were left with Hari. He could be trusted to take good care of them. And as they sat in their hotel room in Kathmandu on the final night before their departure, Kat, Dogi and Leatherfoot questioned their preparedness. Did they have enough? Did they have too much? Were they missing anything?

Dogi's Journal Of Tibet

Part I

Lhasa

GETTING TO LHASA

WELCOME,

Here begins a travel journal that will take you through Tibet. A journey that is sure to produce many smiles and, no doubt, one or two tears. A journey that has dominated my dreams, both waking and asleep, for some time now. I will feed you a diet of as many of the day-to-day happenings as my energy allows, and, hopefully, throw in a little informational and philosophical spice as well. We are in the spiritual land of Tibet after all! So, LAUGH, CRY, SHARE and ENJOY!

Nearing evening of my first day here, I am sitting on the flat rooftop of the Yak Hotel somewhere near the center of Lhasa, surrounded by what I'd have to call mountains, but in the grand scheme of Tibet, they are only hills. Directly in front of me is the Potala Palace, perhaps the greatest and most well known building in the region. It is a magnificent structure in both grandeur and design. Built atop a hill, it has no uniformity, rather it sprawls this way and that in a jumble of square, rectangular, and cylindrically shaped portions, many of which have groupings of windows. Mostly whitewash on its exterior, it is trimmed along the top edges of most sections in a rusty brown. Its upper reaches have several walls of mustard yellow and brick red, topped overall with a lot of golden trim. Probably due to its age, and no doubt a good dose of bombing during the Chinese Cultural Revolution, it seems kind of crooked, yet still exhibits a sense of good balance. Staring at it, one wonders if a Dalai Lama will ever take residence there again.

I would like to hope so, but cannot envision it anytime in the foreseeable future.

Lhasa is not a huge city, though it is the main city and capital of Tibet. Tibet itself has gone through many phases in its history both influencing and being influenced by Mongol culture, and various Chinese cultures. It has seen the influx of Buddhism from India, and spawned it in its own unique directions. There has even been some western influence, namely British amongst others. It has in more recent history been taken forcefully into the Peoples' Republic of China during the time period surrounding the Cultural Revolution and now exists as a political state. This is not something that was welcomed willingly by the Tibetans, and so, like all political land border disputes the world over, has caused both internal and international issues. The requests and ideas of the most recent Dalai Lama, the spiritual leader in exile, have been widely publicized throughout the educated world, though sadly much of what he wishes has fallen on deaf ears amongst those who would have enough political influence to do something about the situation.

Most of Tibet is a huge plateau, bound and isolated by several ranges of mountains, most notably the Himalayas. Other than being bordered by Chinese provinces, it keeps political borders with Nepal, India, Bhutan and Myanmar. The average altitude above sea level in Tibet is 4000 meters (13,200 feet), giving rise to its extreme and unique environment, both culturally and physically. Here in Lhasa itself, I sit at about 3600 meters (11,900 feet).

This rooftop perch is amazing. Being on one of the highest structures in the central part of the city, I can see down onto many of the other rooftops. Most of them are flat useable spaces. The overall tone of the surrounding landscape is brown and rugged. Within the city area, there are quite a number of trees, but on the hills beyond there are none. With the buildings being shades of off white brick trimmed in variations on brown, it is only the clusters of prayer flags and the narrow strips of curtain across the tops of windows that provide colour. The prayer flags come in red, green, blue and yellow, as well as white. The curtain strips are white based, variable, goods always require thorough scrutinizing, and prices, always inflated, are subject to intense bargaining.

Already equipped with their own sleeping bags, they set out to buy a tent, a stove and some fuel canisters, some basic cooking gear, a water filter, and some extra warm and protective clothing. Most of this they found in the small shops, but some they were able to get from other travellers. One traveller in particular who they met had quite an assortment of items mostly suited to mountaineering. Among them was a neck warmer made of a stretchy fabric that was long enough to be pulled right up over the head. Though it was not with him, he said that this particular garment had been to the top of Mount Everest. True or not, Kat decided that it looked and felt warm, so they bought it along with a pair of striped footless stockings that shared the same story. As a bonus, the traveller gave them a small bottle of tea tree oil, which he said might be useful for what they were undertaking. Finally, they stocked up on some food, including oatmeal, nuts, and a variety of dried fruit.

The balance of their possessions that they would not need in Tibet were left with Hari. He could be trusted to take good care of them. And as they sat in their hotel room in Kathmandu on the final night before their departure, Kat, Dogi and Leatherfoot questioned their preparedness. Did they have enough? Did they have too much? Were they missing anything?

Dogi's Journal Of Tibet

Part I

Lhasa

but have blue, yellow and red stripes running across the top. The flags, in particular, give off a most pleasurably serene feeling.

Only half a day spent here, and the encroachment of things Chinese is quite obvious in many ways. Their buildings and shops already dominate the cityscape. At street level many seem hard working and kind enough, the displacement of Tibetan people obviously not the fault of any of the individuals trying to live and do commerce here, yet it is difficult not to call it a shame. A most stark example would be another smaller rock pinnacle in front of me. Once upon a time, I'm sure it had upon it an awesome monastery. Now it is home to a large ugly chunk of metal that is some kind of a communications tower. Here but a very short time and already I find the bitter pill of irony coursing through my mind. What are human rights? What is progress? In Kathmandu, the same shops that are selling stickers and T-shirts saying FREE TIBET are also selling Internet service for $X/hr. Yes, the Chinese are building more "communications" towers, and the same people who are screaming FREE TIBET are "communicating" it to their friends and family.

As I look out in a new direction again, I see a couple of more interesting rooftop sights. Most intriguing are the large, round, slightly concave solar reflectors. It appears that they are using the intense sun to dry things and even heat or, possibly, boil water. Such a simple and direct use of energy. Though perhaps not as time efficient as a plug in the wall, I often wonder why more sophisticated versions of such things are not found in more developed countries. As I scan further, on one roof in particular I see a huge pile of raw wool, and a couple dressed in more traditional Tibetan clothing who stare at it contemplating their future of spinning and weaving. A young mother dressed in more modern clothes has just appeared through the entrance carrying a small baby. On yet another roof, sitting amongst old boxes, baskets, bike tires and scraps of wood, is a young woman wearing a white blouse and blue dress, holding a pink rimmed hand mirror. She is intently dabbing some kind of cream onto her face.

I believe it is Tuesday May 12, 1998, if that is of any relevance. Kat, Leatherfoot and I awoke early this morning in Kathmandu, Nepal. In front of his shop, we met our local travel agent Hari, who was looking pretty classic dressed in some red and white striped pants and a purple and green jacket, as he rolled in on his small motorbike. Being the gentleman he is, he even offered Kat a ride down the street to the place where we hooked up with a few other travellers, loaded onto a small bus and got brought out to the airport. Ahh, Hari from Freak Street, travel agent and friend, it should be a fun month until we see you again back in Kathmandu!

Blindly leading and following various other travellers and "official" tour guides, we made our way through the disorganization of the Kathmandu airport and onto our plane. Our one anxiety going through the security process was the pressurized fuel canisters that we'd brought along for our camp stove. It would have been preferable to buy them in Lhasa, but we weren't sure whether they'd be available there or not. Being so fundamentally important to our trip, we didn't want to take that chance. Unsure of the current rules of carrying this sort of thing on the plane, we debated whether we should put them in our checked baggage or carry on. All I knew for sure was that I shouldn't be the one to carry them. For some odd reason, likely the long hair, I have an unfortunately high rate of being searched at security checks. In the end, we felt that carry on would be safer, and Kat carried the majority, with Leatherfoot, who is much more clean cut than me, carrying the rest. Fortunately, they got through unmolested.

The majority of the passengers on the small aircraft appeared to be Europeans or Japanese. Judging by the snippets of language, quite a few were Germans. I was unfortunately not blessed with a window seat, but did manage to stretch my neck across a few laps to take in some of the spectacular scenery. Flying over the Himalayan Mountains sent a feeling of giddiness through the crowd. What began as a wall of rock and snow on the approach from Nepal became a huge rough sea of white peaks spreading out to either horizon. Just as the excitement seemed to settle for a while, the pilot came on announcing that Mount Everest (Qomolangma in

Tibetan) was visible out the left side of the plane. The reaction in the cabin was quite comical as everybody on board piled over each other all at once just to get a look! I wonder if the pilot had to over steer the other way just to compensate for the weight shift. Not that it looked a whole lot different from all the other mountains down there, but somehow we humans are attracted to superlatives, and it is the highest point on this earth. I didn't get much of a look myself, but at least got my camera sent along with the many others passed to one of the people with a window seat.

Waves of different emotion passed through me during the short flight. First was pure excitement, but as we neared that turned to some nervousness and anxiety. As I stared across laps over the peaks and the great plateau beyond them, my dream overtook me once again. Soon, very soon, I thought, I will be riding a bicycle along some road down there that winds its way through those mountains and over some huge mountain pass! At least, I hope that is the case. It has never been a sure thing. What awaits us as individual travellers is still a mystery.

As you might imagine, the procedure to get ourselves here to Lhasa involved some wading through chest deep BULLSHIT and freely relieving ourselves of US currency, but sitting here in the midst of this wonderful city surrounded by the vastness of hills and space has already made it worth while. Thus far, I am happy that we were able to resist the travel agents in Kathmandu that suggested we were not allowed to be in Tibet as individual travellers these days. With our guidebook understandably sitting on the fence on the issue, due to the ever changing political climate, coming here without being on a tour was a difficult decision. Not even Hari could tell us what to expect for sure after we got on the plane. He said stories change all the time. So we entered on this "official" tour that Hari had included with our flights. In actual fact, our tour only included the ride from the airport into Lhasa and two nights of accommodation. There was another group of five who we met on the bus to the airport this morning that we also knew to be on this version of the tour, but even with them we spoke very little of the details, not knowing who should know how much of what. It wasn't until after landing in the Lhasa airport waiting in the immigration line that we discovered there were four more, making an even dozen of us using this tour as a means of getting in to travel independently if possible.

Most of the passengers were let through quite quickly, but the dozen of us were held in line at Chinese immigration for several tense moments longer. As we handed over our passports, we were requested to pay an extra $10 US for some kind of special Lhasa stamp. Bureaucratic *hooey* for sure, but we had been warned by Hari of this possibility and recommended to donate and get on with it, rather than make an issue. It represented the second time in four border crossings that we have been asked for what Kat likes to call "presents." A little extra gift for the border guards just because they can. Bribery, extortion, presents, call it what you will, it's a fact of life around the globe, and the scope of it goes far beyond just border crossings. Such behavior has deep roots in government, and business too. If you scratch my back, I'll ease your way. Somehow it's human nature to take advantage of situations of power or leverage. As philosophically wrong and emotionally frustrating as it feels to be on the abused end, the consequences of not playing along are usually not worthwhile. Though greedy, people who extort money or favours from other people are usually wise enough to know not to ask for too much.

Ten bucks. It's irritating in principal, but being so close, I certainly didn't want to sit in the same plane for its return journey to Kathmandu, so I pulled out a twenty for Kat and myself and Leatherfoot extracted his ten. Of course, out of a dozen, there just had to be one in the group that felt the need to rock the boat. In this case it was a bold German girl who didn't feel like giving up her ten dollars and insisted on making a scene, which put all of us on hold for much longer than necessary. There was no arguing back by the Chinese officials. They just sat back and waited while she grumbled on. Though the rest of us had paid our ten dollars already, we were not going to be given our passports back until she paid also. It was all or none, which made the rest of us put pressure on her to play along, which she finally did. SMILE AND PAY AND BE ON YOUR WAY!

My mind so focussed on getting through immigration, I didn't become too conscious of the thinness of the air until walking out of the airport terminal. It was one of those moments when I felt like taking a long, deep breath, but discovered that I couldn't! I knew the feeling of being at altitude, having been at over 5000 meters (16,500 feet) before, but that was a more gradual ascent during a hike. This was an abrupt change from about 1000 meters (3300 feet) above sea level in Kathmandu to somewhere close to 4000 meters (13,200 feet) at the airport. That kind of sudden reduction in the amount of oxygen in the air is shocking to the system. I liken it to a deep chest cold without the phlegm. You feel like you simply can't expand the lower portion of your lungs.

Fortunately, the bus ride from the airport into Lhasa was a little bit downhill, easing the feeling slightly. Even so, there was one point along the ride that I felt the urge to sneeze, and drawing in as much air as possible, I still couldn't get a deep enough lung full to do it! What a bizarre feeling. Several times I tried as the tickle in my nose wouldn't subside, issuing forth only something resembling a cough at an opera. The scenery along the way from the airport into Lhasa was amazing. Being a bit of a cloudy, misty day, the light that did penetrate created an array of tantalizing reflections, and silhouettes. The scale of the landscape here is unbelievable. Until you see an animal or person standing on the foot of a distant hill, you have no concept of the size of the area by which you are surrounded. I can't wait to inhale this landscape for days on end!

All twelve of us were brought to the Yak Hotel, and the three of us have been put in a dormitory style room with a few others. The shared bathing facilities here are functional if not glamorous, and the room is dark, frigid, and somewhat musty smelling. Fortunately, we have this wonderful rooftop on which to hang out until we are ready to sleep. After settling in and getting acquainted with the hotel, we headed out for an afternoon walk. First exchanging some money and eating a little, we then headed off to the old Tibetan quarter. That sounds funny now that I write it. Tibetan Quarter. It seems to me that having a China Town in the midst of the capital city of Tibet might be more appropriate, but that is most certainly not the case. The distinction between the two cultures is

35

profound. Whether a quarter is an accurate measurement of the Tibetan's remaining area is difficult to tell, but it's probably not far off. The majority of the city has been taken over by the Chinese and any newer growth is also Chinese. Sadly, this would suggest that the Tibetans will become more and more of a minority in Lhasa as time moves along.

Though I have been to many Asian markets in recent years, the one today in the Tibetan Quarter, known as the Barkhor, was special. My first impression of the Tibetan people here in Lhasa has been totally positive. They are radiant and wholesome looking. Though they look like they lead challenging lives, it is done with great acceptance and contentment. The difference between the Chinese and the Tibetans is obvious, not so much by face, but by mannerisms and mode of dress. The Chinese here in Lhasa wear clothes that would seem quite normal to us. Sweaters, slacks, suits, leather jackets, and loafers. The women sport hair of varying lengths and styles, while the men all wear theirs short. The Tibetans on the other hand, though some have already gravitated towards the more Chinese style, are generally dressed quite differently. Many of the men and women have long thick hair, beautifully woven into tight braids. The women entwined with various coloured stones and jewels, the men woven through with tassels of red or black which they often wrap around their heads. Their clothes look heavy and are made of sheep skins and wool. The women in long skirts with shirt and jacket, and the men in shirt, pants and a cloak. Also worn by the women are beautifully woven striped aprons. Footwear is anything from leather boots to cheap old sneakers with holes in them. Finally, in contrast, there is the look in the eyes. The overall demeanor. Many of the Chinese people who are here are either government, military, or the adventurous who have been drawn here with thoughts of a new life. Though there were exceptions, on many faces I saw arrogance, and on others a look of want. The Tibetans, on the other hand, appear far more neutral and innocent. Simply happy to be alive.

Also in the market area, and along the maze of streets in general, was yak meat, yak cheese, yak butter, yak oil, yak skins and belts and a million other intriguing things. Jewellery was also abundant in the form of beads and stones, silver, turquoise, and amber. From one old lady, I bought a chime whose sound resonates with wonderful purity and longevity. The bargaining process took a while, but I haggled what I think was a decent price, with a big smile on my face. With the fresh air, the mountain backdrop and the great energy, I felt the fascination and wonder of a kid out in the first snowfall of the year, grinning all afternoon!

Monks of all ages were another common sight around the colourful Tibetan Quarter. Some would pass us by with not even so much as a glance, shuffling along their way, while others would flash big smiles and wave. At one point, one of the younger monks with his shaved head and burgundy robes walked straight up to me with a purposeful stride, proceeded to full on hug me and then buried his face in my chest. So out of the blue, it was a rather peculiar feeling, and I was left with my arms sticking out wondering what to do next. Then, pulling back only slightly, and with a huge radiant smile he proceeded to beg me for money and continued to hang on to me for ages! Leatherfoot and Kat were just shaking their heads and laughing.

Dinner was the final adventure of the day. We went into a Tibetan restaurant in the neighborhood of our hotel which, judging by the English menu, was somewhat used to tourists. What jumped out at the lot of us was the yak burger. Pretty plain looking on delivery, it turned out to be one of the fattiest burgers I've ever eaten in my life. I don't think I'll be trying it again.

Well, it has been an incredibly full and wonderful, but tiring day. Kathmandu seems like forever ago, but it was only this morning that we left Hari's smiling face behind. It's not just a word anymore, a place on a map, a dream. We're actually here! Lhasa, Tibet. And so far, it's all good.

LOOKING FOR BIKES

OUR FIRST NIGHT OF SLEEP HERE IN LHASA WAS DEFINITELY restless. The dormitory room was freezing, and the shock of suddenly being 2600 meters (8600 feet) higher in altitude was harder on the body than anticipated. The thick pile of wool blankets did do well to keep us warm from our chins down, though they are a great deal heavier than duvets or down sleeping bags and don't allow for much turning about while sleeping. The combination of the altitude, the cold air, and the weight of the blankets made it feel like having a bad chest cold. We're definitely going to pull out the sleeping bags for tonight.

Beyond the bodily discomforts, the sheer excitement of being in Lhasa also kept my brain buzzing for much of the night. Visions of what I saw on my first day here mixed with thoughts of looking for bikes and riding out onto the plateau. Though not really physically refreshed, I awoke feeling energetic and looking forward to the day. Leatherfoot too woke up on a high. Kat, on the other hand, unfortunately got out of bed with a headache that she has been unable to shake since arriving. In fact, she has been feeling under the weather since all the running around in Kathmandu, and this radical shift in environment has only made it worse. We hope that time spent at the altitude will allow her to adjust and start feeling better.

On our second day here in Lhasa, we walked aimlessly around what commercial part of town there is, looking for bicycle shops and taking in whatever other interesting sights were offered. The process of trying to buy a bike here is reminding me of the time I bought a Russian made motorbike in Vietnam. As I remember, with the help of an interpreter, I paid $500 US for that vehicle brand new, and it broke down almost every day. Communism. Though it may well have been born out of some good philosophical ideals, mixed with the human condition, producing quality products has certainly not been an end result of the system. Here in Tibet, we have the choice between bad quality bikes and really bad quality bikes and beyond that the familiar communication difficulties.

The owners of the bike shops are all Chinese, and between Kat, Leatherfoot, and myself, we know all of three Chinese words. They can all be attributed to Kat, and will help us not at all in buying the bikes. Their English is as non-existent as our Chinese, so we are reduced to the wonderful game of Charades. So far, every shop owner has come across as quite pushy and rushed, and they haven't been too pleasant to work with. As forwardness seems to be perfectly acceptable to the Chinese, or at least those living in this area, I just get in there and poke around on the bikes, taking the odd one out for a test ride. The quoted prices are a little more variable than the options, depending on the shop. Obviously, some of the owners are throwing on a little more tourist inflation than others. As a travel rule, I try not to buy too much beyond food and accommodation on the first few days in a new country. It takes time to adjust to a new currency, in this case the Yuan, and get a feel for its true worth in the local market. There is also the cultural adjustment to be made related to the process of shopping. Not all parts of the world subscribe to a fixed price system. In many places around the globe, bargaining is not only accepted, it's expected. One of the challenges on arriving in a new culture is trying to figure out how inflated the first price is, and how far below it you should start. There is a fine line between an honorable and offensive beginning point, and there are so many factors at play. In some cultures, by even beginning the bargaining process, you have essentially made a commitment to buy no matter how long the back and forth banter takes. In others, it is not an issue to walk away. Also depending on the culture, and the mood of the participants, the practice can be jovial and spirited or nasty and aggravated. The guidebook does a good job of giving rules of thumb, and peering over the shoulders of locals engaged can give additional insight, but there is no substitute for experience. Eventually, you just have to go for it, though starting with low priced items is advisable. In the case of buying our bikes, we know that we have several days yet to spend in Lhasa during when we will hopefully find more shops with better options. Thus we have not yet made any purchases.

Having wandered mostly in newer Chinese commercial or industrial portions of the city today, there was not much in the way of architecture that intrigued me, yet I found the mixture of people most fascinating. Of the endless stream of interesting scenes that passed by, there are two that stand out clearly. The first is a particular lady, an old lady. Though I'd certainly never met her before, she was oddly familiar to me. It's as though I've met her distant cousins during my travels in other countries over the years. She's one of the ones that comes up to you and pokes you firmly, though not offensively. Then she grunts a few local syllables and flashes you a big rotting three tooth grin as she tries to sell you a necklace, and then a bracelet. Having no desire for any of these trinkets, I just stood there and stared into her eyes and wondered about her existence.

Later in the day, at a distance across a main road, I saw a man. The scene surrounding him captivated me more than anything else in my first two days here. He was making his way very slowly along the sidewalk... on his knees. In one hand he had a small bunch of incense, in the other a copper bowl with a few coins in it. These he would rattle now and then, all the while chanting prayers. Not only was he unable to walk, but he was blind, and being guided along on a leash. The leash was being very patiently drawn by a pretty young girl, and it is the memory of her that remains most vividly etched into my mind. She felt not ashamed, not rushed, not impatient, not even sad. In fact, she seemed totally at ease, dancing, talking, singing, and smiling in her own little world.

People. Human beings. We are such interesting creatures, so varied and diverse. People are one of the main reasons that travel in foreign lands is so entertaining, and educational. Other travellers met along the journey tell tales that fascinate and stimulate, and they bring with them a wide assortment of cultural backgrounds.

Locals give mind-expanding perspectives on other ways of life. There is so much to be understood and learned.

POTALA PALACE

THE FIRST TWO NIGHTS IN THE YAK HOTEL FIRST FLOOR SHARED walk in freezer were included in our "official tour," but that was more than enough for all of us. Other than the great rooftop and the decent hot showers, we found the atmosphere to be unpleasant. Most of the guests were older European tourists, and they, along with the staff, were not particularly friendly. As prices were also high for what was being offered if we had wanted to extend our stay, we took some time early this morning to search out a new place. What we found was the Kirey Hotel and it is much more to our liking. Being just down the street from the Yak, it is still conveniently located. Hot showers are at a premium, but the second floor room into which we have moved is far more pleasant, as it provides better warmth and light, and the staff here are a great deal more welcoming. The hotel is set up around a large courtyard from where the laughter of children playing can be heard. Leatherfoot and I already joined in on a few of their games this morning.

The Potala Palace. It is an incredible landmark that absolutely dominates Lhasa, and, finally, we have taken the opportunity to explore it. Of massive proportions, it is built atop a big hill in the midst of the city. It surely must be included in the family of the world's most magnificent structures. From every angle, it is a head shaker and a jaw dropper. One cannot help but stand in awe.

After a long wander throughout the sprawling interior, I am sitting in a large room near the top of the palace. Leaning against a column near the center, there is a large Buddha sitting above and behind me. The mostly shaded room is bathed in a few gentle shafts of light penetrating the one row of windows. Smoke from burning incense dances playfully up to the ceiling. Next to me sits a young monk who is trying to read what I am writing. It is he who invited me to sit here. We have gone through introductions and a few basic questions and now he is showing me his English study book and I am helping him with his pronunciation. Considering that he likely has no native teachers other than travellers like myself, he is doing very well. Most impressive is his patience. He listens with great attention and watches my mouth, therefore he is able to pick things up quickly.

It has been quite the adventure meandering through the endless rooms and courtyards that make up this palace. Actually, it all started with the camel in the parking lot near the main entrance. He was an odd sight with the colourful belt draped around his neck and the most ridiculous grin you've ever seen. If I had to choose a name, I'd call him Cheesy. Not really sure, but perhaps he was the Chinese version of a pony ride, though we never did see him in action.

The entrance ticket was pricey, at least in relation to local costs, but I can still say easily worth it. It's my guess that the Chinese tourists pay less than we do, and one would hope that the Tibetans get in for free, but I'm not so sure that's the case. I found that I wasn't as offended by the price as by the fact that the Chinese government is cashing in on the most important of Tibetan cultural sights and one of the few they didn't completely destroy on their uninvited way in, though I believe they did try. It is yet another bitter pill of irony to be swallowed because I couldn't possibly come to Lhasa and not go into the Potala.

I'm still in the same room and have just been staring all around it for the past little while. It is incredible, as have been many of the rooms throughout the palace. The style is heavily ornate, yet not at all gaudy. To me the best part is the brilliant use of colours. Lots of bright orange, blue, yellow, green and red. The interior is a maze of fascinating hallways, rooms and assembly halls. So many statues, pillars, murals, tombs, Buddha figures, mandalas, and endless other items of intrigue and historical value that occupy the spaces. Yet there is a strange feeling of emptiness. The past life and energy here must have been intoxicating, but at present it feels quite void and lifeless. Having been built in several stages, much of it in the mid to late sixteen hundreds, it has been the home to each successive Dalai Lama since the death of the fifth spiritual leader and, thus, the place of Tibetan government. That is until the exile of the current spiritual leader. Once again I find myself wondering if the life that once was will be allowed to flourish here once again. It does not seem likely that the Chinese government will ever willingly give up the control that they have gained over the area, but maybe a future generation of leaders will at least allow Buddhist culture to re-establish itself. If not completely equitable to the Tibetans, maybe a peaceful compromise will one day be reached. Maybe.

I close my eyes and try to feel the positive energy that still lives in the cracks and corners here. With eyes open, however, negativity resurfaces quickly, and at the moment, it is most certainly being brought by the Chinese tourists who are entering this room. There is signage here written in English and Chinese that indicates one is always to walk clockwise around a Tibetan room or temple. In fact, the young monk next to me is also trying to guide people that way, but so far, several of the Chinese have ignored both the signs and his obvious requests. To me, ignorance is forgivable. By definition it suggests that the thing being done falsely or impolitely is due to a lack of knowledge or understanding. As tourists and travellers, faux pas often occur out of ignorance, and I'm sure I have been guilty of them on numerous occasions. Disrespect, however, is something different altogether. Understanding exists, but wishes are not adhered to. I'd like to think the Chinese tourists are simply being ignorant, but with the signage and the young monk here pointing it out, I feel as though it is more so disrespect. The funny part is, my robed friend here seems less frustrated by it than I am. He continues to sit passively, with a resigned grin of acceptance on his face. I feel like getting up and standing in front of the tourists and pointing them in the right direction, but it is not my place. I resist the urge because it would be confrontational and contrary to what the Tibetan culture epitomizes. Though the rationalization keeps me passive, the feeling of frustration does not fully abate.

I think my friend here knows I was writing about him. He has now settled himself comfortably leaning against me, and there is a purity in his affection such that I feel totally comfortable with him there. Now he has popped back up again and decided he wants to teach me some Tibetan: TU-JAY-CHAY is Thank You, KA-LEE PAY is Goodbye when staying and KA-LEE SHU is Goodbye when leaving, and finally, TA-SHI DE-LEK is a general greeting such as Hello or How are you? I wish I could bottle his smile and the twinkle in his eyes and take a sip of it whenever I need a spiritual lift.

Suddenly, I can hear some chanting in the background. It is something that I have heard several times already in the few days I've been here. It creeps into your consciousness and sets an equilibrium to it. My earlier irritation is being washed away. It is a monotonous hum, and it makes me feel *good*. It is meditation. It makes me feel peaceful and aware. Aware that my legs are beginning to fall asleep sitting on this hard floor! I've been hoping Kat and Leatherfoot would eventually come into this room, as I lost touch with them ages ago, but they must have wandered to other corners of this maze like palace. As I am shaking and rubbing my legs to get the blood flowing once again, the young monk is giving me a quizzical look, though he has quickly turned his full attention back to his studies. He's obviously used to sitting on hard surfaces for a long time. His stillness and concentration are beyond those of anyone I have ever met before. Now that I can feel my feet again, I would like to write one more thing before I get up and move on. I will copy it to the letter from the back of my ticket stub:

A BRIEF INTRODUCTION TO THE POTALA PALACE

The Potala palace was built in the time of the Songtsan Gampo in the 7th century. In the 17th century, the 5th Dalai Lama extended the palace to its present size. At this time, it also succeeded in becoming the Dalai Lama's residing place and truned the main political and religious affair. The main construction is divided into two sections, the Red and White palaces. It is 115.703 meters high with thirteen stories. Including living quarters, temples, funerals stupas and monk dormitories. The countless cultural relics in the palace are images, murals, sutras, etc, which of incredible value. These magnificent Tibetan arts and culture are not only classified as national treasures but are also listed by the state council as one unit of the important cultural relics to be specially protected.

I'm not quite sure about "truning" the main political and religious affair, but boy don't I feel all warm and fuzzy inside knowing that Tibetan arts and culture are classified as Chinese national treasures and the relics are specially protected by the state council. Isn't that special. It sure was nice of them not to blow everything up and save a little! Oops, I don't like to linger in that sarcastic tone, particularly in the company of this young monk. I wonder if the concept of sarcasm has ever even entered his brain. Is that thought process innate or learned? In any case, less of it in the world would probably be a good thing.

Having exited out the back, I have worked my way around the base back to the front and am hanging out with the crazy camel. I had absolutely, positively thee best pee in the palace. It was through a hole in the floor in a small room, which was built extended out over a cliff. I wasn't on the thirteenth floor anymore, but still in the higher reaches of the palace, and the drop was WAY past ground floor. I'm sure the pee must have spread into a million little droplets by the time it hit the ground. Very cool, assuming you have faith in the structure. I don't think I'd have enjoyed it nearly as much if I'd had to go number two, but that's probably enough toilet talk for now.

As a final thought on how the Chinese government is currently treating the Potala, I came across a sign inside. It was large and rimmed in yellow, with a multi-hued blue background, underscored with red and white stripes. A fancy insignia featuring a handshake and the years 1989-1994, it read:

THE PRESENT RES
ORATION OF THE
ALA PA ACE

The missing letters and hyphen between "rest" and "oration" were barely visible, and even many of the other letters were faded.

I have left the palace area and am in a restaurant. I never did find Kat and Leatherfoot and there is a sudden freak snowstorm outside. Let me share some **RANDOM THOUGHTS** while I wait for my food...

The Pabst Blue Ribbon guy! I guess you could call him a busker. He was sitting outside the Potala on a rock. The area is called the Potala kora, which is the pilgrim path that encircles the palace. The area was surrounded by prayer wheels, which I will describe in more detail later. He was dressed in a shabby, well-worn blue suit that didn't fit him in a classic sense at all. He wore a collared shirt, but no tie and, underneath that, a yellow turtleneck. There between his legs sat a twelve pack sized beer case of Pabst Blue Ribbon. Empty? On his head was a Charlotte Hornets white and teal striped baseball cap, and he was wearing some "groovy" black sunglasses. In this location, he sure looked hilarious. The instrument he was playing was much like a guitar, but with a longer neck and a smaller body. The tuning knobs were long and wooden. Personally, I was more impressed with his look than his sound, so I didn't cough up any coins.

Nice, my food has arrived. Oh, maybe not, that bowl is headed to another table.

Tibetan food. There are Chinese and even western eateries around, but we're trying to support things Tibetan as much as possible. From what we have tasted so far, however, that will be challenging. It's starchy and laden with oil or fat. Animal oils and fats as far as I can tell. I don't think Tibetan cuisine is going to win culinary awards any time soon. It epitomizes basic and using what you've got, which in this case is not a lot. It's neither good, nor bad. What it does do, however, is fill you up.

I try my best to reserve judgement on what is good and what is bad. I'm trying to just accept things as much as I can. "It is what it is." An expression easily voiced, more difficultly understood and yet harder still to practice. It really is a nice ideal, but I still see good and bad and, lately, a bit of both together in most things. Food. That the Chinese are here has many elements of great shame, but one thing is certain to me already. They bring with them a far greater and more balanced selection of food. Though we haven't been outside Lhasa yet, it is my understanding that not many crops can grow in this high altitude desert environment besides the Tibetan staple of barley. Fresh fruit and vegetables have never been much of an option for the Tibetans before the Chinese showed up bringing their planes or trucks full of fresh food from more fertile parts of their country. This extends to things such as fuel and electricity too. Good food, fuel, power, things that many might argue should be basic human rights by now. Are they? Should they be? Would the Tibetans be better off without the Chinese? Surviving on a basic diet with minimal fuel and power? Perhaps the lack of these things is the very reason they have become a people of such strong spirit. Perhaps it is when the material life gets more difficult that one needs to develop a strong faith just to survive.

Well that brings me back AROUND to the prayer wheels again. They encircle almost every temple around here. Outside the Potala there are hundreds. They are usually arranged in a long row, along the side of a path, one after the other at about shoulder height. Golden in colour, they each have several rows of prayers on them which are released upon being spun around. The script used to write the prayers is flowing and artistic. The Tibetans walk by with an arm extended spinning one after the next... spin, spin, spin... around and around.

So many things seem to revolve around the concept of around and around to the Tibetans. They walk a circuitous route outside the temples, spinning the prayer wheels or the hand held versions that many of them carry. Even the interiors of temple rooms are lapped over and over. Cycles. A constant reminder of the cycles of life. It seems so different at a philosophical level from Western thought. Revolutionary rather than evolutionary. Western thought seems so linear. As if there is a beginning and end to things. It also seems so focussed on getting somewhere. To this end, I guess.

Which I'm not so sure really exists. There's something so fundamentally different. It's as if so many Western people are living mentally in the future, striving for... what? Around and around. It seems to have a little more acceptance built into it. A feeling of comfort and continuity, and perhaps even a better relationship with the present. Certainly it will be a topic to observe and ponder as the journey continues.

Okay, my thugpa, which was piping hot when it arrived, should be cool enough to eat now. Thugpa is one of the few choices on offer in the Tibetan restaurants. It is a very basic noodle soup with perhaps a few vegetables and, if lucky, some meat. The noodles are fat and pasty and the overall tone of the broth is oily and salty. Momos are the other common choice on the menu. They are small dumplings that also contain some vegetable or meat. They are either steamed, which is preferable, or fried, which makes them rather greasy. So far, the results on both have been quite variable.

SERA MONASTERY

HERE WE ARE AGAIN, EATING, OR AT LEAST WAITING FOR OUR FOOD. This restaurant has become our usual breakfast place. Though the food is very average, the people working in here are delightful, which is why we keep coming back. There is much to tell. Like about the toilets. I'm not sure how much you want to hear about the toilets, but to us they are a particular source of amusement. In this restaurant there are actually separate mens and ladies toilets, but that is exceptional. The laughing starts when you step inside to discover nothing more than three triangularly shaped holes in the floor. Where the pile oozes to after that even I don't want to know. Other than the stench, it's not too horrible as a male, that is unless you need to unload a dump. For Kat however, who always has to drop 'em, it is not one of the more enjoyable parts of the day.

There is another restaurant where we have had lunch a couple of times that is also a treat in Toilet World. In this one, men and women are together, and in between the usual row of holes are actually some partitions. The only problem being that they are only about knee high. Poor Kat! She always hopes desperately that no one will come in while she's there.

It's a funny thing. Urinating and defecating are about as normal a human function as sleeping and eating, but somehow they are not done enjoyably in company. That said, it is not uncommon in some parts of the world for people to share this odorous experience. I can picture rows of people in India sitting along a railway track, all dropping their stinky piles and having a chat. But with our cultural background, the only desirable company is a good magazine.

That's enough for now. Time to get back to the other end, as here comes our food. Momos for breakfast! They look exceptional this morning. Perhaps we're getting a little extra love being such regulars!

O O O

The Sera Temple complex. That was the name of the magnificent place that we went to yesterday. Or was it the day before? No, according to Leatherfoot, it was yesterday. With so much going on everyday, it seems time has already been thrown in the blender since we've arrived.

What I do remember quite clearly is that I woke up feeling rather nauseated. That came as a bit of a surprise. It didn't feel like it was related to anything I ate, but I thought I had adjusted quite quickly to the altitude feeling nothing the first few days. Never mind, I decided to go anyway, as the Sera monastery is a place we all agreed we must see before departing Lhasa. We caught a morning bus, mostly loaded with other tourists, which took us directly to what was a surprisingly large sprawling complex. We were to discover later, however, that it is now significantly smaller than it originally had been. The majority of the complex had been destroyed several decades earlier during the Chinese invasion. Nonetheless, it was a grand sight, and we were to spend many hours there wandering around. Once a whole community in and of its own, there were several functional buildings, such as kitchens and dormitories as well as an abundance of temples large and small. Let me take you there...

Having been dropped off at the edge of the complex, we are immediately gratified with a striking scene. We find ourselves on a long, wide, tree lined boulevard, which has upon it thousands of granite blocks. They are all standing on end like row after row of dominoes. Each chunk of rock is about half a meter square and as thick as the length of a hand. If they need to be moved by human strength, it would take quite a few muscular men to lift one. Here and there, squatted like chickens on the roost, sit men perched on the stones with no more than a hammer and chisel. Tap tap tap tap tap tap. Only a few men, and thousands of rocks. Without a doubt this must be a daunting task, but the men seem to be enjoying their work. I find that when I see rebuilding from destruction at the hands of nature, it does not really bother me, but when the ravage is due to human invasion and war, it is sad. How many hours of labour can be destroyed in such a short time, only to have to be rebuilt again at great expense? Should I ever find myself in Tibet again one day, this will be a place to which I would certainly return. This entrance walkway alone will look incredible when all of these stone blocks are laid.

In unloading from the bus, we realize that we are the only travellers here not associated with a package tour. Our freedoms as individual travellers are still somewhat in question to us at this point. Walking within the city limits in Lhasa on our own, we have been unbothered by anyone official, but this is our first time outside of the city and we are unsure what to expect. At first we feel safer sticking to the heels of the tour group before we feel comfortable enough to slide off into the freedom of our own pace. We can see that the tour group is headed towards one of the main temples in the complex, but we decide to explore the surroundings first. Avoiding some of the areas labelled as "no public access," we head to a nondescript building across from and beyond the temple.

The door is open, and we enter into a fairly large open room that has the feel of a cafeteria. As we wander through to the other side, we discover a large kitchen area, and are suddenly approached by a couple of young monks dressed in their burgundy robes. We hesitate briefly, wondering if we are supposed to be in here, but their smiles are inviting and we soon find ourselves seated on a cold bench in the back of the quiet kitchen area. Promptly, they serve us a drink, which we graciously accept. It looks like tea, but there is a somewhat oily film floating around on top. I take a sip and am surprised by the gag reflex induced before it is even halfway down my throat. I force a smile across my face pretending that I like it so as not to cause any offence. I glance at Kat, who is already on her second sip, and she seems genuinely not to mind it. The smile on Leatherfoot's face, however, is even more forced than mine. One of the monks who speaks some very basic English informs us that it is called Yak Butter Tea. We've seen these big mounds of yak butter for sale around Lhasa, but this is the first we've heard that they put it in their tea. Why would you put butter in tea? It really is pretty gross, and it takes continued effort to conceal the forces trying to contort my face after each sip. It's not even hot, which isn't helping, but for the sake of politeness we hang in there and continue to sip away slowly. It's great to hang out with the monks and have a bit of conversation for a while, but we have to get out. Kat is coping all right, and I am surviving, but Leatherfoot is desperate. He poured his second cup into our half empty ones when the monks weren't looking and declined the next refill. Kat and I drink it up, and fighting stomach contractions with a forced smile, we take our leave.

The other tourists are just filing out as we enter the main assembly hall. The painting and statues rival many of those seen in the Potala, but there is an odd air in the place. The monks here pay us little attention as we wander around. They look as though they are preparing for something, but their mood is somber as they go about their business. We decide not to linger.

There are so many possibilities for exploration, but somehow we are drawn away from the main area in an uphill direction by a few rocks that have large brightly painted figures on them. As we get close enough, we can see that there are a couple of Buddha representations and a couple of other figures that have a devilish look. There are two of these, both painted blue over a yellow background, and the one has a fat human body with a pig like face, long horns and a crazy grin. On the surrounding rocks there is a smattering of Tibetan writing. The whole thing has a graffiti type look to it with the reds and yellows, blues and greens, yet much more complex as it is etched into the stone as well as brightly painted. Whether these evil looking characters are intended to be opposition, temptation, or protection, I am not sure, but I get a definite sense of foreboding.

Now that we have come this far, we can see a lone building at the very top corner of the complex. It doesn't appear as though too many tourists bother with the short steep hike up, and fair enough too, as we quickly find ourselves sucking wind at this altitude. Upon arrival we discover that there are actually two buildings.

As Kat and Leatherfoot head for the one on the left, I drift off alone towards the one on the right. As I arrive, I can see clearly in through the open doorway to a ground level courtyard, but feel unsure as to whether or not I should walk in. It definitely has the feeling of being somebody's residence, but I sense no activity inside. I walk in gingerly and try a few "Hello's" but get no response. I find little except open space once inside, though there are several closed doors. Resisting the temptation to try any of them, I eventually find a set of stairs and take them up onto the big flat roof. Like in Lhasa, that seems to be fairly standard construction here, flat roofs lined with a rock or clay low perimeter fence. I guess an abundance of rain or snow is not a big issue, and the limitation of building material such as trees to make sloped roofs. Funny that, not much rain, not many trees, not many trees, no lumber. No lumber, no sloped roofs, no sloped roofs, no problem... no rain. Around and around. Cultures tailoring their cycles to the local environment.

The view from up here is awesome. I can see down over the rest of the complex and across the valley beyond. The predominant colour is brown. There are definitely a few trees in this valley to lend some green, but they look as though they've been planted and lead fairly challenging lives. I've heard Tibet referred to as the roof of the world, and now I feel as though I'm on the roof of the roof of the world, and it's great!

Suddenly, I hear someone down below. I feel a tinge of anxiety. Should I be here? Should I head for the stairs? Stay quiet up here? It doesn't matter, I am discovered as up comes a monk, and he is a surprisingly large man. He's at least my height, which is over one hundred and eighty-five centimeters (6'1"), and solidly built. He's wearing only a part of his monks robes and a very leathery looking old face as he strides up to me purposefully and throws his arms around me in a great big bear hug. What follows amounts to a full on physical! He squeezes all of my muscles with his strong paws, pulls on my long hair, and nearly yanks off my beard, all the while sporting a huge grin. Apparently, I pass his inspection, and after I manage to recover, we hold a bit of a Tibetan and English conversation in which neither of us understands the other, but which both of us seem to enjoy. These Tibetan monks are quite different from what I expected. For some reason I imagined them to be more physically frail and somber in temperament, but this old man could break me like a twig and he is incredibly animated.

Soon enough, we are joined by Kat and Leatherfoot, who are given a bracing pat on the back, but spared the physicals. At this point I ask him to take a photo of us together, and am shocked as a stern look crosses his face and he holds one of his big hands up with his palm out and then walks off. For a moment I am feeling badly, as I think I have somehow offended him, until he suddenly reappears wrapping the rest of his monk's robes around him and making sure he looks all neat and tidy. Back comes the grin as his arm drapes around my shoulders, and we get a great shot! After, we are emphatically invited into his room.

It is basic and colourful with yellow walls and religious paintings. A small bed sits in the corner below the one window, which has a white curtain with coloured polka dots. Jammed on top of his table are a few dishes and thermoses of boiled water, as well as a radio and cassette player. He has ushered us onto some pillows on the small empty space on the ground while he busies himself with making tea. While we stare at him in wonderment, he continues on in Tibetan, though he mixes in the phrase "holy tea" quite frequently. What he is calling "holy tea" is obviously Yak Butter Tea once again. Poor Leatherfoot is looking very uncomfortable as he watches the oil dance away on the surface of the hot liquid. Our mouths and lips still have an oily coating from the last cup we had an hour or more ago. That this tea could be remotely holy, we beg to differ, but we once again fear being impolite by turning it down. Situations like this are always tough in such an extremely foreign cultural environment. Would he be offended if we don't drink it?

It isn't quite as bad as our earlier serving, as it is at least hot, but it still induces a mild gag reflex. I liken the effect on the stomach to that of drinking cheap alcohol. Kat's okay. I can tell by her face that she still doesn't like it, but she doesn't hate it either. I'm suffering through small sips, but surviving. Leatherfoot is once again desperate. He's hoping I'll bail him out by downing some of his cup when our host isn't looking, but I'm not that nice of a guy.

As time passes, we are all still smiling, but the inability to converse is beginning to get awkward, so he decides to pull out a tray of snacks. They look like some kind of rice crackers, but I get the feeling that they've been in his drawer for about three months. I eat a couple and sure enough they are stale as heck. We wish desperately to be able to talk to him. I think he's absolutely elated to have three foreigners in his little room. Much like an Italian grandma, he's pushing his food and drink on us, accompanying them with one of the best grins I've ever seen. Unlike an Italian grandma, his offerings aren't exactly appetizing.

Suddenly, another monk has arrived. He is a good looking young man, and we quickly learn that he speaks excellent English. What great luck! He has just come from what he calls another Chinese brainwashing session. He says that Chinese officials come and gather all of the monks into the main temple building and feed them endless propaganda. That would explain the odd feeling we encountered down there a little while ago. Apparently it's still going on, but at a bit of a risk, he slipped out and came up here. He says that they know the old monk is up here, but they can't be fussed to walk all the way up the steep hill to come and get him. Our friend, it turns out, is the oldest and most senior monk on the complex. The young monk lives far away and is only here as a visitor. Through his wonderful translations we learn that the old monk has his own private water spring and therefore his "holy water" makes "holy tea." The oil in the tea is, indeed, simply a large spoonful of yak butter, and it is apparently not a big deal to decline it, or not drink it. The young monk finds it pretty humorous that we've been forcing it down in trying to be polite. He has also made us feel at ease about not eating the aged snacks and confirmed that they probably are several months old.

Suddenly, conversation is moving along rapidly, and the young monk has his work cut out for him trying to translate everything. Moving along from more superficial topics, we have gone on to politics. Mostly it is the older monk talking, leaving space for translation, and for the first time since I met him, the smile has been replaced by a rather unbecoming bitter expression. It is difficult for the young monk to relay the details, but in its essence

56

the old monk is issuing a lot of negativity towards the Chinese government. Suddenly, he brings the Americans into the picture and suggests that it is foolish of the president to open economic relations with the Chinese. What he enacts for us is that while the right hand of the Chinese diplomat is extended to shake, the left hides a gun behind his back. With the end of this Charade, there is a moment of silence before his grin begins to creep back across his face, and he offers the snacks yet one more time. Suddenly I get one of those feelings. How the heck did I ever get myself to this place? I stare around the old monk's room and at his leathery face. I inhale deeply...

JOKHANG

Today has been set aside for further exploration of the Tibetan Quarter, in particular the Barkhor and the temple area known as the Jokhang. We arrive early hoping to spend several hours wandering throughout. A buzz of good energy meets us immediately at the outer wall where we see many pilgrims walking in a clockwise direction around the circumference. Most are spinning their hand held prayer wheels, and an endless chanting of prayers floats through the air. It is a captivating scene, and one which we are easily swept along with. It is a kind of micro-world that encapsulates your whole being. You become part of the flow, and there is no need or desire to fight it in any way.

We finally come to rest at the outside of a temple where another form of praying is going on. The participants are wholly absorbed in their rituals. It reminds me somewhat of the way Muslim people pray, yet it is unique. In precise form, they begin in a standing position, drop slowly down to their knees, then, with hands on the ground in front, stretch forward until their whole body lies flat with arms outstretched above their heads. The motion is then reversed, and repeated over and over again. It is not rushed, but is very rhythmic. It looks like both a mental meditative exercise and a good physical workout. We watch for a long time, and many of the people praying have continued the motion for the duration of our stay.

It is not long after we enter the sanctity of the Jokhang that we are joined by a group of playful young girls. Though they do come and go, mostly they just follow us as we wander somewhat aimlessly. The tallest of the three is dressed in a long white gown over a red blouse, while the shortest has it reversed with red over white and rosy cheeks to match. The middle one sports a red coat with white designs embroidered on it. We wonder if they are sisters, but trying to talk with them only meets with giggles. Inside the Jokhang, the intriguing buildings open for exploration by adventurous travellers are many. The girls are a great help in finding fun little spots and interesting rooms, and also let us know when there is somewhere we shouldn't enter.

It is on a second floor balcony of one of these buildings that we witness the most interesting form of discussion any of us has ever seen. We are looking down on a group of monks congregated on the concrete floor in front of an orange and gold temple. All are paired off, or clustered in very small groups. One sits and listens with full attention while the other stands and makes his argument in loud tones following each statement with an emphatic SLAP of the hands. This is done with one hand held out horizontally and the second hand slapping down onto it forcefully. "Blah blah blah blah" WHACK! "Blah blah blah blah blah" WHACK! It is quite apparent, and most remarkable, that the listener is fully in tune to only the speaker. It seems as though his mind is not at all preoccupied with formulating some sort of counter point as is so often the case when we humans talk. I have witnessed so many conversations and participated in just as many (often as the guilty party) where the attention of the listener to the speaker is at half capacity or less. Listeners are so often merely waiting for an opportunistic break in order to begin imposing their own opinion without ever having fully internalized what had been directed to them. We, as a species, are continually increasing our available methods of communication and as such the amount of information moving about surges forth at greater and greater speeds, but are we actually communicating any more clearly? We see some of the monks have finished their turns and have switched positions. We hang out with the girls up here for a little longer enjoying the views across the city, past the Potala and to the hills beyond. Having been so caught up in the wonderful sights around Lhasa the past few days, it is the first time in a while my mind begins to wander beyond the city limits to the big open spaces that we will soon be crossing on bicycles, though I am brought back to the present by one of my young friends wanting to be lifted up high enough to peer over the fat wall down to the street below. Things are bustling down there. Market stalls and parked three-wheeled bikes display their wares. Things for sale include monks robes, trinkets, fruit, and basic household goods. The people are a mixture of Chinese and Tibetan, as evidenced by the fashions. Walking on their own, I can see a monk and a Chinese man engaged in a conversation. I wonder what it is they are talking about.

Moving on, it is in a large room on the ground floor of another building that we see the candles. There are row upon row of them numbering in the hundreds. They are wickless, just burning some kind of oil in their small gold coloured holders. If I had to venture a guess, I'd say yak butter or oil. It is an awesome sight to behold so many candles burning at once, flickering in the drafts of people walking by and accompanied in the background of their glow by the chanting of prayers. We find ourselves spellbound. It's a whole different world in here. I wonder, with the rapid rate of change throughout the rest of the city of Lhasa, how much longer this culture will be able to survive and thrive as it does inside these walls.

After coming out of the Jokhang, we spend some more time milling about the Tibetan Quarter. It is easily the best part of the city. We certainly do not want to add too much extra weight to our cycling journey, but we are drawn in to the markets of the Barkhor area once again. The door hangs, or curtains, are something we've all fallen in love with. Though they come in various sizes and colours, the most common are the ones big enough to cover a standard door opening. White sewn with navy blue trim and Tibetan motif, sometimes topped with red and yellow stripes or small squares. The grade of material is also variable, and we search until we find some nice ones that are a little thicker and sewn well with fairly simple designs. Kat and I buy one and Leatherfoot another. We should quit here, but are captivated by one particular girl and her stall full of jewellery and hair braids. She is fairly tall and strong looking, with a full round face and adorned with red and turquoise beaded necklaces and bracelets. Obviously, she is well practiced at her sales game, so we walk away with a fine piece intended for a friend, and Kat buys another small trinket as well. Finally giving up on trying to sell us any more, she points at Kat and says "same face." We agree that the Tibetans are not that dissimilar looking to the Japanese.

On the way back to our hotel, we witness what I might call a cultural reversal of sorts. It is a group of curious looking Tibetan girls. There are four of them and as they stand leaning in from the edge, they are riveted by something going on inside a small building. All of them have thick, luscious, tightly braided hair hanging down to the middle of their backs and wear their heavy jackets with one sleeve on and the other hanging diagonally across their backs dropping down to behind their knees. It takes Kat, Leatherfoot and I quite a while to figure out why a group of girls would stand so long in such an awkward looking position until we get close enough to see that there is a television on inside the house. This must be as much a novelty to them as the Jokhang was to us, but it strikes us as an odd sight nonetheless, as it is obviously not their house where they are watching.

Today's experiences clarify the realization that we live in a world that is in a state of rapid change. Perhaps at a rate unequalled in human history. We joke about how long it will be before we are all the colour of milk chocolate, speaking the same language, and with no more borders around these things we call countries.

BIKES

I am lying on my cot in our hotel room. It's late and I'm somewhat exhausted, but my mind is still buzzing from the hectic day that was, and from thoughts of what tomorrow will bring. Our time here in Lhasa is coming to a close. We will be waking up early, in the dark, and trying to slip out of the city as uneventfully as possible.

I guess I haven't told you about the *SWIRLING RUMOURS* yet. You know, those snippets of conversation from the hotel courtyards and cafes. The bus rides, and the random encounters all around the city. You see, we have discovered that what we are setting out to do is rare. With the political climate being somewhat sensitive here, most of the other foreigners are doing group tours, including a few days here in Lhasa and then shuttled across the plateau in three to five days in a 4X4. It is the strongly encouraged way. So far during our stay here in Lhasa, we have met only one pair of guys who will also be making a bicycle journey like ourselves. One is Australian, and one is Scottish. They however, unlike us, are well prepared. They have been planning their trip already for years. Somehow they managed to bring with them their top quality mountain bikes on which they have been training for months. They left yesterday amongst all of the *SWIRLING RUMOURS*.

There is also one tour group doing a truck assisted cycling journey from here back to Kathmandu. It was a tour available for purchase back in Nepal, and we had at the time briefly considered that option, but the price was way over all of our current budgets. Besides, we have always liked to do things on our own whenever possible, and we didn't like the pace or the restricted freedom. We want to do it our way.

From what we have heard, many of those like us, whose "tour" pretty much ended upon arrival in Lhasa, have opted for the 4X4 package after all. The logistics of travelling here independently are a little daunting. The choices are hitchhiking, which by nature is highly unpredictable, or taking local buses that run infrequently and don't allow for much sightseeing in between the few major towns. It is those few of us that are subject to the *SWIRLING RUMOURS*.

Those stories of army roadblocks and checkpoints, especially on the outskirts of Lhasa. The rumour of the guy who wore a FREE TIBET T-shirt in Lhasa who was escorted out of the country by the military after refusing to change it. And finally, and most pervasively, the Alien Travel Permit rumour. That's the one where one rumourous wind is trying to blow you into the local governmental office to spend yet some more cash on some piece of paper that might give you permission to travel outside of Lhasa on your own. The opposing rumourous breeze is suggesting that your Chinese visa should be all you need, and by avoiding officialdom as much as possible, you at least don't run the risk of having permission denied. It's a tough choice, but we have decided upon the "Don't ask and they can't say no" approach, which carries risks that are completely unknown if we are caught on our own outside of Lhasa. What's the worst that can happen?

It's all so funny, and yet not. Fear is so corruptive to the mind. It's a valuable emotion, but one that needs to be constantly questioned and tempered. If we heeded every warning ever issued to us, life would indeed become boring and sterile. Many cautions have I ignored over the years, and the consequences have rarely been negative. In fact, it is when I have overcome my fears that I have often felt most alive. What I am feeling now is not fear alone. Many mixed emotions are dancing around in my belly. Many questions are floating about in my mind…

Will our bikes hold up?
Will our packs stay on?

Will we hit a checkpoint outside Lhasa?
What will happen if we do?
Do we have enough food packed?
Will we find enough water sources?
Is Kat going to be all right? (She's still a little ill)
Are we going to make it?
And finally... WHAT THE HELL AM I DOING HERE?

Let me tell you about today. Perhaps that will ground me a little again. It was a day during which we had to buy bikes. That was our main focus this morning. We went back to the bike store that we thought had the best options. We poked and prodded, hummed and hawed, haggled and schwaggled and finally selected the vehicles that will hopefully get us across this vast plateau, over the mountain passes and back to Kathmandu.

Kat's bike was easier to decide upon simply because there were more options in her size range. She said they all felt the same, so we just chose one we thought looked the most sturdy. I hope it works well for her. Leatherfoot and I were having difficulty because of our height. Even the largest frames were smaller than ideal, and even on these, the seats and handlebars couldn't be raised high enough. Though we got different bikes from Kat, the frame sizes are all actually the same. All the bikes look fancy new enough, but somehow the steel doesn't look too strong and the bolts and such don't really either. The gears work okay. You can get to most of them, but they certainly aren't precision. The brakes function adequately enough. All they need to stand up to is one thousand kilometers of what is called the Friendship Highway from here to Kathmandu. They should be able to deal with that.

It was the owner of another shop that earlier in our search had suggested replacing the existing seat post with a set of handlebars off an old bike to extend the height. Of course we tried to communicate this to the guy who we bought the bikes from, but either he couldn't understand or simply didn't want to deal with it. So off we went to the shop of the Idea Man. Naturally he looked a little bummed about getting two seat post jobs instead of selling three new bikes, but he helped us anyway. He found the most solid old handlebars in his leftovers pile, cut them to a suitable length and changed them for us. Thanks Idea Man!

Our next stop was the bike parts shop. You would think they'd be one and the same, but they're not. The bike parts shops were in greater supply than the bike shops and were generally a small narrow space stuffed to the hilt with an amazing array of bike parts. We bought one extra chain, a couple of brake/gear cables, a patch kit, a few spare tubes, a pump, a couple of simple tools and three HEAVY DUTY racks.

Many hours were spent this evening fiddling with the bikes and packing. Fenders and kickstands were removed, and wimpy racks replaced with the more solid ones. All other bolts were tightened more firmly. Being inexperienced at cycle touring, something we never even considered was panniers. We figured it would be easy enough to strap our packs to the racks, but discovered packs are made for backs, not racks. Thus, we've been manipulating them into some pretty contorted sacks. The bags seem to be a little more cooperative with their stiff supports removed, but of course each of them is a different size and design and so a unique puzzle on how to best secure it. Somehow I think it's going to take us a while to figure it out, but we'll get there.

It should prove to be a rather interesting journey. Leatherfoot, though fit, athletic and certainly competent on a bike, has never undertaken a cycling tour of this magnitude. Kat is also an exceptional athlete, but has little experience on a bike beyond a few kilometers here and there in town or city. I have once before been on a long bicycle tour in New Zealand, but that was many years ago and in a much easier environment. The three of us together did rent bicycles for one day in Kathmandu and had a ride around the valley. That was our warm up training! Are we ready? As ready as we're going to be.

It's been a l o n g d a y. I haven't even told you about the meat people - big chunks of flesh on wooden tables out in the open with flies everywhere, or the newest toilet story - pay 2 Yuan and there is poop everywhere, but I must go to sleep now. I'm so beat, yet nervous and excited too. In a few hours, we'll be riding bikes across Tibet! We'll be out into the open country, the great plateau. Into the smaller villages and even getting away from humanity all together, into the waiting arms... of Mother Nature.

Good Night

Dogi's Journal Of Tibet

Part II
The Cycling Journey

THE CYCLING JOURNEY
BEGINS

IT'S EARLY. VERY, VERY EARLY, AND IT'S CHILLY. LEATHERFOOT flicks on a light and we catch each others eyes with a knowing glance. It's time to get up. We are eager, but nervous. Kat lets out a moan and a groan, followed by a few coughs. She's not so ready at this time of morning. Early starts to adventures never suit her, but she understands the value in it and gets up and shuffles out the door and down the veranda to take care of morning business.

Leatherfoot and I finish strapping down our packs. Though we practiced once last night, it still took us a long time. Bungee cords were a consideration, but we figured they probably wouldn't be solid enough, so we are using webbing which we already had on hand. Webbing is a silky flat kind of rope which is extremely strong and durable. We have one long piece per pack and begin at a fixed point winding it this way and that trying to solidify the pack as best as possible. When we finally finish, they feel solid enough, but access to anything in them will require a lot of effort. It's not ideal. Something that is surely fundamental to those who do long bike journeys, but we didn't give it due consideration. Now we'll just have to deal with what we have, and work on improving the process.

We push our loaded bikes quietly down the veranda and Leatherfoot and I carry them carefully down the flight of stairs one at a time. Everyone else in the hotel must be asleep, as it is totally quiet. The stars are still visible from the comfortable confines of the hotel courtyard. We take a few final deep breaths trying to calm our nerves and approach the big gate whose doors are closed. For a brief moment, we realize we might actually be locked in, but the door does creak open and we roll out onto the dark street and into the unknown.

"Are we all ready to leave this world of RUMOURS behind?"

"Yea, let's go. Let's get on with it!"

"Mmmm"

The early start is predominantly in the hope that we can avoid any hassles getting beyond the outskirts of Lhasa. It is an eerie, yet exciting feeling cycling through such a quiet, dark, foreign city. The air is chill and still, and we start out at a very easy pace, mostly because we can barely see the road in front of us. There is nobody on the streets at this hour. Only some sketchy looking dogs, but they fortunately don't appear overly interested in our procession. Leatherfoot and I ride in front together. We both sort of think we know the way, but not exactly. We have only the map from our guidebook and the memory of how we came into the city from the airport a week ago, but enough landmarks show themselves that we are able to figure it out. Kat follows silently. The tension rises as we near the outskirts of the city. I'm not sure who it is that I begin praying to, but somehow I always feel that if you ask the greater surroundings nicely enough, even only in your own head, then your chances get better. Please no roadblock. Please no checkpoint. Come on let us keep on cycling. Nothing, nothing, please nothing.

Nothing! Not a thing. We have clear cycling right on out of the city. The apprehension lasts for a while beyond the city limits, but slowly fades along with the darkness. We are cruising at a comfortable pace now on a long, straight, paved road. The first shafts of sunlight splinter around the distant peaks and our surroundings ease into a soft morning glow.

Sunrise. This time of day always feels special to me no matter where I am. Perhaps it's because I see it so rarely, but I think it's more than that. It's the energy, the calmest, least turbulent energy of the day. It's the promise of light and warmth and opportunity. This morning's sunrise is exceptionally beautiful to me. Finally we are on our bikes. We are on the road riding across Tibet! The seed planted long ago from a few paragraphs in a book, developed its roots and now pokes its head through the surface of the ground.

We begin to see other signs of life. The first locals are on their way into the fields. At a welcoming spot along the road, we take a short break and bask in the radiant warmth of the early morning sun.

"I can't believe it! We're here. We're doing it. What do you say Dogi?"

"Ya! I'm stoked. That went a lot more smoothly than I thought it might. I'm just so glad we didn't get stopped coming out of the city. I lost a little sleep over that thought last night. How's it going with you Kat?"

"Good. My head still hurts, but not so bad. This is beautiful outside city ne!"

We're cycling south, which means the sun is warming the left side of our faces. It's distinct. The left side of me is getting hot, while the right side is staying cool. Breathing at the altitude is noticeably difficult, but we are not pushing the pace. Leatherfoot and I either take turns riding in front or often ride next to one another given the lack of traffic. Kat is content to ride behind. Our first significant rest stop comes at a small lake and a Giant Buddha. It is a place where we also stopped for a break on the way from the airport to Lhasa way back when. The lake itself is quite solitary. We have seen no other bodies of water today, and we take the time to splash it on our faces. It is surprisingly cold and makes a sharp contrast to the hot sun. The Giant Buddha is carved into the base of a high cliff and sits essentially on the water's edge on the opposite side of the small lake. Painted brightly in orange, gold, and blue, it makes a magnificent reflection on the still water. Accompanying the Buddha to his right are three other figures etched into the rock and also brightly painted. Though we have passed some trees and a bit of green in some fields, the only other colours to be found in this area are brown and blue. It's as if the whole landscape has been pencilled in with every shade of brown imaginable, and the sky's blue fills the whole spectrum of the colour from light and creamy to rich and deep. As I look again, I see that there is a cairn atop the cliff with sticks jutting out in multi directions making it look like

71

a bush. The "leaves" on the "bush" are Tibetan prayer flags, but they are so tattered and worn that they more resemble the leaves of late autumn than early.

Over the next couple of hours of riding, we find it good, in fact necessary, to get off the bikes and stretch once in a while. Other than the one half day ride in Kathmandu, it is not a motion or muscle set that any of us have used much. It is during one of these stretch breaks that we play a game of Tundra Frisbee. There are no fences or anything here blocking off "property." Nothing to suggest that we may not be allowed to wander freely over the land at the sides of the road. Our playing area as such is plenty wide open, but on a raw, sandy dirt surface strewn with rocks, small boulders, and a few gnarled plants. Though it is a nice change on the set of muscles we have been taxing, and it provides a good stretch, we find that we cannot play for very long. None of us has the extra energy to chase too many errant throws, particularly while trying to dodge the boulders. Even the shortest of sprints sets our lungs ablaze begging for more oxygen out of this thin air.

We pedal onwards. A slight wind has come up, but it is from the side and at worst throws us into the odd wobble. We keep the pace moderate enough to smile as we ride, while breathing in the landscape. Suddenly, I see a slope off to our right that appears to be pure sand. To get to it we will need to ride a few hundred meters on a narrow, bumpy gravel road.

"Shall we go and check out that sand slope?"

"What do you have in mind Dogi?"

"Sand Skreeing of course!"

"Sand Skreeing?"

"You know what scree is right? The loose gravelly run out on mountain slopes!?! Well check that out. That, my friend, is what you call super deluxe scree! We hike up it, and since we don't have skis, we simply skree it down on our feet!"

I have learned already through the short time I've spent with Leatherfoot that he is always up for an extracurricular adventure, a foray into Randomland. After all, these sorts of opportunities don't come along every day. It is easily the longest, finest, most accessible scree slope I have ever come across. He is not difficult to convince.

Kat, on the other hand, is not overly enthused about the idea. Her energy is already waning somewhat, and she doesn't even like the prospect of riding across the pitted gravel road.

"Okay, I ride there with you, but I no climbing. You guys go ahead, and I catch you up. Leave camera and I take some pictures."

The slope is around thirty degrees and several hundred meters long and plenty wide. The sun at this point is high in the sky and is definitely making its presence felt. We take off our boots and socks and begin to skirt up the edge where the sand is a little firmer, and thus not so much vertical is lost with each footstep. As we look back down to see how Kat is doing, we see that we are joined at the scene by a couple of curious Tibetans. The older man is hanging out with Kat, and the younger one has already taken off his footgear and started climbing straight up the middle of the soft sand. It's most certainly a less efficient place to ascend, but he is still moving at about twice our pace. Imagine the strong lungs these people must develop living at this altitude for their whole lives.

The illusion of distance here is staggering. I thought we'd be able to climb to the top, but once we hit some big boulders about half way up, our legs and lungs alike voice their opinion that it is far enough. Though the young Tibetan man started climbing several minutes after us, he arrives at our rest spot about thirty seconds later. Leatherfoot and I are still trying to catch our breath, while he recovers in no time. We exchange our greetings in Tibetan while we all have a good rest and enjoy the view. Kat is a tiny spec way down there.

Having recovered sufficiently, I try to gain a touch more vertical as I cross out into the middle of the slope. Once there, I squat for a while longer staring at the long stretch of pure sand below me before standing... leaning forward... and...

Momentum is instantaneous... it is all I can do to keep my legs moving fast enough under me. I am beyond even trying to make a turn as this would surely induce an instant wipe out... the slope has no gradual finish, or where it does, there is rock and scrub brush and that is approaching quickly... shit, I guess my only option for slowing down at this point IS a............. **W I P E O U T ! ! !**

73

A simple butt plant is an option, but whether momentum or sheer folly, I decide to go for the full layout front flip. AMAZING! And the landing in the soft sand is so forgiving. I still have so much built up speed after the first flip that it leads straight into a second and a third before a chest slide finish! I come out of it with sand in most of my body crevasses, including my mouth, but once I spit enough of that out, I begin cahooting like a big kid!

"YAHOOO HOOO HOOO!!!"

Leatherfoot comes next followed closely by our young Tibetan friend. Wisely, they both opt for the slightly more controlled big turn decent and finish with equally big grins of elation. Kat and the older Tibetan man give us all a good cheer. Then, with that slightly devilish gleam in her eye, Kat tries to talk us into a second run. I think she just wants a longer rest, but it is time for us to keep going. The Tibetans have already said a casual "Ka-lee-shu" and wandered off.

O O O

The day is moving along and we are well into the afternoon. That little gravel road let us know that our packs are not as well secured as they should be, and we have begun to have some minor issues with our gears. Though our energy has been good, it was an early start and it is our first day out. Add in the extracurricular Randomland Sand Skreeing adventure, and we are getting notice-ably tired. It is time to start looking for a suitable campsite, though we are not really sure what suitable means. This is Tibet. There are no organized campgrounds. What we have is mostly big flat spaces on either side of the road which inevitably end at a distant hill. The flat space is either raw land strewn with rocks and boulders, or it is being used for farms. Most of the farm land looks to be in the plowing and sowing stage. The fact that there are no fences around any of the land really intrigues me. Naturally we don't want to plop ourselves down in the middle of anybody's farm fields, and ideally we'd like to find someplace sheltered both from the wind and from the locals, who, from what we have experienced today, are quite curious about us. Suddenly, we come across a few groves of trees on either side of the road and we stop to survey the situa-

74

tion. To the right of the road we can see some houses further in the distance and there are definitely some farm fields. To the left looks as though there might be less habitation and possibly a small creek. Still on my bike, I head off the road to the left to check it out.

"CRAP!"

"What happened Dogi?"

"I got a flat tire. Oh no, double crap. Now I have two flat tires. The ground in here is full of thorn bushes, so don't come in! Maybe check out the other side, but be extra careful. I suggest walking in without your bike at first."

I push my bike back to where Kat is waiting while Leatherfoot searches the right side of the road. He comes back suggesting that he has found a decent spot for the tent amongst some of the small trees, but that there are definitely thorn bushes around. The two of them walk their bikes ever so carefully through the maze. These flat tires are a bit hard to take after an otherwise successful day, but I'll know to be more careful next time. Plants obviously have a hard enough time surviving in this environment. I can't blame them for defending themselves from being stepped on or ridden over.

"So who has the bike repair stuff?"

"I do Dogi. Why don't I start dealing with it while you guys set up the tent and then maybe you can start on some dinner."

"Good deal Leatherfoot. Hey Kat, I didn't know we brought a handyman along on the trip. That's a bonus!"

We unwind the snake of webbing holding our packs in place, and begin to separate the gear and pull out the tent. We are all tired, but I can see now that Kat is exhausted. It has been a long day. She says she has been battling this on-again-off-again head-ache for much of it, and riding with her head up was less painful than with it down. She noticed it most on that small section of dirt road that was much bumpier, and when the wind had its few little temper tantrums. Feeling as though she needs just a little rest and a hug, she walks up behind me and drapes her arms over my shoulders, resting her head in the middle of my shoulder blades. It is a lovely feeling, and I smile and take her hands in mine. With so much going on to fill my own senses, I really hadn't been aware how much a day like today pushed Kat's limits. For perhaps the first time all day, I let go of all that is around me, all that is in my mind. I close my eyes... relax... and...

"OUCH! AHH, that friggin hurt!... KAT?... K A T!"

"Dogi, what happened?"

"She fainted! Instant dead weight. I was totally relaxed and had no idea it was coming, and she just fell on top of me and I crumpled and bashed my knee into this rock! KAT, can your hear me? Damn, she's totally out cold! Grab some water Leatherfoot!"

" Eee, doko iru no?"

"Whew, she's awake again, but she's disoriented. She has an eerie glazed look in her eyes, and she's talking Japanese. Kat, it's me Dogi. Dai jou bu desu ka? Are you okay?"

"Mmm. I... think maybe okay. Where we are?"

"With Leatherfoot. In Tibet, on our bike trip."

We get Kat sitting up and leaning against a tree. Her brain slowly blows the fog away and we feed her some water and a small snack. That was scary. Fainting is never a good thing, but out here, there is no emergency number to call, there are no close by hospitals, we're on our on. This episode hammers that realization home.

"Are you with us again, Kat? Where were you by the way when you first woke up?"

"In Japan with my family, I think. It was in my old house where I grew up. I was a child. That was weird."

Of course, we tell Kat to rest while Leatherfoot continues bike repairs and I finish setting up the tent. My knee is quite sore, but I'm pretty sure it's only a bruise and it will go away. Hopefully by tomorrow morning. When I'm done with the tent, I check on Kat. She still looks a little dazed, but says she's all right. She gets up to put on some warmer clothes as I begin to prepare dinner.

It's been a long and undulatory day. There were so many high-lights, like the sunrise and Sand Skreeing, but we agree that the day was not without its irritations. Beyond the obvious flat tires, the biggest annoyance was the kids. That sounds extremely odd, I know. We generally all love kids, but these little rascals were throwing stones at us! This wasn't just one brave group one time either. It happened on several occasions and we could never quite tell where it came from. Just the giggles and then the scattering. I must say we never did actually get hit, but whether this was by purpose or luck I'm really not sure. That said, we did enjoy some good interaction with some kids and many of the adult locals today. The further outside Lhasa we got, the more the population became Tibetan and less Chinese. They are curious people. It is quite obvious that we are still very foreign to them, even this close to Lhasa, and so hugely entertaining. Not only our skin colour and hair and features, but the new looking bikes and racks and packs and our clothes too. They were quite at ease to go ahead and touch and check out all of our stuff.

"One woman actually grabbed my pack as I was riding by, but I don't think she wanted to take it, just feel it."

"Yea, I know who you mean Dogi, she did it to me too."

"I see that happen to you Leatherfoot, but she didn't touch me. She just look at me funny. I think many people confused about me. Did you guys see look on faces of tourists that drive by us in a bus?"

"No Kat, I didn't notice."

"Me either, what happened?"

"You guys are ahead me, and they drive by slow. They look so confused on their face. Like they think 'What heck are these white guys doing on their own out here on bikes?' Then they see me and I can see they are talking and have understand look on their face. They must think I am Tibetan or Chinese and sort of tour guide for you guys!"

"That sounds good, Kat. You can be our tour guide for the rest of the trip!"

I feel as though we've done okay with our first campsite in the end. Our tent and some of our clothes really stick out here in their synthetic brightness, but so far we have had no visitors. I just hope we're in an acceptable place. Without any fences around the farms, it's kind of hard to tell what belongs to who. Or does anything belong to anybody out here? What does that mean? Land belonging to humans. We're an interesting species us humans in the way we divvy things up. Naming chunks of land and defending them by fence, wall, law, or might. Here and there we agree for a while on who can use what and how, but there is always someone who wants more. An individual, a group of individuals that rally the cry of a country's name, or a cultural revolution. I suppose many creatures define their territories in various ways and are at a constant struggle to maintain and increase their share, playing this game of life that is not always fair. It seems difficult to freely share our share. It does work towards some sort of an equilibrium though doesn't it? So, are we camped on Tibetan farm land? Are we camped on Chinese government land? Or are we simply camped on land. Dirt, a few hearty grasses, and some thorn bushes. Maybe it doesn't belong to anyone. Any person. Any human being. Wait. Maybe it belongs to none other than Mother Nature, and she says we can put up our pretty little pink and green tent and sleep here for the night if we like. Free. She's not going to impose her ownership and charge us anything. Oh, maybe she already did in the form of those two flat tires.

Nice. I feel good. It is later in the evening, we've cleaned up from dinner, Leatherfoot has patched both of my tires, and sleep is calling. I'm happy that we've not been noticed and have had some peace here for the evening. Our first evening of camping after our first day riding bicycles across Tibet. It's been fun.

PERSERVERENCE

I'M NOT SURE WHETHER IT'S THE SUN FILTERING THROUGH THIS little grove of trees or the giggles of school children that has awakened us. No, wait. It must be the small sticks and stones that are being thrown at our tent, followed up by the giggles. It seems as though we are under siege, but we must get up. Tibet is waiting. Today we are to climb our first mountain pass. Where we are camped, the altitude is about 3700 meters (12,200 feet). The crest of Khamba La is between 4700 (15,500 feet) and 4800 meters (15,800 feet). That's a lot of up!

Khamba La! It sounds slightly daunting, as does climbing out of the tent under the current barrage. Yet, as we unfold ourselves from the tent door and stand up, all but the bravest of older boys back off with eyes bulging out of their heads. You can tell who the mischievous ones are, but the light assault abates when they see us, as we are much bigger than them. It's quite a funny scene. There are about twenty or more children of various ages completely surrounding us. The girls and smaller boys take to hiding behind the bigger ones. After our smiles, greetings, and measured stares at the "troublemakers," we begin to pack and sort out our gear. Their presence, though amusing, is making our preparations quite challenging. They are curious and unabashed. The "troublemakers" are on a mission to touch as much of our stuff as they can. They have gone right into our tent, fiddled with our sleeping bags, stove, bikes, everything. In one sense I feel like saying "GET THE HECK AWAY FROM OUR STUFF," but somehow I don't feel too right about this. At first we were worried that they were trying to steal some of our things, but now it is obvious that they are simply intrigued. All of our belongings are new and fascinating to their senses, just as their world is to ours. I'm not sure I'd simply walk into one of their houses and check it out, but as I write this, I realize I have already done so at the old monk's place at Sera Temple, and he welcomed me with VERY open arms! Though I am a little annoyed by some of their behavior, there is a definite innocence about them. They are just kids.

Thankfully, they finally leave for school. In the end we see only the humour, but it was just a little unnerving to wake up to on our first morning after camping. So who's land was this again? I hope we will be able to find more solitary camping locations in the future. I'm sure the further we get outside Lhasa, the less people there will be. With all the morning fuss, getting through breakfast and packing was a challenge, and now we are attempting to get our backpacks strapped to our bike racks. It is once again proving to be a far greater pain in the rump than anticipated. You wouldn't think it would be so difficult, but somehow it's hard to get them to sit right and tight. Kat holds each bike while Leatherfoot and I work at it. She seems okay this morning, though her headache continues to linger, which is a bit of a concern. The knee that I whacked on that rock yesterday felt a bit stiff and achy when I first woke up, but it has warmed up and the pain has faded amply enough. We are both ready to go, and Leatherfoot is solid. He's looking keen and energetic and is lifting all of our spirits. Let's ride!

We push our loaded bikes as far as the road, being extra careful to avoid any thorny plants. Back to pedalling, our butts are a little sore on the saddle, and our bodies feel somewhat stiff at first, but it's good to be riding again. The temperature is pleasant as the sun has already been up for a couple of hours. There is a third, and even a fourth, colour around us this morning. The farm fields in this area already have a carpet of young green plants growing, which we believe to be barley, and a few fluffy white clouds float gently about the vivid blue sky.

Just as we are craving our first break, we arrive at a crossroads. There is a bridge over a large river in front of us and, before the bridge, the continuation of the main highway. To the right then must be the road that goes westward along the direct route to the city of Shigatse (Xigaze). The direction we want to take, however, is southward, over the mountain pass Khamba La, and down into another valley and a big lake called Yamzho Yumco (Yamdrok-tso). Just to note, information such as altitudes and place names here are slightly variable, and the map which we are using and the guidebook and the signage are not always in agreement. Khamba La or Kamba La is listed at closer to 4700 meters (15,500 feet) on our map and nearly 4800 meters (15,800 feet) in the guidebook. Particularly regarding the place names, it's the mix of languages that makes it all a bit of a challenge. Mandarin Chinese translations of Tibetan, English translations of Mandarin and Tibetan, the fact that all three use different written scripts, function differently grammatically, and the fact that Mandarin is highly tonal, Tibetan mildly tonal, and English non-tonal, it all gets a little discombobulated. I'm not really giving preference to any one source or one way.

So we have crossed the bridge and, facing southwards, we are also facing a cliff. The road here goes left and right, and each way seems equally likely to be our desired direction. There is no signage, and there are no locals about that we could attempt to ask. Our guidebook and map do not show this kind of detail either, so we randomly select going to the right and hope for the best. Riding up a slight incline, we round the first bend and suddenly, we run into another bunch of school children. For the briefest of moments we hesitate, wondering whether we might find ourselves under siege once again, but fortunately there are no incoming rocks or sticks. In fact, they are absolutely delighted to see the likes of us. There is a big chorus of cheers accompanied by pointing and laughing. We stop and hang out and giggle and play with them for a while. We try to ask some of the older ones if we are going the right way, but our inquiries are met with looks of confusion. It had been our intent to study more Tibetan since arriving here, but we have yet to get far beyond basic greetings and pleasantries. We say goodbye, and for the time being continue to ride in the same direction.

We pedal for another five or ten minutes, but don't seem to be getting anywhere positive. The condition of this road is getting worse and shows no inklings of leading towards any mountain passes. We decide to turn around, head back past the bridge, around a bend, and there find ourselves in the midst of a small village. I guess random selection let us down this time. The town is dry, dusty and very quiet, but we spot a place that serves food. We're not quite ready for lunch yet, but this will probably be the last place we can get food for a while and decide it's a good idea to conserve our packaged food if possible. A final good meal before climbing a mountain pass can't be a bad decision.

It's a Tibetan restaurant, which means our choices are thugpa and momos. We order a bowl of the noodle soup each and a plate of the momos to share. Mmmm. It's not greasy like Western fast food, but oily. Scrumptious? Definitely not. Tasty? No, but edible and our bellies are full. Inquiring once again, we follow the pseudo directions of the restaurant owner through the town and out the other end. It is quite obvious now. Before us lies the beginning of the climb to Khamba La! We can see a few short steep switchbacks, and then the road disappears around a corner. Way on a distant hill I think I can see a lighter brown stripe, which may well be the continuation of the road. Deep breaths, here we go.

Plop bouncebadaboomboom uff badaboombounceboomba-boom. We have hit gravel road now. This was unexpected. Our fancy map has it labelled as "highway," which I assumed would mean paved. Did the guidebook say anything about this? Probably. Oh well, perhaps it's just this mountain pass section. I hope so. This cycling thing is hard enough at this altitude with the weight of our gear. Now add in the uphill and the gravel road and…

"Oh ohhhh."

"Ohh ohhh, we have an 'oh ohh'. What kind of an 'oh ohhh' Leatherfoot?"

"A Flat Tire ish kind of an 'oh ohh'."

" O! That stinks. Three flats in one and a half days. Not bad, not bad."

We're only a hundred meters into our ascent. A flat tire is not a good start to climbing a pass that will probably take us the rest of the day. We stop to deal with it and within minutes have attracted a crowd of onlookers. Kids are yelling to more kids that there is something vastly entertaining going on, and they are running in from all directions. The crowd thickens and presses further and further in on Leatherfoot and his bike. Kat and I literally have to pull them away and box them out just to give him enough room to get his tire off.

"Do you think you can do something to keep these kids away?"

"We're trying Leatherfoot. We're trying. Hey Kat, do you know where the Frisbee is? Did we keep it handy?"

FRISBEE! Our little plastic friend is such a great entertainer! It is an item I have used many times over the years to play with people. Such a small simple toy that does such a wonderful job of bridging a cultural gap. Everyone likes to have fun, and if not well, almost everyone can throw the plastic disc. In this case, it's not just about fun, but distraction. Like a mother with a crying baby, we need to find something new for these kids to focus their attention on. Kat and I begin taking turns throwing the disc as far as we can and the entire group of kids gives chase. It's like dogs in a park with a tennis ball, with giggles instead of barks. No matter how many times we throw it, they keep on coming back salivating for more. What a great game! Every last child gets involved, and it takes on a festival like quality. Even Leatherfoot's minor irritation has abated, and I can see him grinning at the scene.

There is one local, however, who is not participating in the game. It is an older man who has taken a keen interest in what Leatherfoot is doing. He, like his surroundings, is various shades of brown. His tattered hat, his leathery face, his shirt, tunic, shoes, everything except his earrings. They are several beautiful shades of blue. Whether it is what they wear, or what they do artistically, it is the people here that add most of the colour to the landscape. I would describe him as handsome, though he is tragically serious looking. He has not even batted an eyelash at the Frisbee chaos going on around him, so engrossed is he in Leatherfoot and the process of patching his tire tube. With the disc back in my hands once more, I throw it as far as I can and watch the throng chase wildly after it before giving Leatherfoot a hand putting his wheel back on and reefing his pack down once again.

"KA-LEE-SHU! BYE BYE!"

Do these kids not go to school? Is school a morning thing only? Or were we interesting and educational enough for them to take an impromptu field trip? Though a few do follow us for a short distance, the mass of kids disperses, and the stragglers drop away soon enough. We are back up on the bikes again and moving. Slowly. Very v e r y s l o w l y. We are in first gear and each pedal stroke is a grunt. The hill is already too steep for Kat to ride. She is off her bike, bent over at the waist, and pushing. I am heating up fast in this sun, and Leatherfoot? He suddenly gets **another** flat tire!

"Are you serious? The same tire or the other one?"

"Same one. Maybe I should have let the patch dry longer, or maybe there was more than the one hole or..."

"Maybe you're just unlucky! Let's throw a whole new tube in, but save the old one and patch it later if it comes to that."

This is not the kind of start one would hope for. There was some humour in the first one, but not this time. Not irritation yet, but no humour. Fortunately, we are far enough up the hill already that the kids won't bother to climb, which means we can focus on the task of repairing his tire AGAIN. At this point Kat decides that she will push onwards, knowing she doesn't have enough power to ride up this incline on gravel. We agree it's a good idea, and off she goes, head down, pushing her bike. Leatherfoot and I operate together, and fairly quickly this time. It's his fourth tube repair in the last twenty hours. He's experienced. Though we don't love the idea of digging into our supply so soon, we do opt for a new tube rather than a patch. The day is moving along and we've made little headway up this pass which we are hoping to get up and over today. If there was any notion of a schedule, we're well behind it already.

Riding again, Leatherfoot and I are working hard to catch up to Kat, who we can no longer see ahead. The village has fully disappeared behind us, and the switchbacks have given way to a longer stretch of winding up the side of a bank. The road has not been cut at a gradual rate, and with the heavy tail ends of our bikes, we can barely ride. Our thighs are at full capacity, and air is taking the direct route in and out through the mouth only. I'm wondering...

"AHHHH SHH UGAR!"

"WHAT NOW? And by the way, watch that vulgar language, there are kids about."

"I don't know what it is yet Dogi, but I can't ride."

"Whadaya mean you can't ride?"

"It's feels like the chain fell off, but it didn't. I heard something go CRUNCH."

After yesterday's two flats, I figured I was cursed with the lemon vehicle, but now I'm feeling like it might just be Leatherfoot. Two flats for him in a ten minute span, and now it seems as though he has stripped the bearings in his back wheel. Something like that anyway. Maybe there is a more technically correct way of saying it, but basically what this means is that he can pedal all he wants, but he isn't going to move anywhere. I've never seen this happen to a bike before. Flat tires, bent rims, broken cables, chains that fall off or break, but not this. It seems that the combination of the load and his power were just too much for the obviously cheap mechanism. We both stare at it for a while, fiddle, and scratch our heads, but there is nothing we can do. It looks as though we are going to need a whole new back tire rim.

So here we are. It's not much past the middle of our second day, and we are four flat tires and a broken bike into our cycling trip standing on a dusty gravel road at 4000 meters (13,200 feet) above sea level at the base of a mountain pass with no one else around, and the third member of our group is by now way out ahead. It's not funny, but it is laughable! Lhasa now represents the closest option to get a new wheel, but it is a day and a half away. If Leatherfoot goes back on his own, that would split the group up awkwardly for several days. Yet catching up to Kat, and then all turning back and adding three days of cycling to the trip doesn't sound like a pleasant option. If we forge on, we're looking at the town of Gyangze as the next possible place to get a new rim, though there is a small town called Nagarze along the far end of the lake Yamzho Yumco which might have one, but that is unlikely. Gyangze is at least three days riding and two mountain passes away on a functional bike, and we're not even sure that we'll get a suitable replacement part there. Truthfully, I think we both feel that going back to Lhasa is the most sensible thing to do, but the fact that Kat is by now well ahead of us really skews the thinking, and the more we think, the further out in front she'll be. We have decided to go forward. Maybe we can get over the pass and down the other side and then spend some time and actually fix the thing. We'll sort something out. We'll deal with it.

With Leatherfoot now reduced to pushing his bike, I decide to pedal long and hard until I finally catch up to Kat. She has a smile on her face when I find her and has her arms around three of the filthiest, but cutest kids I've ever seen. She says she feels good and is having fun. Imagine that. What these children are doing here is a bit of a mystery. There is one crooked shack somewhat off the road, but that's about it. There are no adults in sight and no animals either, but maybe they are around. Perhaps they are nomads. There are still humans that live a nomadic life here.

"I am surprised you take so long to catch me up."

"Leatherfoot broke his bike! Something in his back wheel went crunch and we can't really figure out how to fix it. It's not good, but maybe we'll be able to sort it out later. I like your new friends. Where did they come from?"

"I don't know. I thought I should wait for you guys, and then the girl just kind of showed up. Then the boys came to her. They look curious but maybe a bit afraid, but then they come to me. Now we just have fun. We make silly faces and play tickling."

We continue to chat and play with the kids while we wait for Leatherfoot to catch up. The two boys are perhaps three and four, and the girl maybe seven or eight. Their skin colour, at least on their faces which are the only exposed parts sticking out from under their thick clothing, is a darker brown than the dirt surrounding them, but lightened a few shades by it. Their pants, shirts, vests, hats, everything exposed to this vastness of dirt is tinted a few degrees toward it. Even Kat has a thin layer on her already.

Though Leatherfoot still hasn't caught up, I leave Kat to cycle up ahead for a bit. The road snakes endlessly up this barren valley. Here and there it disappears and comes back out again. Where is the top? Though I would like to keep riding as I have a good rhythm going and my energy is good, I know I should stop and wait for the other two. I lean my bike against a rock and do some stretching. Taking a few sips from my water bottle, I can taste the grit of dirt washing down my throat with the liquid, and as my breath calms down, I realize it is the only sound I can hear. Now there is nothing around me but undulating brown hills. I see no people, no villages, no animals, not even a bird in the sky. What I can see, at certain angles, is that shimmering of reflected heat energy off the surface of the rock and dirt. I look around for a shady spot, but there aren't any. I would like to drink more water, but am beginning to wonder about our water situation. I don't think we'll get a chance to refill until the lake on the other side.

Kat comes into my view, though she doesn't notice me with her head down pushing. Leatherfoot follows soon after, and even he is in a surprisingly good mood considering all of his bike woes. Kat doesn't rest long, preferring to plod along slowly and steadily. After Leatherfoot has had a brief rest, we push on together. Pushing is a literal thing even for me at this point. The road has gotten steep enough again along most stretches that I no longer have the power to ride it. Besides, I don't want to do what Leatherfoot did to his bike. To break the monotony and use slightly different muscles, I switch sides once in a while. Leatherfoot has found a good rhythm pushing from behind his seat while managing to coax his handlebars to stay going straight.

"So Leatherfoot, are you glad you came to Tibet with us?"

"You know Dogi, this whole trip is shaping up to be one of your Randomland adventures!"

After a time, we see that our pace is now a little too quick for Kat, so we each take a bit of her weight to balance out the situation, and we push on… and on… until eventually, the light begins to wane. It's beautiful. The shadows, the silhouetted ridge lines, the birth of the orange glow, but we can't see the top. All we can see now are switchbacks.

> *Switchbacks above and switchbacks below*
> *With no idea how much further they go*
> *How many more until the end*
> *Just what is around that last bend*

Okay, now it's getting a little unnerving. The sunset colours, which have been dazzling, are slowly giving way to darkness. That reflected heat, so omnipresent in the middle of the day, has all but disappeared skyward. I can feel the temperature dropping by the minute. We assumed we would be up and over this pass today, but as it is, we're still in the midst of this maze of switchbacks. We haven't seen any signs of life since the kids, and that was hours ago. No people, no animals, no vehicles, there aren't even any plants to speak of up this high. What should we do? I suppose we could just bundle up a little more and keep pushing on into the night. It's not like we can make a wrong turn. This road is it.

"There it goes. The last hint of purple. The sunset colours have faded out and now it's pretty much black."

" "

"The silence is sweet isn't it Leatherfoot. Pure. I love that."

"Wait Dogi, the breeze is whispering something."

"Yea, it's saying…"

"I'm get cold. I must start move again, but I don't know I can push my bike anymore."

"My legs are pretty spent too Kat. I think we should forget about the top and go at it again tomorrow. I doubt it's too much further, but I don't fancy sleeping right on the road. I don't remember many options in the last little while though and I don't want to lose ground. Can we all try to push a little further and look for something?"

"Sure."

"I try."

It's hard to start walking again. The legs complain vehemently for the first few steps, but it does shake the chill that had set in. Finally, we see a little hole dug into the side of the road. It's shaped like a ditch, and other than the road itself, it's the only reasonably flat surface we've seen in ages. We figure we must be at 4400 meters (14,500 feet), but it's hard to say for sure. What we are very sure about, is that the air is getting extremely thin up here and we are getting increasingly tired and cold. This ditch at the side of the road will be our bed for the night!

Everything comes out of our packs. We layer the ground with the tent and fly and the two thick cotton Tibetan door hangs that we bought in Lhasa. Every layer of clothing that we have along goes on. The extra socks, scarves, hats, rain gear, all of it. We settle into our sleeping bags, lie back, take as deep a breath as we can, and laugh about our long and crazy day. We're physically exhausted, but our spirits are high. We are warm enough for now and the sky full of stars is unbelievable!

OVER THE HUMP

WELL, WHAT A CRAZY PLACE TO SPEND A NIGHT! A COUPLE OF trucks passed us in the last hour or two of trying to sleep, which was a little shocking, particularly the first one. A distant rumble turned into a ground shaking vibration, followed by the headlights. I wonder why they drove up and over this pass at night? Perhaps driving during the middle of the day heats up the engines too much. Thank goodness we did find a place off the side of the road to sleep. Even still, it was rather unsettling. As it is now, we wake up to nothing. Nothing besides us, thin air, and cold hard dirt. Crawling out of the sleeping bag is a challenge. We're stiff from the restless sleep on uneven ground and yesterday's exertion. Also it's still cold, but the only way to remedy that is to get up and get moving. Once we do so, we begin to feel better. Breakfast is much the same as dinner last night. We put some peanut butter onto crackers and eat a little dried fruit. We don't bother firing up the stove. The increased altitude would make water even more difficult to boil, and besides, we don't have an abundance of water at the moment. It's not at a worrisome level yet, but we do need to be conscious of the situation. As we finish breakfast, and begin putting our gear away, the whole scene around us becomes bathed in the morning light. We have the full view back down the valley we have been climbing, and can see well out onto the plains below. The road we have climbed looks like a brown line, and it snakes in and out of view. The scene above? Well, it's switchbacks, switchbacks, and more switchbacks.

I suddenly experience one of those moments when I feel as though I'm another person looking in on my own current scene in life. It's a funny scene. There are three travellers stuffing all of their possessions into three sacks. They knew, in a vague sense from previous adventures, what they were getting themselves into, but they are not well enough informed, or prepared, to know the extent of where this particular adventure might lead. The three figures are tiny on the landscape, and they are exposed. The degrees of exposure can get much higher, but they are exposed. Altitude. No shelter but their layers over the cold night. Wind, with few impediments, funneling to this mountain pass. A sun, welcome in its early rays, but ready to stare down on them with conviction. On bikes that were not designed for these conditions. Powered by legs that have seen almost no bike conditioning. They are exposed, though they are not uncomfortable. They have been travelling already for a couple of months. Through India on trains and buses, surviving the crazy road culture, the extreme heat, different beds every couple of nights, noise, variable food and water, and a thirty hour bounce-fest in a bus crossing Nepal, with innards threatening to fall out on arrival. Now, over a week spent in Tibet, they are highly travel conditioned, but not yet travel worn out. They are exposed, but are they ready?

I snap out of my reverie at a request by Leatherfoot to help him strap down the packs. We get Kat's cinched down quite effectively today. That's an improvement in the process, which is always good. A system is never perfect, so all we can do is keep working at refining it a little more each and every time.

"Packed and ready Kat. Off you go."

Leatherfoot's and mine don't go so well, probably because we've taken a little extra gear, but we get the job done and begin pushing right from the start. Kat's legs give her no choice, Leatherfoot's bike gives him no choice, and I think pushing is actually better energy use per distance gained, though I do ride the occasional flat section just to change muscles and break the grind. The road climbs steeply up and across the barren hill, turns sharply, and climbs the other way. It does this over, and over, and over again. I begin to feel quite small and helpless. Though I know where I am, I feel somewhat lost. Strangely, my mind oscillates between this being a positive experience, and a ridiculous one. One second, I feel like I know why I'm here, the next I wonder why the heck I'm doing this to myself. There are brief moments of clarity, when I feel as though I can solve the world's problems, and other moments, when I can barely understand myself. Am I breaking myself down so I can build myself up even stronger later?

HEAD DOWN... PUSH... UP AND AROUND THE NEXT SWITCHBACK AND?... HEAD DOWN... PUSH... UP... AROUND... AND?... THE SAME. IT LOOKS THE SAME!

As the number of trips back and forth across this slope mount, it is impossible not to wish for the top of the DAMN pass, but it does not come. We were not as far along yesterday as we'd hoped, and Kat is hurting. Though her headache seemed to be a little better yesterday, she woke up with a nasty recurrence of it today. She didn't say much about it at first, but she's let us know that the further we go up, the worse it is getting. I guess her body simply doesn't deal with the altitude well. It's a tough situation. She had that fainting episode only a day and a half ago, and we have all read on several occasions how dangerous altitude sickness can be, but we keep thinking the top must be near. I'm sure that's what most people are thinking when they get altitude sickness. She literally can only do five steps at a time. Then, she needs to stop, until her head is finished pounding.

FIVE STEPS... STOP... FIVE STEPS... STOP...

The day is moving along. We're still ascending this ever bending, never ending, nasty old pass. Mercy Khamba La, mercy already! Kat is now sitting in the middle of the road crying for the second time today. It's a combination of everything. The physical pain of leg and lung burn. The headache, and the mental anguish of not knowing how far to the bloody top. Though Leatherfoot and I are getting parched too, we get her to drink a good dose of our remaining water.

"Do you think there is a top Leatherfoot?"

"I'm beginning to have my doubts Dogi."

"Okay, I'll bet five peanuts and three crackers that there are only three more switchbacks!"

"I'll raise you two peanuts and one cracker it's four."

Kat is oblivious to our attempt at humour. She looks up, smearing the tears across her dirty face. After one long deep breath, she stands up, and without saying anything, she starts walking... without her bike. I've seen Kat endure quite a bit. She's not one to give in easily, but it has obviously become laborious enough for her just to walk. Leatherfoot and I look at each other, shrug our shoulders, and start pushing our bikes as far as the next switchback. Just before we pass Kat, I suggest to Leatherfoot not to say anything to her. Just let her be. We'll get all three bikes up to the top of Khamba La. We can do it. Leatherfoot sets his bike down and walks back to get Kat's. When I get to the next switchback, I leave my bike and head down to pick up the extra. We continue this way taking turns doubling back to get the third bike. Walking back down the hill is kind of nice. The legs get to relax and stretch, and I notice details in the scenery that I hadn't noticed before, like the big river that flows lazily across the flat plain below. Each time up, however, becomes more and more arduous, though Leatherfoot and I keep each other going. When we pass each other, one of us empty handed going down, there's always a smile, a joke, a ten second shoulder massage, or a comment on the fine view below. We do anything to keep each other's spirits up. Kat is silently trudging, though she is at least keeping pace with us. There is no fun there. She is in hell.

Finally, we hear, and then see, some other signs of life as two trucks pass us, kicking up clouds of dust. Then, they stop briefly to have a conversation. The first is the Kathmandu bike tour group. The one we had considered, but passed on. They will be travelling essentially the same route as us, but it is a guided and assisted affair. Some of the group have been on the truck for the whole way up the pass, while others were dropped off a few switchbacks below for the satisfaction of riding to the top. The idea for them, over a two week span, is to ride some portions and be carried on the truck for others. They have total equipment support, which means that they don't have to carry any gear other than their daily needs. Water, meals and lodging are all provided. Ours has obviously been a tougher road already, but we like this more solitary and adventurous approach. At least I think we still do. The tour group leader is not the friendliest chap in the world, but he is kind enough to inform us that the top is very near. Perhaps three more switchbacks.

"Three more Leatherfoot. Three more. Did you hear that Kat? We're almost there!"

"Shall we push our bikes all the way up and come back together and take turns pushing Kat's bike up Dogi?"

"Sounds like a nice change Leatherfoot."

HEAD DOWN... PUSH... UP AND AROUND THE NEXT SWITCHBACK... HEAD DOWN... PUSH... UP... AROUND... AND...

There are few feelings quite as euphoric and relieving as getting to the top of a hill that you have been climbing for a long, long time. I dare say it is orgasmic. All I feel like doing is hugging someone, so I grab both Kat and Leatherfoot, and we have a well deserved group hug, feeling on the border of laughter and tears. Kat's perseverance has been remarkable, and Leatherfoot has been inspiring throughout the whole climb. With all the bike woes included, his positive attitude never wavered.

The view from the top is nothing short of spectacular. The valley we have just finished climbing is immense, and barren. Brown and blue. Earth and sky. HUGE. We bring our bikes across the short stretch at the top to the other side. The view down the new valley is even more picturesque, and it offers more than two colours. There is a huge meandering lake below that is a deep rich blue. It is surrounded by hills of brown, but farther in the distance, snow capped mountains can be seen. It has the quality of a fairytale. Though the wind is blowing forcefully up here, the surface of the lake is like clean glass. We can see the distinct shadow lines of the hills of the far bank, and the reflection of the broken white clouds drifting along the water. There is an hilarious road sign here at the edge of the descent into the new valley, and it is the first sign we have seen in the last two days. It is a pictorial representation of switchbacks! NO KIDDING. Even Kat has a laugh at this one as we lean our bikes against it.

"Dogi look. One more sign over there."

"Let's go check it out Kat."

94

"Look at prayer flags blowing in wind."

"It's nice to have the colour, but they are so tangled and tattered. The wind must howl up here all the time. Hey, can you read the Chinese part of the sign?"

"Kind of... mm... First, 'Name of the lake', then 'Marsh Area', then ..mm.. how do you say it .. maybe 'Nature Reserve Place'."

"I guess you can't read the name of the lake..."

"Well, I can't say it, but I can understand meanings of characters. It says 'Sheep .. Table .. Something I don't know and .. Lake'."

"The English part says 'The Natural Protective Area Of Yang Zhun Yang Lakes'. I wonder how the Tibetan version at the top would read. It's the most beautiful of the three scripts don't you think?"

"So desu ne. Can we go lie down?"

As the wind is far stronger howling up this new valley, Kat and I retreat to the other side, have a bite to eat, and settle in for a nap, while Leatherfoot takes the opportunity to look for a solution to his broken rear wheel. It's quite sheltered where we are lying, and the sun is, at the moment, quite comforting. With the rest, some food and a little more water, Kat says her headache has settled a little, though it is still there. We probably shouldn't linger up here too long. Getting all of us to lower altitude would be healthy, and there is a big lake there waiting to give us fresh water to drink. We are hoping, however, that Leatherfoot will have some luck with fixing his wheel, particularly with the well supplied tour group truck still lingering up here as the guests also enjoy the view.

When he returns a little while later, we get the story. The leader, who we guess has a spare wheel or three for his tour group, is shockingly unsympathetic to the situation. Particularly after he informs us that Nagarze will definitely not have a spare wheel, though Gyangze should. Though I realize we didn't pay to take his tour, you would think that in this environment, and under these somewhat dire circumstances, he would be helpful. We would have happily paid for the spare wheel, which he could have then replaced again at the next opportunity. I'm not sure if I'm right to feel this bitter about it, but I think calling him unsympathetic is too nice. How about pathetic. We are rather happy to see the last of him.

The other vehicle that passed us was a big dump truck, which looked like it carried local supplies. It also happened to have on it two independent travellers, and their bikes, who unloaded at the summit. Not surprisingly, they are Germans, and kind and helpful. At least trying to be. Theirs is an interesting story. They had attempted this ride once before in much the same way as we are now. Locally purchased bikes, trying to ride from Lhasa to Kathmandu. A brief account of their previous journey tells of repeatedly broken down bikes, hellishly big mountain passes, and finally bailing out. Literally, just leaving their bikes by the side of the road about halfway through the trip, and hitching on the next available truck back to Kathmandu. And that's why they are back. They want to finish the journey. This time around, better equipped and prepared. Having also ridden and pushed up this mountain pass their first time around, they knew how harsh it was, and that's why, even on better bikes, they had opted to hitch.

Hanging out now in the sheltered area near us, they spend some time together with Leatherfoot, and improvise as best they can, jamming various things like tinfoil into the mechanism, but they can't come up with any solutions to make his bike rideable again. Apparently, they are quite regular cyclists, and even they have never seen this happen to a bike. We chat a little longer, and thank them for their effort, before a good journey is wished all around and they ride off.

The ride down is a SHAKE, RATTLE and ROLL affair. It's fast, freaky and fun. After plodding excruciatingly slowly up the hill for so long, it is all we can do in some sections to keep from losing control of our speed. It's a little frightening. Given the frequency of our bike woes, I am expecting someone's brake cable to go ping at any time, but it never does happen. We bounce our way down the final section, and are relieved to be alive, and a little shocked at how quickly it is over. In relation to the climb, the decent was not long, but it was enough to breathe a little easier and shave another few edges off Kat's headache.

What we have now is flat road winding along the shore of this huge lake! Flat gravel road that is, and it doesn't look like it might be paved any time soon. Oh well, it's nice to cycle on a flat road any which way. Kat and I ride along slowly, side by side, smiling and chatting.

"EXCUSE ME!"

"Leatherfoot come on. Where .. oops."

"What Dogi?"

"Leatherfoot can't ride remember. His bike is broken. He could coast down the hill just fine, but he can't pedal."

We wait for poor Leatherfoot to catch up. He tries to muster a dirty look at us for forgetting, but he can't suppress the twinkle in his eyes.

"Sorry Leatherfoot. How do you feel? You too Kat, what's your mood?"

"Maybe I can ride a little but not so far."

"I'm not much in the mood for pushing Dogi. Why don't we keep our eyes open for the first good looking camp spot. Maybe I can still try to work on this thing."

"It looks like there are a few good sandbars not too far along. Shall we head for one of those?"

Yamzho Yumco. That's what our map calls this massive lake. The water is gorgeous. The shade of blue is strong and impenetrable, yet pure and clean. The sand that we find at the first good looking "beach" is soft, and it will certainly make far superior bedding to last night's ditch. Kat and I get a pot of water boiling, and then pitch the tent and cook an edible meal, while Leatherfoot works away patiently on his broken bike.

The chill sets in quickly as the sun sets, but the evening light is most playful, and our surroundings are peaceful. We are tired, but feel relieved and happy. We joke a little as we play back our first three hectic days of riding… and pushing. The physical and mental ups and downs. The highlights, and the hell. Perhaps two of the toughest days of physical labour any of us has ever endured, but our will and our company is strong. I'm so glad Leatherfoot is along. Kat and I alone would have had a hard time to even endure this far. We complement each other well, and are thus far cooperative to a high degree. Though his broken bike is a definite issue…

REST

So, it is then our fourth day of cycling across Tibet, though today we are taking a much needed day of rest. No outhouse? No trees, or even boulders to hide behind? What do you do when you need to POO? I finally had one! The first since Lhasa. A poo with a view. Who needs a house, when out is as beautiful as this, and there is no one else around? That's a little odd, three days without a poo. Sometimes the anxious nature of the start of a new adventure will do it. Perhaps spending so much time on bike seats stuffed the situation up a little too.

It is the middle of the day, and the sun is beating. I am in the tent to escape its raw tongue. There are no other shade options. No trees are anywhere no be seen. There is just sand, dirt, rock, and the lake. Everything in the environment is retaining and reflecting heat, and nothing is diffusing it. Kat likes it. Baking in the heat. Leatherfoot would probably rather seek shade too, but he seems less affected by it than me. He's lying on the outer edge of the tent, which is supplying him with some shade. Fortunately, we have this great big supply of water here, though we do have a new issue in the form of a dysfunctional water filter. Though it was already being somewhat temperamental yesterday evening, it did work. Today, however, it has decided not to work anymore. It's as if the O-ring on the pump shrunk in the altitude or something. There is no more suction being created. We tried putting a layer of duct tape around the ring to see if we could create a seal, but not even that mighty friend could rectify this dilemma! We haven't really budgeted enough fuel to boil drinking water, and it is unlikely we'll be able to get any new canisters to suit our stove, so we'll simply have to drink it as is. From this lake, that idea certainly doesn't bother me. Though there are grazing sheep, and thus, sheep feces in the area, I don't think significant amounts are making their way into this huge body of water, which looks to be otherwise uncontaminated in any other sense.

It's been a full and interesting morning. We've had some VERY friendly visitors. Two Tibetan men and their small flock of sheep. They just came into our camp and started checking everything out, while their animals grazed in and around the area. Much like the kids on the first morning, they were looking in the tent, poking through our packs, fiddling with the bikes, the stove, everything. It's becoming a recurring theme, and we are getting used to it, though it still feels somewhat uncomfortable. The urge to get them to stop was there, but we resisted it. We watched them for a time, but it was obvious that they would take or damage nothing. They were like kids in a candy store, attracted to the bright colours and the new shapes.

When their curiosity was finally satiated, we ended up hanging out with them for a couple of hours. We played both Frisbee and cards. It wasn't the same version as with the kids at the base of the pass, though they played it with just as much enthusiasm. We spent a little time showing them the throwing techniques, which they caught onto surprising quickly, though we still had to run and chase their throws much more than they did ours. As such, our lungs and legs were screaming "ENOUGH" rather quickly. Though we've been in Tibet for about ten days already, the altitude is still very much noticeable. My guess is that we're still over 4000 meters (13,200 feet) here at the lake. At rest, I don't notice any shortness of breath like the first few days, but even with a mild level of exercise, it is quickly obvious that the lungs aren't taking in as much oxygen as they are used to. In a sense, it's kind of frustrating. You have to temper the pace at which you do anything. That's why, as fun as it was, throwing the disc quickly gave way to a game of cards.

Finding a common card game between new players can be challenging enough amongst people who are from the same culture and speak the same language. With our Tibetan friends, the idea seemed futile, but we tried it anyway. It was hard to tell whether they'd even seen playing cards of this nature before or not. When they first sat in our circle, they stared at them in a way that would lead me to believe not. We tried to teach them the card game called Hearts, which is one that we enjoy, and one that is not overly complex to learn. One of the two men actually seemed to be catching on to the idea after a couple of hands, but the other one simply never had a clue. As such, the game quickly evolved to random cards being thrown here and there, accompanied by big smiles and laughter. Eventually, the game turned into a lesson in how to count in Tibetan, which was quite welcome and useful for us. *Chik, nyi, sum, shi, na, dug, dun, gye, gu, chu.* Coincidentally, some of the numbers have a similarity to Japanese, which helped us to grasp it more readily. It's amazing that the five of us could sit in a little circle in the sand for so long, and have so much fun playing WITH cards. Meanwhile, their sheep milled about the area, closing in around us and our tent, with their banter providing some interesting background music.

Next on our agenda was some laundry, as we had time, energy, need, and a great big lake to work with. Our local friends stayed on to watch the process, which amused them greatly. We would throw our dirty clothing as far out into the water as possible, then, getting psyched up, we would dive in, grab the clothes, dunk them under, shake them around and swim back really fast! Chasing the clothes was, truthfully, the only way we could coax ourselves in. The water was almost heart stoppingly cold. It can't be too far removed from being snow melt. Standing back on shore after the swim was the best part. The tingling on the skin is sensational. The antithesis of the drudgery we were feeling yesterday in the middle of switchback hell. Kat, not believing our rave reviews on how splendid the water was, cautiously dipped a paw in to see for herself. One test was enough to make her shudder and go back to her warm peaceful resting spot. Perhaps the greatest amusement was the reaction of our Tibetan friends watching us swim in our birthday suits. We were a little unsure of stripping down in front of them at first, and, fortunately, it didn't come across as a cultural faux pas. They just did a lot of pointing and laughing at the whole production. Feeling clean and refreshed, we also lay naked in the hot sun for a while, which they also seemed not to mind, though, surprisingly, they did not immediately vacate and leave us our privacy either.

BOOM! The only other entertaining note of the day was the self *EXPLODING* lighter. Though Leatherfoot and I were still at the lake at the time, the two Tibetan men had moved back to our tenting area where Kat was hanging out. Kat said the noise made them all jump pretty high. We theorize that it couldn't deal with the heat, causing it to explode. After it happened, the Tibetans came over to check it out, and one of them pointed at the "Made in China" sign on it, and they both had a good laugh. Fortunately, we brought some extras, and we'll be sure to try and protect them a little better from the midday heat.

O O O

It is late evening now, and the chill is creeping in quickly once again. It's been a great day. Quite relaxing. Just us, and this huge lake and massive open space. Oh, and the shepherds, and the sheep, who are still grazing on the super slim pickings in the area. Thankfully, the animals are far enough away from us that we can't hear them, and the shepherds are also letting us be. I wonder where they are all going to sleep tonight?

Leatherfoot has been working at his bike for much of the afternoon. He has managed to jam some tinfoil in his rear wheel, and, apparently, it is rideable again. If it works, that will be a huge load off of our upcoming days. Otherwise, I don't know how we will get a dysfunctional bike around the lake and over the next mountain pass to Gyangze. It's at least a two day ride away, even on working bikes. Let's hope his repair job holds.

Still a bit tired, but very happy.

PULL PUSH PREGO

WE COULD EASILY STAY ONE MORE DAY RESTING ON THIS BEACH, but we know that it is time to move on. We wake up early, and see that the morning has brought along some new visitors. Unlike yesterday's, these two shepherds are not too inquisitive. They pay us some attention from a distance, but are more concerned with herding their sheep. What little was available in this area in the first place was surely munched clean by yesterday's flock, so they look to move the animals along. They use no dogs for their herding. It is a human task. A long wander day after day across these wide open expanses. They throw small rocks to provide guidance to the flock. Not at the animals, but rather to the side, to drive them the opposite way. It is simple and effective.

The shepherds do begin to look on more attentively as we begin our morning camp chores, though there is little expression on their faces. It is as if they are watching television, and we are the show. The firing up of the camp stove creates a momentary stir and a small conversation between them. The disassembling of the tent, and packing it into a bag, widens their eyes ever so slightly. The strapping of everything onto the back of the fancy looking bicycles? Well, that probably offends them, being the unrefined process it still is. They fade into the distance as we saddle up ready to ride.

"SHHH UGAR!"

"I take it your tinfoil special didn't hold after all Leatherfoot?"

"This sucks."

"I totally agree. In fact, it sucks so badly you could even say shhhit. But you know, it is what it is, and we have to find a way to deal with it. Any ideas?"

"Touché to your cliché Dogi, but I have no ideas."

It is what it is. Certainly that is cliché, but it's not just some hippie, or philosopher jargon. Here and now, it's as applicable as ever. It's not a good situation, but we got ourselves here, and we need to accept it and make the best of it. Acceptance. That's the root of it. When time is past, it's history. It can be learned from, but nothing more. Why does that seem so easy when you think about it, write about it, and read about it, but so difficult when you try to live it? I could sit here and say we should have gone back to Lhasa, or we should have taken the more direct route to Shigatse, but we didn't. We made a decision, and we have to live with it. Just like the time you were drunk, and said something stupid, or you were playing a team sport, and made a poor pass that got intercepted, we make foolish decisions all the time in life, but we only know they are foolish after we have seen the consequences, by which time it's too late. Then, the only tool we hold to effectively deal with it is acceptance. This is it. How can we best go forward?

We search our minds for options, but there are so very few. Hitchhiking? That is definitely an option, though yesterday we saw absolutely no traffic go by, and the day before only those two trucks. It's also a passive option that doesn't seem too likely to be successful, particularly with three of us and bikes and gear. How about pushing the bike for the next ninety kilometers (55 miles)? We could take turns, and always have two riding, but that would take a long time. Probably four, or even five days in this environment.

"How about towing Leatherfoot?"

"Towing?"

"Yea, towing. Do you think we can actually pull the weight of another bike and person?"

"Euchh! That doesn't sound pleasant at all, though it might work."

"Kat, you got any better ideas?"

"Not really."

We sit in silence for about another two minutes, but come up with no options better than the idea of towing. With that realization in place, we decide it would be best to reconfigure the bikes so that the broken wheel goes on Kat's bike, and her good wheel goes on Leatherfoot's. This way, Leatherfoot and I can take turns doing the pulling. We consider trying the operation without removing the strapped down packs, but quickly come to the conclusion that they must be removed. Leatherfoot leads the way, while I act as the surgeon's assistant. Kat chips in as the anesthetist by holding each bike firmly in place as we operate. Things go smoothly with the change over, and we get the bikes righted and packs strapped back down. Now, we must face the next dilemma. How are we going to attach the broken bike to one of the good ones?

"We do have one spare piece of webbing."

"That would certainly be strong enough Dogi. I can't think of any better options."

"Shall we try it and see how it goes?"

It's hard to know where the best place to tie it would be, or how long to leave it, so we'll just have to experiment and improve. That's it isn't it. Try it. If it doesn't work, try it again. If it works, try to figure out how to make it work better. There is always a way to improve a system.

"That's quite the hectic looking rig. What do you think Dogi?"

"**The Rig!** I like it Leatherfoot, the name I mean. The Rig. I think it positively looks like a bad science experiment, but I think it might work."

So here we are, riding at over 4000 meters (13,200 feet) altitude, on a hellishly bumpy gravel road, on lousy bikes encumbered with full packs. As if all this isn't hard enough, we now have to tow a broken bicycle with a person sitting on it. This is nuts. Purely ludicrous. But do we have any better choices? We have a lake full of good water next to us, but our food supply won't last that long, and who knows when the next vehicle might pass, and whether it would even stop for us. For now, it looks as though we're either pushing or towing. I volunteer myself for the first attempt, giving my legs a little extra shake and stretch, as Kat settles in on the trailer bike. The Rig! Here we go...

"BREAK!"

"How is it Dogi?"

"Holly Crap!... the sheer... weight of the load... is hellish on the quads... and the lungs, but perhaps the worst part... of the towing is the slack... and SNAP!"

With the road as bumpy as it is, and, of course, going up and down a little, the webbing between the bikes isn't staying constantly taut. It gets slack, which is nice for a few pedal strokes as the extra weight is gone, but when the webbing goes taut again, the jerk is painful. Initially, it feels like I might launch over the handlebars, then the next few pedal strokes are excruciatingly heavy. Once some momentum is gained, it is somewhat tolerable, but it never lasts long as there is a constant variation in the pitch of the road. Even a slightly uphill slope increases the weight tremendously, and even a slight downhill slope starts a whole new cycle of slack and snap.

"I know you guys probably think it nice back here but it's hard to stay on the bike. It feels strange with pedals lose. Makes hard to balance, and when SNAP thing happens, I feel like maybe I fly off back!"

We keep the webbing attached to the seat post of the lead bike, and the post under the handlebars of the trailer, but adjust the length to make it slightly shorter. I wonder whether a more rigid link would work better, but without a moveable joint on it, I don't think it would. Besides, I can think of nothing to make this out of.

Leatherfoot takes his turn at towing and does an admirable job on his first shift. Then it's my turn again. There is no preset distance. We go until we can't anymore and then switch. Any time the incline gets too much, Kat jumps off and pushes trying to keep up to the slow moving lead bike, or, more often, both get off and push to the top of the rise. Settling in again after any short downhill requires extra concentration because of the wobble induced by the snap of the webbing. It is slow going. Very slow. This lake is huge, and the road stretches alongside it for as far as we can see. Perception of distance here is still deceiving. We are making progress, but it doesn't seem like it as we round each bend and things look the same. Hours go by, and still we are beside the lake. No vehicles, no other people, no animals, no trees. Space, and three people and bikes moving at a snail's pace.

When Leatherfoot is on his turn, I can ride leisurely, but even watching the two of them struggle is painful. It's best to let them get out in front while I recover from my turn, and then catch up to them again. When I'm on the pull, it is an intense kind of misery like none I have ever known before. Even the switchbacks of two days ago are beginning to pale in comparison. All of my focus, attention, and energy goes into pushing down on the pedals, and trying to stay in any form of harmony with Kat and her bike. The load is bad enough, but the slack and SNAP adds a horribly uneven quality. Rhythm is impossible to attain. It's irritating. Curse words escape my mouth at times, even a scream just to let out the tension.

"AHHHH!"

"Time to switch Dogi?"

"Mmmm… the .. next .. bend… I'll get .. around .. that…"

It's hard to talk between breaths. The mouth is fully preoccupied with sucking in as much oxygen as humanly possible. It is one breath per pedal stroke. A sharp exhale as all body weight and leg power heaves down on a pedal. Forty three more of these and I make the next bend, cough, splutter, and plop down beside the free bike Leatherfoot has left in the middle of the road. The middle of the road. My butt is on a pile of gravel, and my feet rest in a deep pothole. I stare back at the stretch I have just ridden, and my mind fades into the endlessness. It is true that things look the same around each bend, but the scenery really is stunning. It is the saving grace in all of this physical torment. As I finish catching my breath and my heart calms down, I dream that this road were paved and my bike had a motor. I ride it back and forth, and again. Ahh the motor. It's good, and it's bad. It makes many things easier, but it's stinky, and noisy. Oh well, I have a bicycle, and legs, lungs and a heart that work well right now. The Rig has disappeared around the next bend, and it is time for my turn at "leisure riding" until I catch up to Kat and Leatherfoot again.

LUNCH! Prego! Prego! Boiled eggs, fresh apples and oranges, bread, potatoes, and even one chicken leg! We are stopped at a good flat pullout on the road with a fine view across the lake, and are in the middle of our own gourmet lunch of peanuts and crackers, when up pulls a small bus, and out jump a bunch of Italian tourists. A few of them pull out their cigarettes, and others walk towards the lake to take in the view, but a small group of them come straight over to us. They look to be in awe of us and our bikes as they babble on excitedly in their own language, and one or two of them starts conversation with us in very broken English. With heads shaking in disbelief, they generously hand over all of their lunch leftovers, which include fresh fruit and vegetables. We haven't eaten food like this since Kathmandu, and we consume it ravenously. Though we are all hungry for a dose of fresh food, we are not yet like a pack of wild dogs, so we do share the one and only chicken leg as equally as possible. Even Leatherfoot, who leans towards vegetarianism, is happy to have his morsel. Fresh food is so good. That's the difference between taking a tour and going it on your own. With a tour, you can, to a certain extent, stay within the comfort zone of what you are used to. You see the culture, the environment, you taste a little of it, hear some, smell some, feel some, but you don't experience any of these senses with the same depth. It's a case of relativity. We're getting a deeper experience being here on our own, and for longer, but unless we actually lived for years amongst the culture, we still wouldn't know what it's truly like. As many of the people from the tour look to be over sixty years of age, I admire them for coming here. This must be a special experience for them.

Prego, prego. We must have heard that a hundred times already, as more of them come over to us with their handouts. I'm sure half are truly fascinated and impressed by what we were doing, and the other half think we were crazy, but all of them can see our sincere appreciation for their offerings. We turn absolutely nothing down. Prego, prego! They file back into their bus, to the fate of a driver that pulls out aggressively and starts ripping down the road. I guess they are on a tight schedule. In a minute or two, the cloud of dust settles, and the drone of their engine fades. We are alone again. We decide to try the water filter one more time to see if it has changed its mind about working, but it hasn't. Oh well, this water does indeed come from a higher source, and it tastes more amazing than any I have had in a long time. Replenished, and refreshed, we get back to the grind.

I'd like to say one gets used to the towing, but that would be a lie. The lunch break provided some extra energy, but that wore off after the first shift and a half of pulling. At this point, we are shortening our turns as our legs get more tired and we heat up from under the cloudless midday sky. We need another break, and find a decent place to access the lake, because we want to take a swim. There is no hesitation today. I am so hot that I feel like I can't get my clothes off fast enough to jump in. Leatherfoot follows within seconds, and though she does pause a little, even Kat joins today. The contrast from the hot sun to the cold lake is extreme. From overheated to instantly cool, and quickly on to cold if you stay in for more than a few seconds. The water is only a few degrees more than it was when it melted from the snow and ice above. INVIGORATING!

After hours of towing, we are exhausted, but we feel like we must push on. At least we have to get to the end of the lake today. It does end, I'm sure of it. In fact, I think I can see the end of it, though I don't want to give myself any false hope. It's tough to get re-motivated after such a refreshing swim. The heat of the day is just on the waning side of maximum. Leatherfoot takes his place at the helm of The Rig, and Kat dutifully takes up her perch. She reiterates that just trying to keep balanced and minimize the slack and snap is hard, but we're not sympathetic to her just now. This towing business is worse than any exercise either of us has ever done. We are just about to restart when we hear another motor. We can see that it's a 4X4 coming from behind, so we decide to wait until it goes by and the dust from the road settles. Just after it passes, however, it comes to an abrupt halt in a cloud of fine dirt.

"Hey, how's it going?" says the first passenger to jump out.

"No way. No way. I can't believe it!"

Our spirits immediately soar. Of all people, it's the five who we met that were also on Hari's "tour" and on our airplane ride from Kathmandu. One of the guys is Australian, two of the girls are Swiss, and the last two are a Dutch couple. It's unbelievable to meet them again out here. The last we had heard from them, which was still when we were in the Yak Hotel, they were talking about possibly hitching.

"So, what happened to hitching?"

"Well in the end we found a pretty good deal with this local driver/guide."

"Nice. How is it?"

"Well, it's only our first day. It's a bit cramped in the car, and hot, but so far we're having a great time."

We noticed when we were in Lhasa that there were several tours on offer. Essentially, they were much the same as what was being offered in Kathmandu. Four or five days in a 4X4 shuttled across the plateau from Lhasa to the Tibetan side of the border with Nepal, at a town called Zhangmu. These tours usually take the more direct route from Lhasa to Shigatse, though they do often include the side trip up to Mount Everest Base Camp. Amongst other lesser available tour options to other locations in Tibet, there is also a seven day version from Lhasa to Zhangmu. This takes in the lake we are currently next to, the town of Gyangze, which is meant to be nice, a side trip to the town of Sakya, which is reported to be unique, and, of course, the drive up to the base of Everest. It is this version which our friends have negotiated.

They are in absolute disbelief at seeing us here on bikes. Perhaps we never told them of our idea, or it never really registered with them. They are even more amazed after hearing about the four flat tires, the broken wheel, and the night on the pass. Looking at The Rig, they just shake their heads.

"That's crazy. I can't believe you guys are towing a bike down a road like this. How far are you going? Let's see if we can take Kat and the broken bike along down the road for a bit, and save you guys some strife."

"Oh, that would be fantastic. Thank you so, so much!"

They chat it over with their guide, who is an extremely nice fellow, and he is agreeable to the idea. It takes a fair bit of reorganizing, seeing as they already have six people and gear in the vehicle, but the driver takes control and sorts it out. He finds a few extra ropes and manages to get the bike strapped to the outside of the car. A few other pieces of luggage will need to rest on laps in order to squeeze Kat in, but everyone pitches in and they get it done. This might be the luckiest thing that has happened to us all trip. Once gone, we come to the realization that we didn't even take the time to get a photo of everyone and the incredible packing job.

Leatherfoot and I suddenly feel incredibly liberated. For the first time since the morning of the second day, we will actually be able to ride unencumbered at a regular pace. This proves to be most enjoyable. Freedom. Wind blows gently though the hair as we leisurely wind our way along the lake shore. It's a wonderful feeling to be able to keep our heads up and enjoy the views of the lake and the distant snowy peaks.

"This is a little more like it eh, Leatherfoot."

"Definitely more along the lines of what I was expecting."

"How far do you think they're gonna take Kat?"

"Who knows, but the father, the better."

Eventually we round a bend, which leads us in a more southerly direction, and not much further along, we find Kat looking content and relaxed. It was about fifteen kilometers, which isn't a lot in the grand scheme, but would have seemed an eternity had we needed to continue towing. At this point, we're only a few kilometers away from the next small town of Nagarze. Kat says they offered to take her right into town, which is where they will stay tonight, but figured we would prefer to camp, and this is an excellent location for camping.

"Did you have a nice ride Kat?"

"Oh yea. It's a little squished, but everybody so nice. They say maybe they come back to visit us tonight if they have enough energy."

"That would be cool. Speaking of enough energy, who wants to cook?"

"No cooking necessary. We have leftover oatmeal, Dogi, remember? We made way too much this morning."

"Mm Mmm. Looking oh so forward to it, Leatherfoot. Shall we at least brew up some tea?"

There is not a lot burnable around with the total lack of trees, but we have managed to collect enough dried shrub twigs and such to make a very small fire. We are enjoying the waning light, and talking about our day and the great fortune of our friends showing up when we were in such a time of need, when we begin to hear a distant hum. As it turns into a loud rumble, the noise is almost deafening in contrast to the silence that we've been indulging in. It's a 4X4, and it stops at the edge of the road right above our camp.

"Hey, we're glad you guys have the fire burning, otherwise we'd have never seen you down here. It is so dark out. Driving was kind of weird."

"Where's your guide?"

"He's back at the hotel, probably sleeping already. It took some convincing, 'cause he didn't wanna drive, but he finally let me take the car."

Apparently, there's not a lot to the small town of Nagarze five kilometers further on where they are staying the night. They say it's already all dark and quiet there, and there's nothing going on. As they have brought along some Chinese wine, and a few snacks to this wonderful locale, we suddenly have an impromptu international party. Being the most common language, the English conversation provides good laughs, mixing the different accents and ways that the non-native speakers talk. Both the Dutch and the Swiss have such a wonderfully musical lilt in the way they speak, and, of course, the Aussie, the American, and myself the Canadian have good fun joking around with, and trying to imitate each others accents and expressions. Kat is on the quiet side, but she has a grin, and a glow, from the few sips of wine. It tastes like cheap port, but it is certainly drinkable, and sets a great mood. The sound waves of laughter carry out across the huge open water, and it turns into a great evening. When they finally depart, there is a tinge of sadness. We won't see them anymore. As a last request, the Dutch couple, who are particularly big on photography, have asked if we happen to have any extra camera batteries as theirs has run out. We don't, but between the three of us, we do have two cameras, and one will do for now, so Leatherfoot takes his battery out and gives it to them. They give us the name of a guesthouse in Gyangze where they say they will buy one if possible and leave it for us. They are absolutely delighted, and we feel good to be able to give something back.

As the hum fades after their departure, the silence penetrates deeply once again. Silence, and deep darkness. The only light is the soft glow from the dying embers and the billions of tiny little stars. It's incredible. No artificial lights, no cars or trucks passing, no motors of any sort, no people, not even sheep. It is utter silence. Pure. To me it is the most beautiful sound in the world.

CLOUDS

ABOVE US NOW ARE DARK CLOUDS, WHICH SEEM ALMOST CLOSE ENOUGH to touch. Way at the end of this huge dry river bed, on which we are camped, the sun pokes through, and shadows play on the numerous peaks and valleys. The wind teases, occasionally showing its fury, and just as often its kindness. Enough mini hail storms have fallen on us in the past few hours to let us know that Mother Nature is in control. Yet, she laughs gently and leaves us our peace in what is surely only a pin prick in the vastness I can see, and less than an atom in the vastness I can feel.

This morning started with a lot more pulling. Leatherfoot was very motivated on his first turn .. turn .. turn .. turn... If there actually is a thread of rhythm to be found in such a process as gravel road bike towing, then he found it this morning. His loud breathing was the dominant sound in the area, followed by the early whispers of the wind. Kat was quiet this morning. She took her place as the towee on The Rig without even a sigh of resignation, and, thereafter, had a look of stern concentration etched on her face. When Leatherfoot finally gave in, I was ready to go.

"Are you set back there Kat?"

"Mm."

We changed nothing of The Rig's system from yesterday. It is still one piece of webbing attached from the seat post of the front bike to the base of the handlebars of Kat's bike, but something did feel a little better. Maybe now, we are the most experienced "gravel road bike towers" in the whole world! Then again, maybe the road was just flatter and the wind hadn't come up yet. As it was, my shift on The Rig took us the rest of the way to Nagarze, the little town

113

where our friends had spent the night. Nagarze. The main street was lined with one and a half meter weathered mud-brick walls. There were a couple of short side roads, and houses and buildings on either side, though not many of each. Wind battered Tibetan flags could be seen poking out from the tops of many of the structures. For the most part, the town looked to be purely Tibetan with little or no Chinese influence. And, although we were pretty sure that there wouldn't be one, we did have a quick look around the town for a bike or bike repair shop, but there was nothing of the sort. There were almost no shops to speak of. In fact, all we found was one tiny hole in the wall place where we were able to buy some crackers. An interesting thought, a town with no shops. The community must be largely self sufficient. I wonder how much money is exchanged in a place like Nagarze. A small amount of electricity does go in, and at least one supply truck did pass us in the past four days, so there is outside influence, but it is minimal. I wonder if everyone takes their supplies straight from the truck, or if there is some kind of community warehouse or shop that we couldn't notice?

It was a two way street called Fascination in Nagarze. Though they do see a handful of foreigners who stay on occasion, we were a huge curiosity to the locals. Loaded down cyclists would be a rare enough sight, but I'm quite sure they've never seen a bike TOWING another bike with a person on it. What a strange sight we must have been. The attention only grew as we stopped and pulled out our map. Though we were fairly certain which way we needed to go, we had absolutely no desire to pull an inch more than necessary, so we wanted to double check. The locals were intrigued by the map, and we realized after a short time that they have probably never seen a map of their own country. Their reaction was something along the lines of "Tibet? Really?" as the younger ones craned their necks to have a look at the shiny flat object with red lines, black words and blue spots all over it. It didn't take long before the map was circulating the small crowd, none of the lookers aware that we were hoping to figure out which direction we needed to go. Once we were able to re-secure it, we folded it away and simply proceeded to say the next big town name of Gyangze a few times in different accents. Finally then, we were pointed in the direction that confirmed what we had thought. I left feeling as though we would be the talk of their town and area for the next little while. Episodes like this must be exciting in such an isolated place. An amusing and unusual scene in their everyday worlds.

The town ended as abruptly as it had begun, and the road that lay ahead of us was flat, straight, and l o n g. Gravel, rock, dirt, and a row of telephone poles as far as the eye could see. Way in the distance rose a diamond shaped peak with a wisp of snow on the top. On either side, further distant, more snow capped mountains. Somewhere through those mountains lay our road, and our next pass, Karo La at over 5000 meters (16,500 feet).

Of course, we continued to entertain thoughts of hitchhiking. At least Kat and the broken bike. The prospect of riding/towing/pushing up another huge pass was hellish, but not a single vehicle had passed us all day. What choice? Onwards we towed, onwards we rode. At least on this part of the road, the grade was flat and consistent, thus minimizing the effects of the slack and SNAP. Leatherfoot took his turn, then I took mine, then one more each, and the road in front didn't change much. If it weren't for the town fading behind, and finally disappearing, we might have thought we were on a gravel road tread mill. It was just us, the various shades of brown, and the telephone poles.

R R R R R R R U M M M M B L E

A truck! A BIG truck! A BIG DUMP TRUCK! A BIG EMPTY DUMP TRUCK! Emphatic would be an understatement in how hard we tried to flag him down. Three people standing at the edge of the road waving arms frantically. Thank him, god, and everybody else, he did stop. Not much was said. Not much needed to be. The driver didn't even get out of his vehicle. He just waited patiently while we disassembled The Rig. Leatherfoot jumped up into the back of the empty beast, and Kat and I lifted the bikes, with baggage still tied on, up to him. Then I boosted Kat up, and I jumped on board too. "BANG BANG," I rapped my hand onto the side of the truck when we were set. It seems to be the universal symbol for "we're ready," and off we RRRUMMBLED!

What a ride! The big tires grinding over the road and the rattle of metal were loud, but the wind blowing past us so quickly felt amazing. We were beaming as we watched the remainder of that long straight road pass behind us. Soon enough, the incline began, and along with it came the curves, then the river, then the waterfalls, LANDSLIDES, GLACIERS! The scenery had made a dramatic shift, and was suddenly eye-filling. Rivers born out of glacial snow snaked down the mountain sides by the dozens. Some of the patterns in the rock were dazzling. Suddenly, we were almost sorry to be passing so quickly, but not so sorry that we volunteered to get off. In fact, our ride ended sooner than we'd hoped. Sooner, that is, than the top of the pass. This was where the driver was working, somewhere halfway or so up the pass. A little deflated, but still happy and thankful for what we got, we unloaded and began to push.

Above us now, a lone dark cloud in the distance has transformed from a piranha into a shrimp, and now it is a hand reaching for a distant mountain peak. This is why I came to Tibet. VAST, CRISP, and POWERFUL, even feel like weak words to describe what lays around me. I am in awe.

Pushing. Towing was no longer an option on the incline, and there was no need to separate, so we all pushed together, and between breaths commented on our surroundings. It was not two or three curves in the road later, however, when we came across a small group of Tibetans gathered off the side of the road. They were some sort of roadwork crew, though their equipment was minimal. There were rakes and shovels, and a few other hand tools, but no machinery. Enthusiastically, they waved us over to where they were gathered around a small fire. There appears to be little formality to greeting with the Tibetans. There were no handshakes, no bows, not even the hands together "namaste" seen in Nepal. They simply rearranged themselves to make space for us in their midst, and encouraged us to sit and relax. It was so welcoming, making it comfortable and easy to join. We were made to feel like friends. Before we were even fully settled, they were offering us the "deluxe" beverage know as Yak Butter Tea! With thirst being an almost constant out here, Kat and I, who have gotten used to the warm oily liquid, accepted. Leatherfoot, who would need to be literally dying of thirst before drinking it again, politely declined.

What we offered in return was peanuts. It was either that or crackers. That's what we have left to eat for lunch. We have no cheese, no meat, no vegetables or fruit. They were happy to receive peanuts, and a chance at looking through our binoculars, which were absolutely marveled at. Pure childlike expressions of fascination. Around and around they went, some even taking a third turn. The beauty of experiencing something completely new and foreign. The purity and power of emotion. Feeling like a child. It always amazes me how little it takes. We come from societies where artificial stimulation is prevalent in massive doses. Artificially flavoured food, electronic gadgetry, media... It is so easy to get sucked into a void of bigger, better, faster, more. One gets quickly used to the level of a particular artificial stimulant, and the only way to re-attain the feeling of fun or happiness is by "upgrading." It never ends. The bigger television needs to keep getting bigger, the faster computer needs to keep getting faster, the food that is real tastes boring in comparison to the candy or chips. Out here, the people have experienced very little sensory distortion or artificial stimulation. The binoculars, even the peanuts, gave them such joy. I suppose, it's all a kind of relativity.

With grease coated mouths and lips from the lovely Yak Butter Tea, we took our leave feeling good about our communication with these people, even though we were able to exchange less than a handful of words.

The purples are starting to come out now as they seem to during most evenings, and a huge manta ray floats across the sky.

So there we were once again, pushing our loaded bikes up a hill with no end in sight, and no solid idea of how far it was to the top of the pass. But, we felt okay. We felt good. The footsteps were tiring, but the sights and sounds, as we slowly wound our way up this river valley, continued to be grand. Waterfall after waterfall cascaded and crashed down the cliffs feeding the swift flowing river. The echoing quality of the canyon, further swirled about by the wind, was both loud and musical.

Suddenly, a new noise. A motor. Another truck? That would be nice! No, not a truck. It was a fully loaded tourist bus which passed us by, giving no inkling that it might stop. Yet, around the next bend, there it was! Not stopped for our sake, but rather at a nice viewpoint. The tourists had already disembarked and were milling about. To us, it represented a golden opportunity that needed to be tried. Just getting Kat and the broken bike to the top of the pass would be hugely helpful, as then Leatherfoot and I could ride. We approached the guide and explained our situation, happy to find that he spoke English well. Unfortunately, however, though sympathetic, he was unwilling to impose on the clients of his tour and take Kat along to the top. What could we do?

We nodded and smiled at some of the tourists who I could clearly tell were Germans. Naturally, curiosity brought a couple of them our way, and I was able to shake enough rust off my German speaking abilities to tell them of our journey, our bike difficulties, and then our desire to get Kat and the lemon bike to the top of the pass. In the end, one gentleman in particular was very sympathetic and convinced of our need for assistance. He pleaded our case to significant others in the group, and, in true German fashion, once it was decided, it got done! Kat and the broken bike were puzzled into the front area of the bus, and off they went, leaving only a cloud of dust in their wake.

According to the guide of the tour bus, we had six kilometers left to go to the top of the pass. Leatherfoot and I settled onto our mounts and began to cycle. The road became very winding at this point up the valley, and the wind direction would change as we rounded each corner, but, prevailingly, it was in our face. Once again, it was tough riding. Leatherfoot is proving to be the stronger rider of the two of us, and I had to work hard to keep up to him.

A few kilometers later, the third and only other vehicle we saw today also pulled over shortly after passing us. It was a 4X4, and out jumped a couple of Japanese tourists along with their guide and, of course, their video camera! They had the most incredulous looks on their faces.

"What you do here on bicycle... oh, this clazy!"

"So desu ne. Clazy desu ne! We can video you please?"

The funniest part was their looks of stunned disbelief when we responded "sure, go ahead" in Japanese, and then continued talking to them in their language. What an hilarious scene, Leatherfoot and I being "interviewed" by Japanese tourists in the middle of a mountain pass in Tibet. Naturally, we told them also of Kat, the third member of our group, being a Japanese girl who they would find at the summit of the pass. To this news they were also flabbergasted, as were we at the whole spectacle.

Amused, and somewhat refreshed from the short rest, we plowed onwards into the increasing wind, and up the winding gravel road. As I rounded each new corner, I realized that I was falling further and further behind Leatherfoot, until, I rounded one corner and he was gone. This was disheartening, and though I knew I didn't have too much further to go to the top, I felt a strange pang of loneliness. Stopping for one more brief rest, the loneliness morphed into a silent communion with the greater surroundings and a small smile crept across my face, until it was promptly wiped off with the next blast of wind! No choices. Get back on the bike, pedal, and endure.

We found Kat at the summit of the pass hanging out, once again, with a small group of Tibetans. Welcome to 5000 meters (16,500 feet) above sea level. Awesome! It's the prayer flags that tell the best story of life up there. Brightly coloured small pieces of cloth with prayers written on them, they are attached to sticks that are jammed into a big pile of rocks at the side of the road. All Tibetan passers by will either jam in a new stick, or tie another flag onto an existing stick. They are the only visible splash of colour in the midst of the dirt and rock, and most are faded, battered, and tattered to the point that their prayers have been carried off into the winds. Regrettably, we had no prayer flags with us, but I made sure to go and touch one and leave my own thanks for seeing us to the top, and requests for a safe descent.

Kat, all bundled in her wool hat and warm gear, was pretty relaxed and smiley looking as she hung out with the Tibetans. Once again, it was a bit of a mystery to me as to why they were way up there, but they seemed to be having quite an enjoyable time together, especially Kat and the kids. She had them laughing and giggling, and there were smiles on the faces of the adults too. If it weren't for her clothes making her stand out with us, she would, with her dirty and weather beaten face, have blended in completely with her new local friends.

WOW, a funked out prehistoric seahorse kissing as alligator… ahh clouds!

We lingered at the top of the pass for a while longer, letting the picturesque views around us penetrate. It was the glacial aspect of the whole area that was most captivating. We found a spot not too far afield where we were able to refill our water bottles and enjoy the fresh melt water. It was the kind of liquid that makes you shudder as the freezing sensation seeps through your teeth, but once it settles, makes you feel alive. Being such a lovely spot, we could have easily lingered longer, but the afternoon was wearing on. It was time to move along to what may have been the most joyous part of the whole day. The realization that we could actually leave our towing system undone, and let Kat be free. The wheel still spins fine as long as gravity is on your side.

The ride down, though rough and bumpy, was exciting. Kat, so happy to be free of being dragged and able to coast, was going unbelievably fast. I must admit that I was a little worried about her wiping out, but, of course, she didn't. Maybe my few words with the prayer flags helped. You never know. And much like most downhill thrills, the ride ended sooner than hoped for, and, as the terrain mellowed, we began to think about a campsite. We'd been through enough for one day, and were certainly not in the mood for any more towing. It was then that we saw a sign for a very small monastery pointing down a narrow little side road. Though we certainly didn't want to add too much work, we thought it might be a nice, relatively untouched experience. The narrow gravel road went up and down along the waves in the terrain of the lower slope of the valley. Up and down, just like the day, just like the whole cycling journey so far. We all pushed together and chatted, and tried to stay on the road, which, at times, became more like a path. At least twenty minutes passed, and still there was no sign of the monastery, at which point an ominous, thick black cloud drifted overhead and brought with it a hail storm. The pellets came in droves, and were somewhat painful, but not intimidating. Not that I would have wanted the storm to last too long, but it was a nice change from straight sun and wind. And, as the one big black cloud blew past us and up towards the pass, we came to a sudden sharp drop in the road cut through some wind eroded towers of dirt and rock. Being such an appealing spot, we laid down our bikes and explored the area. At the bottom of the short hill, we found that the road ended at a huge, wide, completely dry river bed. The water carved banks working in wonderfully with the wind sculpted towers. It didn't take long for us to agree to camp here for the night, not only for the beauty of the area, but for the shelter it will provide. This, then, brings me around in the day's journey to where I am writing this now, sitting in a naturally carved dirt chair.

This might just be Tibet at its most beautiful. Mother Nature changing cloaks, her heavy breaths and oppressive stares giving way to more playful moods as she weaves her favorite colour fabrics through the evening skies. Her only voice now coming through the odd cry of a hawk, and finally the symphony of stars that builds slowly to a magnificent crescendo!

EXTREMES

WE AWAKEN IN PEACE. THIS REALLY IS A MAGNIFICENT SPOT TO have camped. Our tent looks tiny as it sits nestled against the cliff that is the side bank of this massive dry river bed. I try to envision water pouring down here in another season. Often, I wonder of the many different faces this land must have at various times of the year. It is not a gentle place, even now, but I think we are here during one of its gentlest seasons. The wind, which is at rest at the moment, has carved some unique shapes into the surrounding landscape. Nature is still the most talented artist.

Leatherfoot has unraveled himself from his cocoon. The tent would fit all three of us, but it is more comfortable for all when he sleeps outside. Dressed in his warmest clothes, and stuffed inside his sleeping bag, he then wraps himself in the tent fly, which we do not need to use. His outer most layer is usually his backpack, and a protective rock wall barrier, which he builds diligently before bed each night. He loves it, sleeping under the stars, and why not. The stars are here by the bazillions to behold. There is no artificial light anywhere close to drown them out. The only thing he needs to protect himself from is the cold, which penetrates deeply through the night. There are no "predators" to fear. None, at least, that we are aware of.

"Kat, the stars were brilliant last night. I wish you could have stayed awake long enough to see them. They were so beautiful."

"I wish too Leatherfoot, but I was so tired, I can't even keep my eyes open. Only I can think sleep."

"How did you sleep?"

"Pretty good, but it was cold middle of night again."

"Yea. How do you feel now?"

"Mm. Okay, but not great. My neck and shoulders are sore. It's hard to keep bike going straight when being pulled. I know you guys laugh, because you think it easy back there, but it's really exhausting. Anyway, how you sleep Leatherfoot?"

"Pretty good too. I agree that it was cold last night, but wrapping up in the tent fly definitely helps."

Our bodies are stiff, even after the nice exchange of massages we still managed late last evening. But, that is not a surprise after yesterday's cycling, and a long frigid night. I suggest a game of Frisbee to loosen and warm us up. Frisbee. The great entertainer. Particularly with local kids. Multifunctional when used as a plate. One of the ultimate travel companions. A dear friend that goes along on all voyages. It's such a great location for throwing the disc anyway. We do need to exercise caution not to turn any ankles on the rocks and boulders, but it is so wide open, and the disc travels so far in the thin air. Nobody chases the first few errant throws, but we do settle into a nice rhythm for a while, and do, indeed, warm up well enough to deal with packing.

We are ready to head off in the early morning sun, and push our bikes across the width of the dry river bed to the continuation of the path on the opposite side. Another twenty minutes along, and still there is no sign of the monastery. At this point, we decide to give up, and leaving any remnants of pathway, we ride in a generally downhill manner across the rough open plain, angling back towards where we assume the main road lies.

"Ha haa! Check out all those little gopher-ish rodents and rabbitty things scurry away in a frantic wave at our rumbling through their world. That's hilarious!"

"Are those technical terms Dogi?"

"Do you know what they really are Leatherfoot?"

"I think they're marmots, Kat, and the 'rabbitty things' are called pikas."

"They make funny noises. I think they are yelling at us."

A look behind reveals curious little marmot and pika heads sticking back out of holes. We're hooting and hollering to accompany their chattering as we ramble down the hill having a grand old time! Eventually, however, the roller coaster ride ends, and we reconnect with the main road. Here a stronger dose of reality settles over us once again, and our laughter fades into knowing smiles. We still have quite a way to go until we reach the main town of Gyangze, and we still have a lame bike and Kat to pull to get there. Fortunately, we remind ourselves with positivism, the overall grade should be downhill as we are still heading away from yesterday's pass and further down this new valley. We re-connect The Rig. Though we have made some minor improvements as to how we strap our packs to the racks, we have come up with no improvement modifications on our towing system. The Rig will have to function the way it is for one more day, assuming, that is, we can make it all the way to Gyangze today. If a replacement part for the bike cannot be found there... well, we'll think about that then. We look at each other pensively, and saddle up.

Our first stint on the yank goes well. On the slightly steeper downs, Kat has been able to coast, on the steeper ups, she has been pushing hard, and on anything flat or gradual, Leatherfoot and I continue to take turns pulling. He has just started his shift, and rather than hanging back with them, I decide to ride out in front and enjoy some peace and solitude.

Soon, I am riding down a slight hill, when on my right I can see a rather fancy looking property. One could even call it an estate. The structures are Tibetan looking, but I get the impression it's probably a wealthy Chinese abode. But why out here? There is nothing else around. In a sense, it's an attractive house, but it is certainly odd and out of place looking, and... SHIT... DAWGS! Two of them. Nasty, slobbering, snarling beasts barreling down on me full tilt. Where the hell did they come from? They're half way down the long driveway just as I'm approaching it. They're scaring the hell out of me, but I zone in and start pedalling furiously. I get by the driveway just before they get to the end of it, but the hell-born brutes turn the corner and give chase. They're not far off my ankles and I don't even have time to think about anything but pedalling. Pedal. Pedal. Pedal. That's not totally true, there is a part of my mind that is prepared to give them a good boot in the nose if I have to. Back off you bastards!

Fortunately, I do have enough speed to outlast their pursuit, but what about Kat and Leatherfoot? There is a slight downhill approach, but they can't move as fast as I did. Maybe the dogs will be freaked out by The Rig! No, not likely. Maybe they'll be too winded from the long chase after me. Poor Kat. She doesn't care much for dogs in the first place, and she's afraid of most of the docile ones much less these kinds of creatures. Where are they? I didn't think they were that far... Oh here they come .. and here come the dogs. I'm ready to go back if I have to, but I sure hope I don't. Go Leatherfoot go! Come on Kat, hang on...

"You guys made it! Are you all right?"

"That was crazy. I so scared. They run at us so fast and bark so loud and I can see their teeth! I want to pedal but I can't. All I can do is concentrate to stay on bike. My fate is totally in Leatherfoot's hands!"

"More like in my legs, Kat. I don't think I've ever cranked bike pedals harder in my whole life. Sorry, the slack and SNAP got pretty bad there for a while, but you did a great job keeping it together back there."

"Oh don't be sorry, you were amazing. I don't want to hit brakes with those ugly things right beside me, but I almost hit you on your back wheel a couple of times."

"I don't even want to imagine the consequences if one or both of you had gone down. Mean old doggies! I hope they go after a truck whose driver has as nasty a disposition as they do next time! Come on Leatherfoot. Let's switch again."

So this is rural Tibet. When I'm not the one pulling, I get a chance to look around. Interestingly, structures are often built on the hillsides, or even on top of hills. The huge expanses of flat land are in the early stages of preparation for farming. Animals, mostly sheep and yaks, are seen in far greater abundance than people. As I round a bend in the road, I see that we have arrived at a point where the road drops steeply, goes across a small bridge, and rises again steeply on the other side. If only we could jump a few hundred meters, we wouldn't have to go down and up again at all. This is no place for The Rig. Kat is on her own here. She can enjoy the coast down, but she'll have to push this one up by herself. Leatherfoot and I need to conserve as much energy as possible to continue this towing business. We coast down the hill, across the bridge, stick it into first gear, and arrive atop the other side huffing, puffing and sweating.

"That was a tough hill Leatherfoot."

"Yea, but still not as tough as towing. I hope we can make it to Gyangze today."

"Hey, can you hear that? We'd better get off the road."

We think we hear a truck approaching, but are surprised to see Kat show up sooner than expected, accompanied by an old Tibetan man and his son who is driving a very basic looking farm cart. The machine, with its exposed engine, is generating quite the roar, and the young boy in control of it is wide eyed and smiling. The older man is pushing Kat's bike!

"What happened Kat?"

"Well, I am about halfway up the hill. This man and his son catch me up. They drive this machine thing. It is really noisy, so I try to ignore and keep my head down and keep pushing. Then, when the machine is next to me, old man jump off his cart and grab my bike and push. I'm little shocked first, but he is so happy and friendly. I can't believe it. He is sweating and breathing so hard, but he just keeps pushing. Once I recover a little, I start push from the back too, and we get to top of hill together. He's so nice."

"Hey, do you think we should give them a Dalai Lama picture?"

"If there was ever a time to give a picture of the Dalai Lama to someone, this is it."

Dalai Lama pictures. Can you imagine that all pictures of the exiled spiritual leader are currently forbidden in Tibet? A picture of a person is illegal to possess because of the desire of a government to suppress a culture. Is this acceptable, or ludicrous? This is a fact we knew before leaving Nepal, and we took a chance to get them across customs, and, it is even a risk to carry them while here. We also understand that it is a risk for the Tibetans to accept and retain the photos, but that it also represents a very precious gift. We would like to provide them opportunity and freedom to choose whether or not to accept. To risk potential punishment out of love for their culture, loyalty to their true spiritual leader, and hope that he may one day be allowed to return. Being the first time to give out a Dalai Lama picture, which we have in the form of postcards, we are unsure of what kind of reaction we might receive. What we have right now, however, is confusion, as we ask them to wait while we dig in our bags trying to find them.

"Here they are. Hey Kat, I think you should give it to them."

Confusion turns into instant gratification. A look of greater happiness I may have never seen before. The young boy, whose eyes were already bulging at the likes of us in the first place, stares in awe at the photo as his father tells him who it is. Surely it is the first time he has ever seen a photo of the Dalai Lama. The man clutches it tightly in both hands, looks up at us with a huge smile, and then back at the photo, almost in disbelief. Suddenly, he looks around with a slight trace of nervousness mixed into his emotions, as if "big brother" might be watching. Then he touches it to his head several times and stores it up under his hat!

There are a few clouds passing over today, and we are thankful whenever one decides to doodle in front of the sun for a while. The sun is such an amazing thing, and its definition may have no greater clarity than in a high altitude desert. It gives so much, and takes so much away. It gives energy to the land, the body, the mind and the spirit, but at certain times during its journey across the sky, it robs all of these same things of that same kind of energy. When there is not enough sun, we crave it like few other things in life. When there is too much, we try to avoid it with great desperation. And, as no clouds have blocked the sun for a while, and we are beginning to overheat, we are happy at the timing of a lunch invitation. It is not the first such invitation we've had today. It is becoming a common occurrence. The local Tibetans in these rural areas are always so happy looking and waving us in, whether it's time for a meal or not. Unfortunately, we can't stop every time. Naturally, hunger and the dozen or so smiling, laughing Tibetans are reason enough to stop in this case, but there is one more thing that draws us in to this particular group. It is the shade of a grove of trees. I feel as though these are the first trees we've seen since our first night of camping a week ago. Trees. These ones are not too green or lush, but it is so nice to be sitting under their shade. I have missed them more than I realized.

Lunch is a whole new culinary experience today. It's an amazingly extensive "menu" with five items. Boiled rice, flat breads, tsampa, some yellowish coloured chunks of something that looks and feels like rock, AND, Yak Butter Tea. The boiled rice tastes like boiled rice, but it is very welcome to us nonetheless, as are the flat breads, which taste like no more than flour and water. The real adventure starts with the tsampa. Tsampa is probably the most basic and common everyday food for the Tibetans. Particularly, those outside of the urban areas. It is roasted barley flour. That's it. We've seen some of the nomadic looking Tibetans stick their hands into a little side pouch, and put something into their mouths, which we have assumed is tsampa, but this is our first opportunity to try it. Our guidebook suggests that they sometimes mix it with yak butter, but they offer it to us as is. Flour. Powder. I don't know why I wasn't expecting it, but the second I put a handful into my mouth, it soaks up all the saliva so fast that I feel as though and can't breath and I've gone cross-eyed. Liquid! I need liquid! Oh god, how I wish we'd brought a bottle of water up from the bikes, now all I have to drink is Yak Butter Tea! The Tibetans are laughing their heads off at the look of my contorted face. I don't see the humour myself until I get some "lovely" tea in to re-hydrate my parched mouth, which probably only rearranges the contortions. It is pretty funny, and we all have a hoot.

After barely surviving my first tsampa experience, I am eyeing the yellow rock chunks carefully. Unless, perhaps, it came from a candy store, it is not something any of us would ordinarily put in our mouths, but they are all sucking on it, and offering it. The Tibetans are amused some more by my thorough inspection, rubbing it in my fingers, sniffing it, and finally sticking it between my teeth to test it out before closing my lips around it. I do cross eyes and funny faces just to maximize the reaction. Their laughter is so pure. The "rock" does feel like jagged candy, but slowly dissolves into a fatty substance, rather than a sugary one. Yet another form of yak fat, we assume. Maybe you could consider it cheese. Add in the perennial Yak Butter Tea, and the thick oily coating on the inside of our mouths may last all day. Next time, Yak Rocks first, tsampa second!

Though very generous with everything else, there is one thing that this group is unwilling to share. That is the dried meat stuck to bones on which many of them gnaw. On some of the pieces, it seems like you can still see bits of the animal's hair. It's impossible for me to tell if it is yak, or lamb meat. Probably they eat both, but would share neither. It is obviously too precious for them. It is a part of the scene that resonates deeply with me, as I watch one particular lady work the end of her bone. How many times in wealthier countries have I seen people leave meals, including meat, unfinished? These leftovers going in the garbage. Meat. An animal is born. During its life, it consumes energy provided by the land by grazing on grasses or eating grains, which have been grown through the time and energy of people. Then the animal is killed, skinned, and butchered, all requiring the time and effort of people. Then, finally, it can be consumed. The energy, having entered the animal though what was provided by nature, and manipulated by people, is now stored in the organs, the skin, and the meat. That stored energy is now available for recycle to the people in the form of clothes, blankets, and food. Nutrients. Energy back into the body so that the whole process can continue. The process that is a cycle, and here in Tibet, there is no waste. No energy, stored in the form of food, sits on the side of a plate only to be swiped into the garbage. It is all kept in the cycle. Energy potential is maximized. The tendons, the cartilage, the marrow, anything that has nutrient or other value will get consumed.

All in all, it is a meal that many from wealthier nations might consider barbaric, yet we love the experience. It gives us some much needed nutrients and energy, and the company is splendid. And, as if eating, making tea, and cooking with yak butter aren't enough uses, some of the Tibetan ladies in the group also insist that we rub it on our dry skin. I can just picture it in some fancy bottle with an ad that reads "New Secret Tibetan Formula - Two in One Sun cream and Moisturizer!" These people are so kind and generous. They particularly goop a lot onto Kat's lips, the lower one of which has begun to form a nasty looking sun blister.

As much as you might try to guard against it, the elements of sun, wind, and altitude are mightily taxing on the body , particularly the skin. The people here all look old and weathered, and after spending only such a short time here ourselves, we too are beginning to look old and weathered. We try to be good about drinking enough water, and using good sunscreen, but our faces are beginning to crinkle. Maybe, we need our own supply of yak butter! What we have been given, is a handful of yak rocks to go.

"Tu-jay-cha... Ka-lee shu."

"Ka-lee pay."

"Do you think we should learn more Tibetan?"

"Yea, if we have enough energy to study, but we're getting by okay with the basics."

So, off we ride again from our wonderful lunch companions, with yak butter coating the inside of our mouths, the outside of our mouths, and our cheeks. We are protected, at least for a while, from the elements.

Do human beings count as one of the elements? The sun, the wind, the rains, the plants, the animals... the humans? This one still confuses me. I guess we could analyze it in terms of the classic elements. The sun, the great fire, builds and destroys. The wind does much the same. It erodes, cleanses, and blends all parts that make up earth, as do the rains, the rivers and the oceans. Water mixes and perpetuates the great flow going around, and around in its cycles. But humans? Are we simply a subset of earth, one of the four basic elements, or are we something else? We work so diligently at trying to control the flow. Control? We might think so, but control of an environment is a fallacy. We can strongly influence a micro-environment over a micro-time-period, but we cannot control. Perhaps, manipulate is a better word. We manipulate all the elements to our own benefit. Much of what we do is brilliant. We have figured out ways of manipulation to derive copious amounts of energy from the elements, yet we are wasteful. We use far more than we need to, simply because we can, and we are no longer educated well enough to notice that we do. And though we are trying hard to sweep it under the carpet, we are leaving little byproducts of mess all over the place. No matter what we do, however, the great flow of the elements will continuously work towards an equilibrium. One thing will lead to another. We are not walking in a line, or up a hill, rather, we are going in a circle. All of what we do will affect things in the cycle in ways that we cannot foresee. Humans. We are imaginative, intelligent and inspiring, yet, we are also disgusting. This all becomes perfectly evident as we, and The Rig, arrive at the "Asshole of Tibet."

The Asshole of Tibet is not on our map. That's why I have gone ahead and named it myself. I hesitate to call it a town. It is, rather, a conglomeration of all that is sick about humanity, and it is so very unexpected here in the middle of this vast emptiness we have been meandering through for the past week. It is gross. It attacks every sense grotesquely. The sights are awful, the noise is horrible, and it stinks. Everything about it feels revolting. It is a town seemingly taken over by the Chinese army, and a Chinese power corporation, who are in the middle of building a huge hydroelectric plant. The massive machinery kicks up clouds of dust and dirt, which the intense wind plasters into our faces. Buildings in the town are raw and colourless, and garbage is strewn everywhere. Broken glass, paper, plastic, food... everywhere. I feel nauseated. The people of the town, Chinese and Tibetans alike, all seem evil. Any love and spirit that must have once existed here has been crushed by the big machines. Electricity. Power. There it is. That is the beauty that all of this hell will bring when it is finished. Harnessing the energy of flowing water, and distributing it to a great number of humans in order that they may be able to cut down significantly on their work loads. The ability to pump water rather than carry it. The ability to create heat with which to cook food, clean dishes and clothes, bathe, and stay warm during a cold night. These things are beautiful. They most likely will be very beautiful one day to those who have never known them, but the process of building it that is going on right here, right now, is foul, and we have no choice other than to go through it.

Pulling Kat and her bike through this will, unfortunately, be futile. There is way too much headwind to tow right now, and too much chaos. We disconnect The Rig, and, for a while, we all push together, trying to ignore everything going on around us as much as possible. Every lung full is thick with dirt. After a week of so much silence, the noise is deafening, and the people, the humans, those beings in which we have seen so much kindness in the past weeks, are gone. They are replaced by shadows of horror. We must push and ignore. Push and ignore.

There is one thing, however, that we cannot ignore. It catches our attention through all the surrounding hell. It is the mournful crying and wailing of a little lost sheep. Its cry penetrates the rest of the chaos, though it takes us a while to locate the poor animal wandering in utter confusion on the bank of a small hill to our left. Never can I remember hearing as much anguish and distress in the voice of any creature. I don't know how many animals, or humans in the world are more miserable than Kat, Leatherfoot and myself at this point in time, but this poor solitary sheep is definitely one of them. Its cry makes me feel a lot less sorry for myself, and, after tearing myself away from watching its plight, I resume my own, with head down and new vigor.

Leatherfoot and I begin to ride. We try to stay in touch with Kat. We wait a couple of times, but the desire to get out of hell is just too strong, so we ride ahead and leave her to deal with it. The air is so thick with dirt that I stick my face into my shirt up to my nose to act as a filter. Finally, we are nearing the end, when we see one final obstacle to deal with before being farted out of the Asshole of Tibet. It is a Chinese army checkpoint, and it represents our first since leaving Lhasa and all of the "Swirling Rumors" behind. A sudden wave of anxiety flows through us. This would not be a fun place to have an official hassle.

We keep a little distance and await Kat before we approach what is mostly a group of very young men. There is testosterone in the air, though a look of confusion and uncertainty is in their eyes as well. In a sense, I feel a little pity for them, as I wonder which part of the country they have been sent from to man such an obscure outpost. We approach together and await instructions. They ask to see our passports, and we reluctantly hand them over. Trying to be helpful and respectful, I flip mine open and hand it to one of them. As he is inspecting it, I realize that it is on the page of my old Indian visa instead of my Chinese one. Should I try to tell him? No, he doesn't seem to be able to tell the difference anyway. We have an exchange of words. They speak to us in Chinese, and we answer back to them in English. We totally can't understand each other, but it is the tone that is important. It feels like a test of our patience, a game, a show. It is our job to let them know that they are superior, yet we must retain an air of confidence. As the slow seconds tick by, it becomes quite apparent that they have no idea what to make of us. They have some discussion amongst themselves, while we smile and wait without signs of agitation. Finally, some "official" piece of paper appears, and we are told to write our names and passport numbers on it. This is given one final inspection, and we are let on our way. We walk the bikes along the road for a few minutes to clear the noise and stink.

"Whew, that was a bit tense. Are you okay Kat?"

She doesn't look good at all. As it turns out, she had the worst time of the three of us going through the Asshole of Tibet. Maybe even worse than the sheep. She got hassled a lot. Grabbed, yelled at, and, at one point, someone even tried to steal the pack off the back of her bike. Fortunately, she was brave and strong enough to pull away from the situation. The Asshole of Tibet. It's part of the cycle. The shitty part. Like the manure that becomes compost that one day becomes a carrot or a flower. I wonder what this town will be like in five or ten years. What will the power be used for? Who will benefit? What will happen to the flow of the river and the micro-environments upstream and down? Progress!?

Feeling relieved and recovered, we reassemble The Rig. As the road is mostly flat, or even a slight steady downhill, and the wind has eased considerably, I manage to get into a good rhythm towing Kat. The closer we get to Gyangze, the better the condition of the road, though it is still gravel. Suddenly, we come upon some more green. The road is lined with trees, which we take as a sign that the town must be quite near. Their life gives us a last boost of energy, and anticipation grows. I feel so good that I suggest to Leatherfoot to go ahead, and scout the town and accommodation options, while I keep towing. He does so, and even rides back to us and offers to tow the last section, but our rhythm is still there, so it isn't necessary.

GYANGZE! We have arrived. As much as I am exhausted from the extremes of the day, and the workload of towing, a wave of excitement washes through me. Yet so early in the journey, but I feel like we are coming to a kind of end of a cycle. The end of towing a broken cycle is the hope. No, not just the hope, the necessity. We can't possibly keep dragging this thing, this rig, all the way to the next bigger town of Shigatse. If it hasn't already been folly, then to continue surely would be. The Rig must be laid to rest in Gyangze. Not that I can look around too much as I follow Leatherfoot to our hotel, but, at first glance, this is a very pleasing town. From what Leatherfoot has said, and what we can see thus far, it appears to be mostly Tibetan. The immediate impression is pleasant and serene feeling, with added splashes of colour. It is a welcoming place after such a long and crazy day. We ride our mini-caravan into the compound of the hotel chosen by Leatherfoot. In fact, it is the hotel which was suggested to us by our 4X4 friends. Much like the place where we stayed in Lhasa, it is built around a big open dirt square. The person who comes to help us get settled is as shabby as the rest of the place, but he radiates a friendly smile through his dirty face. He points out the room where we can store our bikes, and then points to a room on the second floor for us to sleep.

Entering the room, we plop ourselves down on the beds, which all respond with various melodies of creaking, and look around at one another with knowing nods of our heads. Then comes the wave of tiredness, that slightly woozy feeling that strongly suggests going from sitting, to lying, to closing the eyes and drifting off to a far away place.

"Kat. Don't go to sleep yet. We need to get something to eat and drink."

"Just five minutes."

"I don't think so. If you fall asleep now, you won't want to get up anymore. Come on, let's go straight to the hotel restaurant."

"Mmm"

RELIEF

THE ATMOSPHERE IN THE RESTAURANT LAST NIGHT WAS SUPERIOR to the food, and it had ragged, dirty drapes, a crooked floor, scratched up tables, and smoking patrons. We liked it. It was our first restaurant meal since that lunch before the first pass, back on our second day of cycling. We ate the Tibetan basics of thugpa and momos. There might have even been a bit of meat in the momos, but I can't say for sure.

The first half of last night's sleep was deep and blank. The time between getting horizontal, and being unconscious, must have been no more than a few seconds. There were periods in the later hours of rest, however, that were somewhat more disturbed. The intermittent sound of stray dogs howling was one reason, but mainly it was the creaking of the cots every time one of us would move, and the fact that they are so saggy and uncomfortable. Our whole room is worthy of description. The walls, where they are not peeling, are half poo brown, and half lime green. The ceiling is drooping so much, that we're afraid a chunk might fall off at any moment, which would mean a horrible floral pattern falling on us. And, our three rickety old cots, which are also way too short for Leatherfoot and myself, rest on a broken up concrete floor.

The rest of the hotel is just as basic. The communal toilet consists of a hole in the floor, or you can just go wherever you want for number ones, like in the corner of the big courtyard. There are no showers, though buckets of cold water are available. That all said, the place overall is clean and tidy, and it represents to us a wonderful place to rest and recuperate, which is what Kat and I are continuing to do.

Leatherfoot has gone into town this morning to look for a bike store and a replacement wheel, and we await the results rather anxiously. We start a conversation about what we should do if he doesn't find one, but decide that there is no point in thinking about that until we need to. Rather, we take the bikes out of storage, and begin to clean and do some other minor maintenance on them. They have taken a beating, and, not surprisingly, we find a lot of loose parts that require tightening. What little oil remains on the chains is thick and dirty, and we take to cleaning off as much gunk as possible. The only other patrons at the hotel are a couple of truckers, and one of them, who has been watching us off and on, suddenly comes striding over. He brings a can of grease with him, and indicates we should use it on our chains instead of the oil we had dribbled on. Figuring he must know what he's doing, we accept it, and proceed to lubricate as best we can. Just as the trucker is wandering off, Leatherfoot comes prancing through the big open doors into the courtyard.

"Kat, he's back. Here he comes! So? So? So? So? How'd it go? How'd it go?"

"We are the proud owners of a brand new back wheel!!! And, I even bargained a good price."

"Oh Leatherfoot, you are so great. We love you man."

This is the happiest news we can imagine. We all give each other big bear hugs, and I break into a ridiculous song and dance.

"NO MORE TOWING!!!

NO MORE TOWING!!!

THE WIND WILL KEEP BLOWING, BUT NO MORE TOWING!!!"

The trucker looks up from the engine in which he had his head buried to see what the commotion is, gives a little chuckle, and goes back to his work.

○ ○ ○

With the completion of our bike repairs, we have the time to explore Gyangze, and discover it to be a wonderful place. It is a mostly Tibetan little town built around a lot of cobblestone streets. It reminds us of the Tibetan Quarter in Lhasa, though it is quieter.

Small trees line some of the streets, and many of the buildings look to be in good condition. Though there are not many of them about, the locals we do see are going about their everyday business. After some aimless wandering, we are pulled through the Tibetan old town and towards the dominant feature of Gyangze, the area of the Pelkor Chode Monastery. It sits at the end of a long wide cobblestone street back dropped by brown hills, the nearest of which has a large wall built along the top. I am sitting here at the base of what is known as a stupa, or a chorten. It is a common style of architecture related to Buddhism, and this one is called the Gyangze Kumbum.

A somewhat crazy monk has suddenly appeared. My image of monks has certainly changed since arriving in Tibet. Somehow, I expected them to be calm, quiet and withdrawn, but from what I have seen thus far, many are theatrical and curious. They are interested in learning, not just from their Buddhist scriptures, but about life in general. Seeing someone foreign like myself must provide them an opportunity for unique learning. They are very much human, and their individual personalities are on open display. This young man, wrapped in his dusty robes, has squatted in front of me drawing pictures on the rock with a chunk of dirt, and has begun to ask me questions in very broken English. I try my best to provide answers in simple clear language, but his next question leads me to believe he isn't really understanding much. His questions are totally random. If he wasn't a monk, I'd say he's been into the chang...

This stupa, which I have already finished touring, is fabulous. From the outside, it rises as though in giant steps, before you get to a tall rounded top section. On top of this is a square room with a set of Buddha's eyes on each wall, that stare out in the cardinal directions. They have an even more penetrating gaze than others I have seen before, making them particularly mesmerizing. The crown of the structure is a massive and intricate golden dome. Walking up it in a clockwise direction, there are an endless amount of mural paintings over the four floors. For one who has the patience and interest, they must tell some wonderful stories.

The crazy monk now has his face closer to the page of my journal than my own. Also, a young boy wearing a Chicago bulls cap has wandered over and sat unashamedly touching against me. Unfortunately, he smells rather badly. Though I'm not sure about the monk, I'm assuming that the smelly boy can't read what I'm writing. There is also an old woman with a beautiful long braid, who is walking around and around the stupa, chanting and praying. By the gaze in her eyes, her mind appears to be floating. As her sound fades, a skinny battle worn dog shuffles in, sits in front of me, and begins gnawing viciously at his fleas...

The one mural that remains etched in my mind is the huge painting of the evil looking blue faced character with three eyes and a crown with five skulls, surrounded by a robe of fire. We've seen him, or depictions like him, in other monastery areas, and I have learned that he is some form of protector deity. After a while, however, I found rooms to be similar, though there was one near the end of my tour where I did find some intriguing sculptures made out of coloured yak fat. One piece is an upside down skull with deep red eyes, and one green worm coming out of each pig-like red nostril. It has pink teeth, and a red tongue sticking out. Green ears sit low on the jaw line, and beady black and orange eyeballs are attached near the bottom of the chin. From the very base of the chin, a staff sticks out, off of which hangs a blue bag with a red ribbon. On the staff, between the bag and the chin, is a small orange plate. I found it to be a unique and rather disturbing piece.

The crazy monk, satisfied with my journal writing, and having finally exhausted all of his questions, gets up and moves on. Fortunately, the smelly boy has tagged along with him, and I sit alone again waiting for Kat and Leatherfoot to finish their tour of the stupa. The old lady continues to walk around the stupa, and, at the same time, spin her hand held prayer wheel. She is beautiful. Not in appearance, as she is weathered and wrinkled like all of the older people here, but in aura and demeanor. Just watching her go around and around makes me feel so at peace.

"Hey Dogi, have you been waiting long?"

"A little while, but never mind, I find it just as fascinating out here as in there. Did you guys have fun?"

"Yea, and I think I got a half decent photo of those Buddha's eyes too."

Leatherfoot did manage to collect a new battery for his camera from the hotel staff left by our 4X4 friends. We wander only a little more, taking one more photo of a giant pole that must have a thousand prayer flags attached to it, before we make our way back to the hotel. Though Gyangze is a lovely town, it is also very small, and it has not taken long to exhaust the sights that we have taken an interest in. As such, we have decided to leave later this afternoon. Though we are adhering to no specific time schedule, there is the possible issue of our visa running out, and we feel as though we are quite behind what we expected because of the whole broken bike fiasco. We'd really like to make it to the city of Shigatse by tomorrow night, and getting some kilometers behind us this afternoon will help us cut down on the length of tomorrow's ride.

The Rig is dead! And, we hope, never to be resurrected again. I cannot begin to describe what a huge relief it is to have the third bike operational again. One more day of that towing business would have been the death of us. There was no humour in it at the time, none at all, but looking back, I can have a little laugh. I start in on my silly song and dance once more, but only long enough to get some dirty looks from Kat and Leatherfoot.

Packed, strapped, and ready, we begin our late afternoon ride on a paved section of road. This, coupled with having all three bikes rideable, leaves us feeling happy and energized. In due time, we find ourselves riding next to a local man. I am in such a jovial mood that I begin to talk to him. In English. He can't understand me, but he smiles back, and retorts in his own tongue. These kinds of conversations are fun. We learn absolutely nothing from each other, yet positive feelings are exchanged. At least I hope so. Perhaps he's actually saying "get the heck away from me you foreign freak," but I don't think so. He peels off the main road just as it turns back into gravel. Unfortunately, our much too familiar acquaintance, Mr. Head Wind, has also greeted us with authority. Though this doesn't bother Leatherfoot and I too much, it is particularly hard on Kat. She says that her leg muscles are screaming, but she does her best to plod on.

We were hoping the late afternoon would be an ideal time to ride, but it has proven to be slow going. Kat, who has never really had the chance to gain any sort of cycling conditioning, continues to struggle against the wind. That said, we have made some positive ground, though, as the light is fading quickly, we find that we are not yet clear of the outskirt farming area of Gyangze. Riding in the cold and dark is not appealing, so we begin the search for a place to camp where we might be relatively undisturbed, but the options are few.

With the sky turning purple, we finally decide to pull into a little driveway, which is home to a small square building made of clay bricks. We have a quick dipsy doodle around the area, and it appears that we are alone. In behind the building are farm fields, but there are no longer people working at this late hour. It is the sound that is the most striking feature of the area. A strong channel of water is flowing directly under the structure, suggesting that this is probably a grain mill, and perhaps a storage shed too. At first, we think about pitching our tent behind some bushes at the side of the building, but after standing on a sidewall, we are able to see that the surface of the roof is flat and rimmed with a very short wall. It feels somewhat intrusive, but we figure our chances of remaining hidden from discovery up here are much better than if we set up our tent. We love to hang out with the locals, but early morning discovery is not really ideal, and we have a chuckle reminiscing about our morning attack from the school children after our first night of camping.

We hide our bikes behind the bushes, and climb up onto the roof easily enough from the side wall. Everything comes out of our packs, and the base of our bed is the tarp. As we have no sleeping mats, we consider unpacking the tent to use as another under layer, but opt against it. Instead, we layer on our warm clothes, crawl into our sleeping bags, and settle in. The water that channels through underneath us is loud, but constant, and it soon fades in to the background of our consciousness as the stars twinkle to life. This location absolutely begs for a bedtime story, and what better than

140

to replay the events of a great day, and the nightly tradition of going over the highlights and the lowlights.

"My highlight is the stupa. I enjoyed all the paintings."

"They were amazing weren't they Kat. I loved the crazy monk and the old lady wandering around the stupa, but my highlight of highlights is still the fact that Leatherfoot found a new wheel."

"Well, I agree with both of you, and can't decide between the two. And, to be honest, I can't think of any lowlights today at all."

"True, there wasn't much to gripe about today Leatherfoot, but I tell ya, that boy who sat next to me was the worst thing I've smelled in Tibet."

"For me, just the riding, the gravel, the wind, it's hard work."

To end, we all agree to add this to the list of one of the most intriguing places we've ever spent a night. Kat and Leatherfoot are lying silently on either side of me staring at the stars as I write this by flickering candlelight. Very cool! Time for me to watch the stars and ponder as well.

GOODNIGHT

EXHAUSTION

It is the jingle of pony and cart that first alerts us that it must be morning, and the roar of the water that passes below, that reminds us where we are. The sun has not yet crested the eastern horizon, yet, it is light enough to see around us. There is still a chill in the air after the cold night, making sliding out of the sleeping bag an effort. One more jingle is on its way, and we peek over the edge of our short rooftop wall to watch the pony trot past, pulling its humans on a very basic rectangular wooden cart. With no one else in sight, we pack our gear, along with the dust that thickly covers all of it, and hop off our rooftop perch well rested and undetected. We still feel chilled, but alive. ALIVE.

Leatherfoot and I get into the pack strapping routine this morning. It's a complex weaving project, but we finally have it figured out. Sometimes this sort of thing is referred to as the learning curve, but I prefer to call it improving, or balancing the cycle. The idea of a curve leaves me hanging out in empty space, where as a cycle is a better representation of a repeated pattern. We must have repeated this routine close to ten times by now. Most things that we do in life are repetitive in nature. We do them again and again. Some things, like walking or brushing your teeth, become engrained to a point we might call second nature. Our subconscious deals with them, and we no longer need to question them. They are cycles that appear to be in balance, though physiotherapists and dentists may not agree. The cycles of footsteps or brushstrokes are most often in good balance, but not great. Some of us may develop footsteps that land hard on the ground each time, causing, over time, stress in the knees, the hips and the back. Others may have the habit of dragging their feet, causing imbalances in other parts of the body. Those things we do with less frequency, like swinging a racquet, or fingering piano keys, we tend to give more attention. We are conscious of the fact that the motion, or the cycle, is not as smooth as it can be. It could be too hard, or too soft. Too fast, or too slow. If it is too "anything," it is not in balance. The professional athlete, or musician, strives continuously to balance the cycles of their craft, or motion. It is an ongoing pursuit. Whether simply walking, or playing in a complex team environment, the nature of time perpetually changes the environment around us, making things dynamic. Thus, there is rarely, if ever perfection. The more dynamic the task at hand, the more one needs to focus on balancing in perpetuity. Like cycling across Tibet. Every day, and every pedal stroke is unique. Our bags are packed slightly differently each day, so we pull a little more here and twist a little more there, trying to balance them as well as possible. When we finish, they are more solid than they have been all trip. We get on our bikes and begin the endless search for a sustainable pace.

For what seems like the first time since the morning of the second day, we settle into what I would call regular riding. There is no pass to climb, no lame lemony bike to tow, and, as yet, no wind battering us into submission. Regular riding. The road is, of course, still gravel, making the riding less than smooth, but we assume this will be the state of things until the Nepalese border.

The first thirty-five kilometers of riding are delightful. The sun is creeping slowly up our backs as we move westward, and we receive pleasant smiles and greetings from the locals sharing the road with us on their way to the fields. Having come out of the stunning mountain scenery into the huge plateau that stretches endlessly between peaks, there are an array of stark background landscapes, worked fields, and colourful Tibetan villages. It is amazing how fertile they can make this sandy, windy, barren environment. We see only a sparse amount of people and animals tending to the huge fields being farmed, and little machinery. Water is diverted from rivers into a network of canals, and it looks as though much of the planting has been done, and the growth is just starting. There are a few more electrical wires, and many of the houses are more neatly kept than those we have seen before. Here and there are even some decent sized trees.

The animals are one of our greatest sources of entertainment. This morning, we see mostly cows of various shades and sizes, yaks, ponies, chickens and roosters. The Tibetans like to adorn the bovines with various interesting head gear. Sometimes things are woven through nostrils and up foreheads, but the most common sight is red tassels dangling from the ears. The ponies or donkeys, and the bovines, are always hard at work. The former pulling the carts to transport the people to and from fields, and the latter pulling the ploughs. Chickens are on about their usual peck and scatter, and we see one rooster perched on the corner of a roof, next to a wind battered bunch of prayer flags, screaming "COCKADOODLEDOOOO" for all he's worth.

For gravel road riding, thirty-five kilometers is a good chunk, but we have at least forty-five to go until Tibet's second biggest city called Shigatse. This means we aren't as far along as we'd like to be for a lunch break, but we have gotten an eager invitation from quite a large group of Tibetans. Though sticking to a schedule does have some merit, we feel like we cannot pass up the opportunity. We remind ourselves that this sort of thing is the reason why we are travelling like this in the first place.

Ten in total, most are younger women, but there are two men and one young boy. They are sitting in a circle on the ground next to a lone structure. There are no tables or chairs. Not even a mat or blanket is spread on the sandy ground, which has a slight covering of grasses. It is a simple picnic. A few of their outer garments are scattered around the area, along with cups, bowls, two big pots, a water canteen and a beat up old thermos. As we dismount, there is a brief scramble as they rearrange themselves to give us space. Once again, we are made to feel completely welcome. We expect the usual fare of grains, tsampa (the roasted barley flour), and perhaps some flatbread, but on this day, we eat in style. We are served a monster bowl of rice, topped with some kind of potato and yak guts stew. It tastes plain, but we enjoy it. A second bowl is offered, and Kat accepts a large helping, while Leatherfoot and I take half a bowl each. By the second helping, the oil starts to permeate.

Add, as always, a copious quantity of the Yak Butter Tea, and once again our mouths become saturated with oil. Leatherfoot has not yet changed his mind, and still abstains from the tea, but Kat and I take in the liquid and the fat at every opportunity. I could almost say that we are acquiring a taste for the stuff, but I'm sure it won't be something I'll serve up at home, even if it was available.

Our Tibetan friends are dark skinned and sturdy looking, wearing heavy layers of clothing, and men and women alike all have long hair. Some braided and tied, some messed and tangled, other heads covered with blankets shielding off the rising sun. They lead lives involving hard and very basic work. Farming land, tending animals, building and maintaining structures, and gathering fuel and water. It is obvious that the women share equally in the physical labour. Other than the monasteries, where the monks are predominantly men, I have noticed no significant difference between the roles of the sexes amongst the Tibetans, though I have not spent time inside any homes. Outwardly, there appears to be genuine respect between all people, old and young, men and women alike, and, though there are no frills in their lives, there is such enthusiasm, joy, and peace in their beings. It makes me wonder about the word poor. They don't have bank accounts, televisions, shopping malls, traffic lights, cars, dish washers, or sushi restaurants, but they do have food, shelter, community, love, and no need for a book of psychology naming a thousand "dis-eases and dis-orders" associated with the modern world. Are they poor? Materially, yes, but spiritually, it seems not at all.

We leave another Dalai Lama picture here. We brought quite a few, and were at first budgeting them, but since giving out the first, have been a little more liberal. The reaction to the gift is comical, and yet somewhat uneasy. They tug and parlay over it as though they were a bunch of teenage boys trying to get a look at a scantily clad photo of the latest super model. The uneasiness arises through the fact that there are a so many of them, and only one photo. Who should be the keeper of this precious gift? It is the first time I can remember seeing even a slight hint of animosity between them.

With no English spoken among them, and our half a dozen word Tibetan vocabulary, it is another case of not much talking, but great communion. As we get up to leave, I make a final gesture by taking out the phrase book and trying "that meal was very delicious" in Tibetan. "Kha-la shim-bu shay-ta choong" which is greeted with a wonderful chorus of laughter. We take our leave with thickly oil coated mouths once again. These lunch invitations are becoming one of the highlights of the journey. It always feels special to be able to spend time with people like this. The convenience of a little extra food and hot liquid doesn't hurt either.

Back on our bikes, we continue plodding along and watching the rural scenes go by. More yaks, donkeys, goats, cows, sheep, roosters and villages. The kids that come running out frequently are endearing, but somewhat overbearing. They are prone to running right in front of the bikes yelling "ELO ELO ELO" and at times have to be fended off. The odd rock continues to be flung in our direction, but from where it originates is always a mystery. So far, however, we've gotten no direct hits, so it is something we have learned to laugh at, if not really enjoy.

We push through some good kilometers on our full stomachs. Kat is having a positive stretch of riding so far today. The midday sun that is usurping my energy rapidly, seems to be feeding hers. Every BODY is an individual. She is an athlete, no doubt, having great natural coordination, power, and grace, but I don't think she's ever dealt with this kind of an endurance test. Mentally and physically, this pitted and potty gravel road allows no rhythm. No groove. No respite.

Trucks are one more obstacle with which to contend. There are more of them along this stretch of road than there were on our route before Gyangze. For a start, they are intimidating. They rule the road, and we are never sure how much leeway they will give us. We have not had any issues with close calls yet, but there are warnings in the guidebook, and have been other rumours that some drivers may choose to make sport with the likes of us. So far then, it is not the space that is an issue, but each truck that passes by kicks up a huge cloud of dry dust. We have choices. Either we inhale it, try and hold our breath while riding through it, or, if it's a particularly huge dust cloud, just stop and bury our faces into our shirts until it settles. It is the size of the vehicle, and the direction of the wind, that determines the best strategy.

Though she is pedalling well, Kat isn't talking too much. I suppose talking period, much less in English, must not be worth the mental energy it would require. She just rides. Leatherfoot and I have brief conversations, but even for us, each breath is too valuable to waste on an abundance of words.

The midday grind begins to wear on us. It's an accumulation of sun, wind, trucks, dust, kids, and plain old fatigue. With thirty kilometers to go to our desired destination of Shigatse, we come across some nice big trees at the side of the road, and decide on taking a break. We each find ourselves a reasonably flat place in the cool shade and crash out for a while. It is a blissful time and place for a nap. It doesn't take long after closing the eyes to start drifting. With each breath, my muscle fibers relax a little bit more, and a tingling sensation washes over me. I begin to float. The thread of attachment to where I am, and who I am with, grows longer and thinner. I feel utterly weightless, blending into the air around me. I think of love, and life, and then death. It's not so horrible, blending and swirling with rest. Then I feel a rock. It's digging into my lower back, telling my mind to find its way back to my body and deal with it.

Leatherfoot and I unglue one eyelid each at the same time, and a hazy glance connects between us. We know we should get up and start riding again. Surprisingly, Kat too awakens without any prompting. After clearing the haze, and doing some mild stretches, we feel somewhat refreshed and manage a few smiles and jokes. We look hilarious as we are all totally covered in a thick layer of dust. I feel like it coats my innards, as well as every part of my exterior. If Leatherfoot and I weren't so tall, skinny and white to begin with, we might even blend in with the locals. Kat, however, except for the clothes, totally looks like a local by now. Her face is dark, dry, wrinkled and covered with dust. She continues to get a lot of curious looks. Is she Chinese? Is she Tibetan? And what is she doing with these two white guys?

Though our nap has done us good, and our spirits are up again, we are still tired and stiff, and thirty more kilometers feels a little daunting. As we remount our bicycles, we agree to break it down into five kilometer sections. Manageable chunks. Like all daunting tasks, it eases the mind to break things down into manageable chunks. As we get set to leave, we realize that we have a light tailwind, which is a welcome blessing.

"Two down, four to go. Shall we have some water and a snack?"

"A snack we can do, but we're getting a little tight on water Dogi."

"Oh, is that our last bottle?"

It's been a bit of an issue today. There simply hasn't been any good opportunities to refill. We've been trying to consume enough, but make sure we won't run out either. I'm sure we can make it to Shigatse on what we have, but guzzling a liter or two would significantly help the energy level. We restrict ourselves to one swallow each and start riding again.

Not much further along, we come upon a side road that we can tell leads to a small town. We discuss the water issue, and agree it would be worthwhile to take the side trek and find water. Kat, who reminds us she hasn't really ridden much since the first two days, says she's exhausted, and doesn't want to add any more pedal strokes than necessary. She decides she'd like to continue plodding along at her own slower pace, which is agreeable to us. Leatherfoot and I enter the town, and we immediately attract a lot of attention. Kids either follow, or scatter to find their friends, to let them know of the "entertainment" that has just rolled in. We scan for water options, and find a small general store. As we fill, drink, and refill, we become surrounded by half the population of the town. Mostly children, but a few curious men as well. This crowd is good though. There are no bike fiddlers. Everyone is just staring intently at the excitement of us filling our water bottles and drinking. Leatherfoot and I throw in a few theatrics and a little animation just for fun. It isn't until we are just about finished our business that we notice... ICE CREAM!

"Hey, check it out Dogi. ICE CREAM!!!"

"I SCREAM, YOU SCREAM, WE ALL SCREAM FOR ICE CREAM!"

"Original. So, who would have thought in such a small dusty

roadside town there would be ice cream, but I guess we aren't too far removed from Shigatse at this point."

"So the biggest question of the day is, do you want one, or two? And what about Kat?"

Leatherfoot and I ravenously lick our ice creams to nothingness as we ponder the idea of bringing one to Kat. We have no idea how far ahead she might be by now, but we must try! Being fresh up on water and ice cream, we figure we can ride hard for a while. The sun is already waning, so it isn't too hot anymore. If worse comes to worst, and it starts melting too much, we'll just have to eat another one!

We get ourselves totally set to ride, order the last cone, yell for the throng of kids to move aside, and begin to pedal to their departing cheers.

RIDE... RIDE... RIDE... Lick, lick... Pass the cone... Ride... Ride... Lick... Pass... Ride... Lick, lick... Pass...

"There she is, there she is!"

"KAAAT... KAAAAT... STOP!"

"Have some ice cream!"

"Sorry, it's half gone, but here eat it fast, it's melting."

I think Leatherfoot and I probably burned off twice the calories of the ice cream just catching up to Kat, but that was great. Great, great, great.

○ ○ ○

Life. It is amazing how quickly "great great great" can turn into "gross gross gross." From ice cream, and pleasant rural scenery, to what is turning into an ever increasing hell. Though the sweet treat and fresh water gave us a short boost, we are nonetheless getting exhausted after a long day. It seems like forever ago that we awoke to the pleasant jingle of pony and cart. The outskirts of Shigatse are horribly unappealing. They don't quite rival the Asshole of Tibet, but they are trying. It looks to be mostly Chinese expansion, which means ugly buildings one after another, glass and garbage aimlessly strewn about the streets, and a truly degenerate looking cross section of both Tibetan and Chinese people. I must note that thus far on our trip, both the Tibetan and Chinese people

149

have been quite pleasant in their own right, but at this point along their historical journey, they are an unharmonious combination.

The noise, the dust mixed with fumes, the miserable looking people, the rabid looking dogs, and to make matters worse, descending darkness. The time of day when the canines begin to transform from skittish second rate citizens of the streets to brave rulers of the nighttime neighborhoods. In the midst of all this, we are consulting our guidebook map, trying to figure out where the hell we are and which way we need to go. There is no time for fear or misery. The only thought is to deal with finding our hotel, and get off these streets and away from the crooked stares of people and dogs alike.

"Ahh! Whadaya think? Should we hang a right here, and then left again at the next main block or... "

"No, I'm thinking go straight a bit more first, and then right, and that should bring us there. If we see this restaurant along the way, we'll know we're on the right track."

It's such a familiar budget travellers scene. Exhausted upon arrival in a city or town at an awkward hour. You kind of want help, but not really, as the help can often add confusion to the chaos, or be ill of intent. Particularly when communication abilities are somewhere between nil, and next to none. The town or city is most often not that confusing once a good night of rest is had and an hour is spent wandering around in the daylight, but the shear foreignness, coupled with the darkness and impaired brain functioning due to exhaustion, produces high degrees of disorientation.

It takes a while, but eventually we do manage to sniff out our desired hotel just before the hounds look like they will start gnawing at our ankles. Leatherfoot and I continue to mesh well in these higher stress situations. Good, straight forward cooperative communication. Kat just leaves us to it, and hopes that we sort it out quickly. She and the dogs are eyeing each other with no friendly intentions.

Once the first door is shut behind us, and we are in a ground floor hallway, we realize just how exhausted and frazzled we really are. We've been running on high doses of adrenaline for the past hour or so. We must fight through the delirium that is starting to set in after coming down from the stress of the long day. Storing our bikes, and then carrying our packs up the several sets of steep rickety old stairs is the final test of our will and determination. The process winds us one final time, but we are elated to find this hotel to be a mini-paradise. The family that runs it has greeted us warmly, and they are kind and helpful as they show us to a very respectable room with three beds. The interior of the building is open and full of plants, breathing life and good energy into the surroundings.

The beds are begging us to lie in them and succumb to the urge to sleep, but we are starving and extremely filthy. Though we had those fast dips in that really cold lake, this is our first shower opportunity since Lhasa about ten days ago. Ten days of riding through hot sun and dust clouds. It may also represent our last until Kathmandu, though there are one or two small towns yet to go where a shower may be possible between now and then. Kat goes first, and comes out looking like a whole new person. Take a truck that has been four wheel driving in the muck all day, and run it through the highest priced wash and wax, and there you go. So stark is the difference. Though she still looks a little wobbly and delirious, she has a big, clean, smile on her face.

"So, how was it Kat?"

"Amazing! Riding is so hard today, but I think hardest thing is turning off hot shower! I never want to stop and get out."

Leatherfoot and I take our turns, and both concur with Kat. Conservancy is always warranted with the use of hot water in a place like this. We know their energy is not cheap to come by, but turning those taps off really may have been the greatest struggle of the day.

Clean and refreshed, we made the long "trek" down the stairs to the hotel restaurant that they graciously kept open late for us. We have just finished gorging ourselves with some rather tasty Chinese food, and are hanging out in our room, which faces out over the main street. It's noisy. Particularly the packs of howling wild dogs. I'd hate to be out there. Kat and Leatherfoot are already sleeping soundly and I am fading fast...

OFFICIALDUMB

SHIGATSE, THE SECOND MOST POPULATED AREA IN TIBET, LIES at an elevation of 3900 meters (12,900 feet). It is located about 250 kilometers (150 miles) southwest of Lhasa, along the more direct route, and has long been an important trading and administrative center. For us, it represents the last major hub of humanity before Kathmandu, and another welcome break from cycling.

Hunger is becoming a constant the longer this trip wears on. Even supplemented by the Tibetan picnic lunches, our camping diet is proving to be less than adequate. Our bodies are depleted after a week and a half on the road. Add in the fact that we are still weary this morning, and we make it no further than our hotel restaurant. They treated us so well last night, that we have no hesitation to eat there again. The menu, which offers both Chinese and Western cuisine, is both extensive and hysterical.

"I'll have, two orang juces, one fly pototo, three bored egges, and a tea please."

Menus in foreign lands are always a great source of amusement. I often wonder how they go about the translation. Is it straight out of a dictionary? No, that can't be right. They must have somehow learned the words verbally and then tried to write them. Then, why wouldn't they ask the help of a native English speaker to get it right? Or why wouldn't an English speaker volunteer to rewrite it correctly? Someone like me, or Leatherfoot? No, we enjoy the humour too much to want to spoil it for others, and it's all understandable.

After explaining what I'd like, the waitress tries to leave, thinking the order is complete for all of us. She looks slightly confused when we ask her to come back, and then, somewhat dubious as Kat and Leatherfoot complete their equally large orders. As she walks away to get started, we continue to peruse the menu for the sake of future reference and entertainment.

"Dogi look. It says kaffee."

"You gotta know it's gonna be instant don't you Kat."

"You think?"

With coffee not being the ideal drink to fit in with endurance cycling like this, Kat and I have not had a cup since Lhasa, which, for coffee drinkers is a significant drought. Though we are coffee lovers, we are also coffee snobs. Even typical diner or gas station coffee is out for me, much less instant. I'm not that much of an addict. Filling our mornings with our own tea has been pleasant, but seeing coffee on this morning's menu does give rise to great temptation, and as the waitress arrives with the first of our huge order, Kat decides to go for it, and it gets delivered promptly.

"How is it Kat?"

"Mmmm, weak."

"Flavoured water huh?"

"Do you think we can ask to make stronger?"

The poor waitress is exhibiting remarkable patience with us. After searching futilely for the words "stronger" or "darker" in our guidebook language sections, we move on to other modes of non-verbal communication. How do you get across the idea that you want your coffee stronger? Verbs are easy enough, and nouns not too bad, but adjectives are tough to communicate non-verbally. Our first attempt results in getting a second cup, but one equally as weak. Finally, Kat has a good idea, taking out a pen and paper and scripting Chinese characters, which actually does get the point across! And, what do we get brought, but the whole jar of instant coffee! What the heck. It's not THAT bad. We each put an extra heaping spoonful in our cups, which makes the coffee so strong that it effectively kills the flavour, but somehow it is still pretty darn good. And, by the end of the meal, the waitress looks pleased as every last scrap is cleaned from plates, bowls and cups. We will make like the Tibetans and waste nothing.

After washing and hanging some clothes, we finally step out the door looking forward to our day in Shigatse. It is a place that I referred to earlier as a city, and in last night's confusion, it sure felt like it, but as we wander with more clarity today, I would sooner call it a big town. That said, it looks to be growing rapidly. The old Tibetan area is being surrounded by ongoing Chinese expansion, such that it is lacking the pleasant character found in Lhasa and Gyangze.

The tallest orders of our day are a trip to the bank, which goes unexpectedly smoothly, and then a visit to the PSB. The PSB is the Chinese version of tourist police, and, we are going there to get extensions on our visas. At our current pace, we're not so sure we'll be able to clear the country before ours expire, which is also why we have been pushing through days like yesterday, rather than camping and breaking it into two days. Travelling too fast somewhat defeats the purpose, but officialdom unfortunately makes it necessary once in a while. Going to the PSB is a tough decision. Without going, there is the risk of an overstay, which holds unknown consequences. On the other hand, actually dealing with the official world at this point in our trip, after we'd tried quite hard to avoid it in Lhasa, harbours its own mysteries. We enter the small, rectangular office, encouraged by the lack of a line, but dreading the conversation with the uninspired official that saunters up to the window once he's good and ready.

"Hi. We'd like ten day visa extensions please."

"Grumble, grumble, here, you fill out paperwork. Names, passport numbers…"

He slides a stack of mysterious looking papers across the counter under the glass. It has only the basics written in English, so we don't really know what we are filling out, or agreeing to. We slide the paperwork back, with the requested fees, and wait… until he's good and ready to come and get it. He passes it first to his associate, who, up until that point, had been doing absolutely nothing. When she is done with the scribbles, he takes over with the stamps, and our passports come sliding back under the window. We are relieved.

"Nice, that wasn't as bad as expected eh, Leatherfoot?"

"There is nothing in my passport." says Kat.

"What?"

"Look your passports. No stamps in there. Look Dogi, you have piece of paper."

"You're right, and it says Alien's Travel Permit."

It's true. An Alien's Travel Permit. That's what we got. A lovely little green and purple piece of paper with a few bright red stamps, and the following endorsements;

1. Travelling
2. Travelling to assigned places, No breaking out any rules and Regulations.

We feel so much better knowing that we have official permission to be aliens, though this piece of paper does not necessarily permit us to be aliens for as long as we'd like to be aliens. We still need visa extensions! Back to the window, there is a small fire of anger burning in the pit of my gut, but I know that I should keep the flame well contained. I don't have a lot of experience with the Chinese culture yet, but I know in most other Asian cultures, losing control of your emotions, particularly anger, is not acceptable. The concept is known as losing face, and you are embarrassing both yourself, and the other party. When dealing with officialdom, the principle holds double. You will never get anywhere positive if you lose your cool.

"Um, excuse me sir, umm, this isn't what we asked for. It isn't a visa extension. We'd like VISA EXTENSIONS please."

"Do you have Alien's Travel Permit?"

"Well, no, we didn't, but I guess we do now, though we still would like visa extensions."

"Grumble, grumble, here, you fill out paperwork. Names, passport numbers…"

We scrutinize this particular paperwork a little more thoroughly, and decide that it is not some other permit with which to officially wipe your butt, but indeed an application for a visa extension. We hand over more money, and spend more time sitting and waiting, before we receive more pretty red stamps. With our visa extensions in hand, we feel better about not having to rush the remainder of the journey. Thank goodness that Kat noticed. Leatherfoot and I would have just walked out of there. As we depart the office, we joke about whether or not this Alien's Travel Permit will ever be extracted from my money belt for the rest of the trip. Guesses lean heavily to the no side.

Finished with our "official" business, we try to go shopping in the local Tibetan market. I say try, because we are literally accosted by super aggressive shop owners. At least that's true of Leatherfoot and myself. Kat continues to be regarded with curiosity and wonderment, though she too says she feels sick from the general bad aura of the place.

"LOOKY LOOKY! LOOKY LOOKY!" This is the cry that comes forth in a chorus from the vendors. STUFF is being stuffed in front of our faces. It is impossible to looky looky and enjoy any of the crafts when the tone is so forceful. It seems so incongruous with the usual Tibetan demeanor. This must be one of the tour bus and 4X4 tour stops on the regular tourist romp across Tibet, which means people who quite happily pay inflated prices for the merchandise. It is not surprising, or unnatural, then, that the locals see us "aliens" and equate us with, in a relative way, a lot of money. Saddening is the corruptive force that begins to fester. It is not an uncommon scene the world over. Those who have travelled to less financially wealthy places are likely to have encountered it. The material inequality creates an ironic disharmony. The extra money seems to breed greed, rather than generosity.

I reach my tolerance limit when one particular lady launches herself over her stall, screaming "LOOKY LOOKY!" and begins to poke me with her wares quite forcefully. I must admit, even after rehearsing this "don't lose your cool" business, that I tripped out a little at her. "STICKY STICKY your STUFFY STUFFY somewhere else!" Physical contact outside the realms of love, friendship, or sport is unacceptable to me, foreign culture or not. I poke her back! It's true. POKE. Not hard, but enough to show my displeasure. Then, suddenly, I am grabbed on the arm! The person grabbing me is neither a lover nor a friend. The contact, however, is both love and friendship. It is a young Tibetan man who is squeezing my arm, and there is no tone of aggression in the gesture at all. His grip is both firm, and, at the same time, gentle. He says nothing, but stares straight into my eyes, and completely disarms my frustration and anger with an immensely calming smile. He counters my anger with love. Without a word spoken, it is one of the most powerful things ever communicated to me. It is a look and a feeling that I am sure I will retain for a long time.

○ ○ ○

Groggy. That's how we wake up from our long afternoon naps. It was one of those naps that lasted far longer than anticipated, but we needed it, and we didn't exactly have the relaxed day we'd hoped for. The food and the hot shower have been wonderful, but Shigatse felt complicated and disharmonious to us. So many of the people here seem to be missing the joy of life that we've noticed elsewhere. We feel like there is something positive somewhere in this city. For example, the Tashilhunpo Monastery, which is a walled town of its own, and said to have weathered the destruction brought by the Chinese Cultural Revolution. With our visas extended for ten days, it would be an option to stay tomorrow, and go and see it, but we all agree that we've had enough of Shigatse, and are content with the amount of time we have spent in other monasteries. We are ready to get back to our Tibet tomorrow.

As the afternoon wears into evening, we consider eating a meal elsewhere for a change, but with the wonderful service, and agreeable prices, we decide to return to our hotel restaurant. Besides, we don't really like the prospect of walking home in the dark amidst the packs of howling canines. We feast once again, as our bodies are still craving copious quantities of vegetables and meat. There are eight variations of potatoes on the menu, and in our three meals here, we have exhausted the entire list. Shocked at first by how much we were eating, they have gotten used to our multiple orders. We feel as though we must eat while the eating is good. Who knows when, or even if, we will be able to eat this much good food again with the lack of large communities the rest of the way.

STILL HAVING FUN?!

"How'd you guys sleep?"

"Not so good."

"Mm"

"Yea me neither. It was so noisy. Was it that loud the night before? The trucks, the horns... "

"The dogs! HOWWWWLING."

We really thought about going somewhere new to eat this morning, but you have to walk by the restaurant here to get to the exit, and we just couldn't do it. Their looks were so expectant. Oh well, the food was great once again, and they know our needs well by now, like the extra strong kaffe. We loaded up, and ordered a big portion of stir fly and lice to take with us for dinner later tonight. There was a lot of confusion over this last request, but we finally got it sorted out and put into a double plastic bag.

It's raining this morning, making it the first precipitation we've seen since that freak hail storm back at the dry river bed. It's kind of nice, but it does inhibit us from being motivated to get an early start. It's still drizzling as we depart, but the clearing is imminent. A few blocks into our ride, we pick up some cheap Tibetan style buns, which will act as lunch and snacks along the way. The problem is where to tie them down without squishing them. Our packs are artfully reefed down, and unless we want to go through the whole procedure again, we are relegated to what we can strap on top, or even onto the handlebars. This means we had better guess right on what we'll need for the day and have it accessible. Once a gap between pack and strapping is created, it's all over. The condition of the road here will make short work of loosening the whole pack so that we have to start reefing all over again from the beginning. Packing to do any sort of travelling is an art. On this kind of an adventure, it comes down to layers, water and food. The day's food rations are kept in a separate bag, that gets strapped on top of our packs, along with water bottles. Some of the layers of clothing come off and then on again in rhythm with the sunshine.

Sunshine. You might be surprised how many layers you keep on when the sun is at its strongest. I've noticed that in many equatorial latitudes and desert environments, locals are usually wearing clothing that totally covers the body. It provides shade and insulation from the sun that would otherwise burn directly exposed skin. The Tibetans are always wearing quite thick, heavy, woolen clothing throughout the day. Warming at night and cooling during the hot midday hours. It is a desert up here. That means extremely dry with huge extremes of temperature. My guess is that the days get well into the twenties on the Celsius scale, though with the direct midday sun, the effect makes it feel like high thirties or worse. The temperature then drops as rapidly as the sun. The middle of the night probably approaches freezing.

Our faces, which are our most exposed body features, are beginning to look more weathered with each passing day. Kat has unfortunately burnt her lower lip quite badly. Apparently, she also has a sore throat and a few canker sores coming on, but she says she's happy to be moving on.

Unlike the way into Shigatse, the town ends quickly on the way out, and humanity is sparse. It feels great to be on the road again, knowing that we don't need to rush things anymore. The space, the hills, the breeze through the hair, the *thud crunch crunch crunch* of the bike tires. The paved road ends abruptly, and the merciless riding conditions greet us once again. The pace slows considerably, but I refuse to let the road dampen my spirit. It's a beautiful day, and I'm going to enjoy every shake and shimmy across the washboard. I think that's the best term for describing this road. Washboard, with intermittent potholes. At least that's the less evil choice. There are choices. The other choice is soft mushy gravel, which doesn't pound as hard, but sucks you in, and increases the load on the legs dramatically. So, really, there isn't much choice. It's washboard and potholes, and a constant search for a few smooth meters. Enough distance to lift your head for a second or two and take in the scenery, before putting it back down to search for the path of least resistance. It is not uncommon for us to change sides of the road, or even ride in the middle. Wherever it is the least rough. Traffic outside of the city limits is not really a concern. It is rare enough, and always either a big dump truck or a 4X4, and you can hear them coming. In fact, you can feel the dump trucks coming. They shake the ground. Honking is also not uncommon. Whether it means "Hello," "I'm coming through" or "GET THE HELL OUT OF THE WAY!" I'm not sure. That probably depends on the personality of the driver.

The truth is, we can only take a good look at the scenery when we're having a break, and it does continue to be superb. The space is perhaps the most striking feature. It's kind of like staring at a sky full of stars, in that you feel so small and insignificant, and yet, somehow connected and interwoven into the grand fabric of life. The space also intimidates and demoralizes you as you get back on your saddle. The road stretches way out to the horizon. Hamster. Wheel. Around and around. Are we getting anywhere? Or is there actually anywhere to be gotten? Maybe, we're just going. Not somewhere, not anywhere. Just going.

Five kilometers at a time usually. We've adopted this as our rule of thumb. Whether it's been a tough five, or an easier stretch, it is a manageable breakdown, and we stop for a rest. We know the distance because there are convenient stone kilometer markers. Most of the time anyway. Perhaps some are missing, or we just pass them as we have our heads down. There are two numbers on each. The larger of the two being up in the five thousand range and growing. We're not sure, but we figure, perhaps, that it is kilometers from Beijing. Our breaks consist of water, sometimes food and ideally some stretching. When someone has the energy, a massage in some form is also given out. Kat got a super deluxe from Leatherfoot during one long break today. He's great in every which way. His energy and positive attitude are unfailing. His skills with the bikes, and his massages are also a bonus. We are so fortunate to have him along.

We've gone thirty kilometers when we agree to quit for the day. It's not a huge distance, but it's reasonable after such a late start. We decide fifty kilometers should be our average goal from now on. That would be a solid day of riding on these rough roads, in this environment. Though that all depends on the wind and the hills, amongst other things. Any which way, we agree that we should always try to quit with enough daylight and energy to deal with setting up camp and cooking dinner. We are here to enjoy after all.

Though the overall land is flat, the ground in this area has a lot more contour than what we've encountered before. There is a network of meandering ditches, and a greater abundance of interesting shrubbery. It requires a longer search, and a small trek with the bikes, before we find a soft flat section in a ditch well off the main road. It's sheltered and nice in that we are quite hidden. We anticipate being undisturbed, though you never know when, and where a curious Tibetan might show up.

We have missed the colourful sunsets the last couple of evenings, and anticipate it greatly as we dig in to our stir fly and lice under the deepening blue sky. Even eaten cold out of a plastic bag, it is delicious. With these surroundings, and my wonderful company, I wouldn't trade this meal for one in a fine French restaurant.

ONE TREE

THE TRUTH OF THE MATTER IS THAT I HAVE NO IDEA WHAT DAY IT is in any sense of the word. What day of this thing called a week? What number in the month? What Day number on this cycling trip? No idea. I suppose I could figure some, or most of them out, but I find no need. I don't care. There is no meaning to any of the answers. It's today. We're a bit BatTeRed and BeaTen but we're okay. We're alive. That's good.

Time... right... it was a few days ago the last time I wrote, but I can remember... no, we can remember together, the three of us. That's six eyes, three noses, six ears, three mouths, and a bunch of hair. Hair takes things in too you know. I wonder how Hari is back in Kathmandu. He's good. He's a happy character. Great smile... I'm drifting... obviously, a bit delirious... let me take you back now... I'll try to keep it together... come on, let's go...

SHADOWS – Long and at our fronts again this morning. They are so stark, so noticeable here. The sky is huge, the background is barren and brown, and the sun is strong. It's a combination that produces distinct lines between light and dark. The silhouette of the distant horizons just before sunrise, or just after sunset, are a delight to the sense of sight. Yet, it is the outline of ourselves, bikes and riders, that is most distinct. Shadows.

"Hello Shadow. How are you this morning?"

"I am   l o n g   and I am thin, and I stretch before you and show you the way. Come... this way... It's time to ride."

My head, my Shadow Head, is far in front and shaped like a twisting banana. Brown, of course, not yellow or green. But I don't see Shadow Head often this early in the day. I am looking down more directly in front of the bike in order to negotiate the micro-obstacle-course that is the gravel road. Continuing westward, the terrain this morning is mostly flat, and the wind is not too hectic, yet, the going is still slow. The condition of the road is getting worse the further away from humanity we get, and Kat is suffering. Her burnt lips are looking pretty gross, half of her lower one badly split and swollen. She says she feels like an old rag.

So this is the Tibetan Plateau. I feel like I am in the middle of it now. Brown rocks, brown dirt and sand, brown hills, blue sky. Beautiful blue sky. It's like the shadows. Sharp, simple contrast. Two colours. Brown, blue. A full spectrum of shades of each, but the simplicity of two. Of course, clouds of white and grey pass over on occasion. Their shade more than welcome in the midday hours, but rarely received. Many of the sheep are black, or have black heads. The white ones are actually brown from the blowing dirt. Just like the people. Just like us. The yaks are also black with occasional white trim. Those bright red tassels hanging from their ears add such a nice splash of colour. I'm no bovine expert, but a yak looks pretty much like a cow with long shaggy hair. Pointy horns too. Much like cows, they're somehow simultaneously ugly and cute. You know, dorky looking, but they make you smile and laugh. They are beasts of great importance to the Tibetans, no doubt. Providers of milk and its byproducts of cheese and butter, pullers of the plough, givers of wooly hair, and of meat, tendons, marrow and anything else edible or usable from their dead bodies. This is surely a culture that wastes nothing at all. Having seen the yaks mostly at work, I haven't noticed what they eat. Grazing in the greater surroundings seems to be reserved for the herds of sheep, and they need to roam far and wide to find enough to eat. I guess it's early in the farming cycle. Maybe they grow grains for the yaks. Perhaps, they eat the same barley that the people eat in flour form.

My Shadow Head is coming back to me. It no longer looks like a banana, more like a big egg. It is connected much more firmly to my Shadow Body. There is still the twisting, and now some shaking too.

"Hey Shadow Head. Are you here to help me?"

"No Dogi, I am enjoying a dance. The Dance of Chaos, with the lovely Miss Road!"

"I can see that. How is it you flow so well with such a difficult dance?"

"I am made by pure light, and my disturbances are few."

I like to talk to my Shadow Head. Kat won't talk while she's riding, and while Leatherfoot and I do converse on occasion, we are often separated by her. One of us tries to maintain a reasonable pace, while the other makes sure she doesn't silently disappear. There are advantages to conversations with my Shadow Head. He's a great listener, and when we talk, we don't need to speak out loud. That way it's easier. I can focus more attention on breathing.

Oh my, it's a tree! A tree! And, a shadow friend. This is noteworthy. Not accompanied by village, or house or significant fellow plants of any kind, it looks so lonely out here. It's the only one we've seen all day. Was it planted, or just some determined seed dropped by a bird or the wind? Its leaves are even green. Oh, and there's a nest in the upper branches. "Tweet tweet, hello, is there anybody in there?" I get no answer, but perhaps it has company of some sort after all. "Bye tree. I hope your friend is nice, and that it rains on you enough. Good luck."

It's the sun that makes me delirious as much as anything. There is always much debate about whether the sun is good for you or not. Some people say never expose yourself, others say it's full of necessary vitamins. I say it's the same as everything else. It has the potential to be both good and bad, healthy and harmful, and the key is to seek the balance between the two. In the dynamic world in which we live, there are no rules that apply to all situations. Only people who work in marketing try to tell you there are, so they can sell you stuff. There are, however, general guidelines that can be applied to the consciousness of yourself as an individual, and the environment you are in. In the case of sunshine; what is the pigment of your skin? Are you near the equator? Are you lying on the grass near sea level, or are you on the water, the snow, or a high altitude desert, where the strength of the rays are magnified? I have made up my own guideline that I think works well in most environments, though I don't mind skewing it one way or the other by a few degrees depending on the situation. It's related to shadow length. When my shadow is longer than me, I don't mind exposing myself to the rays of the sun. During that time, I feel like I am taking its energy in. As it becomes shorter than me, however, I either try to take, or make cover, as this is when the energy is being taken away.

"Shadow? Shadow!? Where did you go Shadow?"

Our shadows are tiny now. Straight under us. The sun is like falling daggers, piercing me. I feel weak and helpless. There is no shade to be found anywhere. The lone tree is well behind us. I NEED shade. It is my single thought. Nothing else matters. I must have shade. I am a French fry. No better than a French fry.

We come upon the remnants of a roadside gravel quarry. The sun is so vertical that its banks provide no shade. Cringing through the process, we pull out our tarp and our tent poles, and with the help of a few heavy rocks, we rig up a small sun shelter. The relief is immense and immediate. The blood in my head drops from a boil down to a simmer, and after a few more minutes to a calm. I can think again, and now that I have shade, I need food.

"No picnic with Tibetans today!"

"Yea, that feels kind of strange doesn't it."

"Poor Leatherfoot. No Yak Butter Tea."

"Pass the water Dogi."

Lunch consists of crackers and a can of mystery sausages that smells like cat food. Oh, to bite into a nice juicy apple. That would be blissful. But we have no fruit. We've had none since that bus load of Italian tourists. That feels like forever ago. I don't think any fruit grows here. Tibetans probably never eat fruit. I'm sure the Chinese will begin to import more. That would be good, as long as they share it nicely with the Tibetans.

The wind has suddenly picked up. There is no warning. Our tarp has gone from being a gently fluttering sail, to being ungraciously ripped from all its holds but one. One rock saved our tarp from a long ride across the plateau. In the destruction, a couple of the other rocks were ripped down from above our heads. They land closely on either side of us, but, fortunately, not on anyone. A rock falling on your head anytime would be horrible, but out here, it would be catastrophic. A tarp shelter rebuild is impossible in the breeze, but the sun has shifted just enough for one of the banks to create a sliver of shade. Lying down, I get my head, and as much of my body as possible in it. Leatherfoot, meanwhile, wraps the tarp around himself as shelter, and Kat, covered by clothes and facing away, says she is perfectly happy to rest and nap, even in the bright sun. The fact that I am lying on uneven gravel and rock, and being intermittently crumbled upon, doesn't bother me at all. Just staying cool. It is enough. It is all I need.

The shadow I cling to grows ever so slowly, and I have fallen into a dull haze. Unwilling to move, there is nothing to do but wait until the sun eases. This ant crawling near my face, housed in its little black body, doesn't mind the heat. It darts about this way and that, as ants do. Aimless in direction, its movements still seem purposeful. People look like this sometimes. Especially in big cities. It's often referred to as the "rat race," but it could just as easily be called "Ant World." Finding stuff, moving it, cooperating with some in the effort, fighting with others. Motivated by need. The ant that is. Humans? Motivated by need, and greed. Are ants ever motivated by greed? Do they take more than they need? The ant has found a nice chunk of something. It tries to lift it, but it is too big to carry. Instead, it drags its find... toil and grind...

Not exactly refreshed, we begin to ride once again, leaving our shadows slowly behind. What more can I tell about riding? It is work, pain, and endurance. It is discipline, perseverance, and forced meditation. We are each in our own mental world now. Each playing our own mind games of motivation. During the hardest spells, like slight inclines, wind blasts, or particularly potty holed places, complete attention is given to the task of riding as straight as possible. When the going is a little better, I have time to think about life, and olives, and Christmas tunes. The bizarre likes to mix with the philosophical.

"What the heck is going on?"

"What happened now Leatherfoot?"

"My bike rack just fell apart. It's only holding on one side. My pack is wobbling all over the place."

166

"You do have the Lemon Bike, don't you. Shall we pull out the repair kit?"

"No. Why don't you guys just keep on riding. I'll repack my bag and carry it on my back for the rest of the day."

"That sounds pretty uncomfortable. Are you sure?"

"Yea, I'll deal with it for the rest of today, and fix it later this evening at camp."

"Okay. See ya!"

Separating a group is never ideal in such a remote situation, but it is Leatherfoot, and he'll be fine. I know he can deal with it, and, assuming nothing else on his bike breaks, he'll be strong enough to catch up to us later. It really is best, particularly for Kat, to just keep going. Going. Pedal strokes. Feet go around and around, knees go up and down, keeping the bicycle in balance.

○ ○ ○

CLANG!

"OUCH!"

"Did he hit you Kat?"

"Mm, just on my leg though. It didn't really hurt too much."

Kids that throw rocks. I know I have mentioned this strange phenomenon before. What is it that motivates them to throw rocks at us? They herd their sheep by throwing rocks. Not at them, but on the flanks of the herd to encourage them in desired directions. Do they think we are sheep? We don't look like sheep. We do look odd, peculiar, foreign, *alien*, to them I'm sure. Our modern looking bikes and more colourful synthetic clothes and packs, but we still must be identifiable as human. Are they afraid? Is it simply a game? Fun and amusement? Ha Ha, I hit one of those crazy aliens with a rock today!?!

I just chase him. The little bugger. I've really been practicing patience too. You know, Tibet, Buddhism, Spirituality, the man from the market who squeezed my arm, but I snapped. True, it wasn't hard, or with a big enough rock to inflict any real damage, but my girlfriend getting hit with a rock thrown purposefully pisses me off. There was only the one boy this time, and I saw him. He knew that I knew it was him. I launch off my bike and

167

run after him, but he has a big head start. His lungs were born at this altitude, mine are soon ready to explode. I don't have a chance of catching him. I get as far as a Tibetan man, who I presume is his father, rant and rave at him for a while, pick up a rock, and pointing at it, give a big sign language "X." The kid, now standing wide eyed a good distance away, receives the most evil stare I can muster. All this energy spent, but I'm still not so sure the message is communicated. The father just stares at me blankly until I calm down. Then, he smiles a little and waits patiently. It's such an interesting reaction, in that there is no reaction, which causes the issue to die. I leave grumbling and defeated.

Residual anger fuels our next little stint on the bikes, but this extra energy is misdirected and burned inefficiently. It was foolish to spend it on anger. How often, I wonder, is there worth in spending energy on anger. Maybe there is a time and a place for it, but not here. We need all our energy for riding. My mind, having finally calmed down again, gives more thought to the lack of reaction by the father. It was so effective. Not the usual ping-pong rally of debate, or argument. No escalation of pitch and velocity of words and actions. Not even an attempt to verbally, or physically calm me down. It was one hundred percent passive. What are you going to do to counter that? Nothing. That's brilliant, and beautiful. Nothing said, and it spoke volumes.

We are about ten kilometers short of our day's goal when we come upon a scenic spot. The folds in the surrounding hills are eye candy. Leatherfoot has not yet caught up, Kat is exhausted, and my energy is, suddenly, waning rapidly. We decide to rest here until Leatherfoot comes. Kat wastes no time finding a comfortable patch of dirt on which to lie down.

O O O

It is evening now. Shadows can stretch no further. They are going to sleep. This is truly an idyllic spot for camping. We are in a canyon with a clean river, a bit of green, and a great view in all directions. We have set our tent on a nice sandy patch amongst all the rocks. Our pink tent. I've never liked that colour much, but I'm happy to have it out here. It adds a little splash of brightness after a long day of all earth tones.

By the time Leatherfoot had caught up to us at our rest spot, our bodies had atrophied, making riding any further extremely undesirable. It hadn't exactly been comfortable for Leatherfoot to ride wearing his pack either. Thus, we let our day's goal slide by the ten kilometers, and agreed that this rest spot would make a wonderful place to camp, and it has.

As Kat made noodles for dinner, Leatherfoot and I used the remaining daylight to attend to the bikes. We repaired his rack, washed everything as best we could, and oiled the chains. It's been a heck of a day. We finish all our tasks just in time to watch our regular evening feature presentation. It's the Light Show starring Sun Setting, Clouds Reflecting and Hills Blazing. It's the kind of thing you never tire of, and we add the sound through commentary, laughter, jokes and story telling.

"So, you say the Lemon Bike is mine now, do you Dogi?"

"It would appear that way Leatherfoot. I think the gods must have sensed early on that I wouldn't have the patience for it. I think you'll handle it best."

"Thanks a lot. Are you sure you don't want it, just for patience training?"

"No, I think it might be best if I just learn through observation for now."

"Goodnight guys. I go to bed!"

"Goodnight Kat. Are you all ready to settle into your cocoon, Leatherfoot?"

"Yea, it's about that time. Goodnight Dogi. See you in the morning."

"Goodnight Leatherfoot. Enjoy the stars."

APPLE STRUDEL

WE SLEEP REASONABLY WELL, AND ARE UP EARLY ENOUGH TO TAKE in the morning version of the lightshow. Shortly after breakfast, we are visited by a curious Tibetan man. I notice the braids. The ones woven for the straps used to carry his sack are tight and neatly patterned. His hair, which is also braided and wrapped around his head, is no longer tightly woven. The only hair stylist that these rural Tibetans would know, outside themselves and family, is the wind. He's harmless enough. As we pack, he just stands and watches us with a very blank expression on his face. When he's seen enough, he readjusts his carrying sack and walks away. There is something noteworthy about the Tibetans, or being here in general. We feel safe. Since the world of rumours, and our first morning of camping under siege, we have had no anxiety. Well, maybe in the Asshole of Tibet, but otherwise, we have felt no threat to our person, or possessions. The Tibetan curiosity can be slightly overbearing at times, but there is no fear. Particularly in regards to the local people. If there is anything to be afraid of out here, it is the environment.

Today we must face our third pass, this one topping out at about 4500 meters (14,800 feet). Kat is in no condition to ride it. Never having adjusted well to the altitude, the accumulation of hard days has worn her out. She'll persevere if needed, but, if at all possible, we will look for her to hitch a ride to the top. Leatherfoot and I would, however, like to ride this one.

No sooner do we hit the road, than we hear the clatter of a big truck approaching. We see that's it's a dump truck once again, and, we are able to successfully wave it down. The back already has some

170

locals in it, but the crew seems to be friendly, and they agree to take Kat along. A couple of the men help to load her bike, and they even tie it down securely, and make a comfortable place for her. This is good fortune, and will take a load off her day, and ours.

Leatherfoot and I wait for the resonance and the dust to settle, and set out happily in the cool morning air. The stiffness is not too bad today. We start in first gear and go easy, until all the necessary muscles are awake. Only then do we click up a gear or two, and settle in to a better pace. Our bodies have just enough time to warm up well before we start riding up a slight incline. The muscles and the mind readjust. The upper end of the valley begins to unfold as we round each new bend, bringing subtle and beautiful variations in scenery. It is the soft morning light that brings out the best in the landscape.

"PAVED ROAD! How exciting is that Leatherfoot!?"

"The contrast to the gravel is simply unbelievable. Night and day."

"It's kind of funny you know. I had no idea that this whole highway would be gravel and dirt road. The guidebook doesn't say anything about it. Well, it probably does somewhere, but I certainly never took note. And that fancy map I bought at home labels it as 'highway,' and looking at the nice fat red line, I assumed that meant paved. Somehow, I guess, I should have known. I don't know what I was thinking. Maybe, I simply wasn't thinking."

"Just not about that Dogi. Me neither by the way. I had no idea."

"But here we are. And we have a paved section!"

Being on this paved section of road certainly is pleasing. We can ride smoothly. Our butts are not getting b b b bounced around for a bit. It's much friendlier on the hands, the wrists, the shoulders and every other body part. We can keep our heads up continuously to take in some of the finest scenery to date. Or, perhaps, the scenery just seems better because the riding is smooth for a change. It's hard to say how these things work themselves out in your head.

The road becomes more winding and the incline increases, but going up on a paved road is still easier than going flat on gravel.

We feel good, and even have enough energy to talk, and smile and laugh. We hear the jingle of a donkey approaching from behind, and look back to see him pulling a cart loaded with a few Tibetans. What a remarkably strong creature to be pulling such a load, and still be travelling twice as fast as us. As he passes by, I grab onto the edge of the cart, and get pulled for a while. The Tibetans have a chuckle at this, though after a while, I can sense the driver is concerned about his animal, and wants me to let go. This is understandable, as the poor beast is obviously working hard enough. Not long thereafter, just as the road flattens, we enter a sparse farming community. The place has a lot of character, and we enjoy the houses and plots of worked land, until, a short time later, the asphalt comes to an unceremonious end.

"So. That's it huh?"

"That would appear to be our one and only gift of the day Dogi. Look up ahead. Can you see it?"

We groan a little as we return to the bump and grind gravel, but feel thankful for as much of a smooth ride as we received. Taking a brief pause, we can see along the rest of the valley, and in the distance what appears to be the pass. Our shadows are almost as short as our bodies, and the wind is threatening. Suddenly, I am feeling intimidated, but Leatherfoot's attitude is positive, and this breathes some energy into me. We slather ourselves generously with sun cream, take a deep breath and begin to ride again.

With Leatherfoot as the pacesetter we gobble up the flat section of the valley quickly, and soon find ourselves at the base of the climb, which does **not** start gradually. Without stopping, we dig in to the first pitch, which is a steep, lung burning grunt. This takes us as far as a small tunnel, under which we rest, until we recover our breath.

"Chocolate, Dogi?"

"Now that's the best idea you've had all trip, Leatherfoot! Let's do it."

"Should we save any for Kat?"

"Mmmm, no. She won't really need it. I hope her ride went okay."

"I'm sure she's relaxing at the top with some more locals."

"This chocolate is good. Oh, to save a piece for later or not?"

The chocolate gives us the little boost we need to get started again. We can do this. We have to do it. Kat is waiting for us at the top. We start out together, and I do my best to keep up with Leatherfoot for a while, but eventually I succumb to his pace, and settle in to my own. A few turns later, I am surprised to see him taking a rest, and though sweat has started to drip continuously off the end of my nose, I am in a good zone and keep on going. As I stop for a rest not long after, he once again passes me, and we begin to play what amounts to a game of tag. I pass him as he rests, and then he passes me. Back and forth, back and forth. Each restart gets more, and more difficult, but every time he passes, there is an invisible force that motivates me to move on. I will not be left behind by myself in the middle of a dusty mountain pass road!

I start to count out one thousand pedal strokes between breaks. The first two hundred hurt like hell, fighting through the lactic acid build up in the legs. The next six hundred are in a good mental groove. This is meditation. Forced meditation. The last two hundred are back to hell. The sweat begins to sting the eyes, bringing salt and dust along with its flow. There is no chance to wipe it. Lifting a hand off the grip would throw off the balance, and thus, break the rhythm, and rhythm is everything. Blowing the drips off the end of the nose, spitting, drooling, maybe even a little head shake... whatever is necessary to keep going. Then the mind begins to waver, the legs feel like they will explode, and nausea creeps in. Sometimes the groove lasts, and I go with it. Twelve hundred, fifteen hundred, even two thousand on one motivated spurt.

Pedal Breath Pedal Breath Pedal Breath Apple Strudel

"Apple Strudel?"

"Yea, with whip cream on it!"

"Where in the heck did that come from?"

There it is, right in the forefront of my imagination. A huge piece of apple strudel piled full of whip cream. It's sitting on a plate all alone on a small round table. I know it's only a reverie, but I cling to it desperately. I stick it out in front of me and chase it. I lose track of my pedal stroke count, but I don't care. I just want some Apple Strudel. It is a strange, but welcome vision. Definitely a pleasant change from the olives that have been making a regular appearance lately. Maybe it's Leatherfoot's white T-shirt that is billowing in the wind as he rides by. Oh boy, now Leatherfoot looks like whip cream. Oh well.

Pedal Breath Apple Strudel Pedal Breath Apple Strudel .

At long last we reach the blustery, wind swept summit. There is a mini-bus there and a small bunch of tourists who are smiling and waving and saying "Hello," but I am so overwhelmed with my arrival, that I ignore them. Instead, I run to the pile of rocks that hold the prayer flags, hug them, and shed some tears of relief, happiness and pride. After my little moment of elation, I settle in, and greet the tourists with big smiles and "Hellos," and then go and give Kat a big hug. She is quite contentedly bundled up in her sleeping bag in a sheltered spot. I wander around the area, and it feels good to walk. Wobbly, but good. I can see way down the valley that we just came up. I think the air is too thin up here for me to give a clear picture with lush words, but the view is awesome. Words, even photos can never encompass this kind of euphoria.

By the time we settle, we realize how famished we are, so we shelter in with Kat, and eat crackers and a can of questionable looking fish soaked in a black bean sauce. It's not Apple Strudel with a big pile of whip cream, that's for sure. In fact, I can't say that it looks or tastes a lot different from yesterday's sausages, and I'm sure that on a regular Sunday afternoon in Canada I wouldn't eat this stuff, but up here, after that climb, it almost tastes good. Every last drop of oil is extracted from the can, and licked from the fingers.

"How was your ride in the truck Kat? Did you have fun?"

Kat had an enjoyable morning on the truck. She says the driver and all the people in the back were really nice, and helped her get settled in. It was a bit cold at first, but she was so happy to have been picked up right away, and not have to ride. Not far along, she saw another foreigner by the side of the road with a bike, and quickly realized that it must be the Dutch girl who passed us with her boyfriend yesterday. Though an unusual occurrence, the encounter was so brief that I didn't even make note of it. Already later evening, they were in a hurry to keep moving, and we found out little other than their nationality.

Kat could see that she wasn't in a very good state, and had her thumb out. She already looked worn out yesterday, as she passed, and with her boyfriend nowhere to be seen, Kat decided to yell to help get the truck to stop and pick her up. She most gratefully accepted the ride, telling Kat that she had no idea how far in front her boyfriend was, and that she was exhausted and hungry. After hopping on, and hunkering down beside Kat, she had more of a chance to tell her own tale.

The two of them also purchased their bikes in Lhasa, but opted for the Chinese style ones. Those bikes ride more upright, and have less gears, but are more solidly built. They took the direct route from Lhasa to Shigatse which, according to her, was flat and not too scenic. They don't have much stuff along because they have planned their trip around staying in towns. Apparently, her boyfriend is a regular long distance cyclist, suggesting that he is super fit. She said he never waits, and he's been like this everyday so far. He just rides way up ahead, and expects that she'll catch up later in the day. Empathizing in the first place with her level of exhaustion, the news about her boyfriend's lack of support even had Kat feeling sympathy for this poor girl.

"She looked so beat. We had little laugh at how horrible we must look. We wonder how do we get ourselves here?"

After a while, the truck stopped to exchange some supplies, at which point everybody disembarked. They were fed some noodle soup, along with all the other passengers. The Dutch girl said that was the first thing she'd eaten since lunch the day before. Apparently, they rode until quite late yesterday, after they'd passed us. Not being able to make it as far as the small town, they ended up banging on some family's door, who, fortunately, let them stay. Can you imagine no tent, no sleeping bags, not even any cooking gear to boil water or anything? They're so lucky. And, can you envision the surprise of that Tibetan family, suddenly having these two foreigners banging on their door late in the evening?

The rest of the truck ride was great. They were unloaded at the top of the pass, and not even charged anything for the ride or the noodle soup they had for breakfast. The Dutch guy was already at the top of the pass, of all things, smoking a cigarette. We are all shocked that he rode the whole way up without even waiting for his girlfriend. To add to the folly, he didn't even have any water left, and Kat had to give him some of hers. As soon as the Dutch girl had her bike set to go, off he went out in front once again. No mercy. With a bit of a desperate and despondent look, she said thanks to Kat, and rode off in her vain effort to keep up.

This couple is being risky enough in not even bringing sleeping bags or a tarp. I know the distances on the map don't seem that huge, but there are large expanses of nothingness out here, and no traffic goes by from late afternoon onwards. Then, he routinely goes ahead and leaves her alone. What if she wipes out, or her bike breaks down? I understand risk. Go ahead and take it, but why not minimize it if you can? Especially when it involves the safety of others who are with you. Even more so when they are weaker than you. It is difficult to find any respect for this guy.

On her own at the top of the pass, Kat pulled out her sleeping bag, found the most wind sheltered spot that was still in the sun, and relaxed, drifting in and out of a nap. She was quite happy, as she was staying warm enough, and hoped we wouldn't arrive too soon.

Kat stuffs her sleeping bag away, and we re-tie her pack and get back on our bikes. After going uphill for most of the day, we are really looking forward to the downhill. The wind at the top is a swirling frenzy, but as we round the first bend, we get whipped directly in the face so hard that it is difficult to even control the bikes. It's not about rhythm this time. It's about staying on the bikes. With the ever changing direction and force of the gusts, it becomes an intense game of balance. Though we are on a pretty good downhill grade, we still need to pedal on many of the sections. It's intermittently horrible, and fun. Tibet. Can anything here be what you think it might be? This place plays my emotions like a concert violinist.

Finally, the terrain flattens out in the valley below, and we can see a bridge in the distance and a set of buildings on the far side of it. We think that one of these buildings will be our destination for the evening. The bridge doesn't look too far away, but we are being blasted ferociously from both sides and the front. The wind simply can't make up its mind which way to blow. It only knows that it wants to blow violently. It's making me feel small, feeble, and insignificant. Knowing that it is blissful as often as miserable, I'm not one to complain about the weather, but this extra endurance test tacked onto the end of an already grueling day is tough to take.

I SCREAM AT THE WIND! "AHHHHH H H G O O O O O A W A Y Y!!!"

It doesn't listen. It doesn't care. It has no mercy. I ask nicely. It blows. I plead, and it blows. Finally I shut up, fight back the frustration, think about my Mommy and put my breath to better use. Just pedal Dogi. Pedal Breath Pedal Breath.

We're spent. That last few hundred meters sucked out all but the last of our energy. Upon first arriving at the buildings, we see no signs of life. No wonder, who would want to be out in this kind of a wind storm? Before we need to start shouting, a young lady does appear all bundled up. I learned the words for "we'd like a room," but they elude me in my state of fatigue. Instead, I tilt my head onto clasped hands and close my eyes, which has always been easily enough understood. I am really enjoying this part about being human. The ability to communicate without words. She waves for us to follow, and we are shown to a room where we can also bring our bikes in with us. It is as basic as most we have stayed in. There are four cots and one table on uneven ground, and there are no windows. It is cold and dark, but to us it is five star beautiful. We don't have to set up our tent and we can cook our noodle soup on a stable platform. It is all we need.

LOCALS

"BREAKFAST IS ALMOST READY!"

"Oatmeal is good for breakfast every day. Oatmeal is good for breakfast everyday. Oatmeal is good for breakfast everyday."

"Good idea, Dogi. Keep telling yourself often enough, and you'll start to believe it."

"Kind of like the Chinese trying to brainwash monks that communism is better than their Buddhism, only a *little* different."

"Yea. Maybe a little different."

I am remembering back to when we were sitting with the old monk at the Sera temple, and the young monk came in. It was the term he used at the time. Brainwashing. He explained that, at a certain amount of risk, he had snuck out of the Chinese brainwashing session going on. Now that I think about it, I find it funny. The Buddhist monks live such a basic and communal life, which, in its essence, is the communist idea. Commune. Community. Communal. Communism. Only with the communist ideal, there is meant to be no religion attached. Brainwashing. It's an interesting term. Washing your brain. I think almost all of our brains have been washed to a certain degree. It's not only the current Chinese government washing Tibetan Buddhist minds, but most governments throughout history have done so to their populations, though, they would never refer to it as such. Arguably, it can be a good thing to a certain extent. Washing everyone's brains to a common way of thinking, so that we can coexist more smoothly. Population management. The human race might well be a lot more chaotic without any brainwashing. What does brainwashing really mean? Is it thought alteration? Where is the line between what is valuable brainwashing, and what is unethical? Lines. Always lines between good and bad. Perhaps, that which we refer to as "education" is meant to be on the good side of the line, and that which we refer to as brainwashing, on the bad side. Yet, the same act can be interpreted both ways. To the Chinese communist movement, they truly believe that they are educating the Tibetans in what is right and good. The Tibetans think it is brainwashing. As with all lines, there exists that grey area over which we are in perpetual struggle. The line is by no means clear. In fact, it is invisible, though we are constantly searching for it. The media is a prime example of the grey area, particularly as you get into the field marketing. What of the corporate jingle? To many, advertising is seen as a useful tool for driving what we call "the economy," to others it is the devil of greed in colourful disguise. How about religion? Is it valuable education, or is it brainwashing? To the Christian, it is obviously one, and to the atheist, the other, though they both may be good human beings and even friends. Perhaps "choice" is a key ingredient in the mix between what is defined as education, and what is defined as brainwashing. Choice. Academics is a good example of how choice helps define the line. To large degrees, it is something which we have choice to participate in, at least, in democratic societies, though we are not encouraged to believe this is the case. How about the news? This might be the pre-eminent topic exhibiting the grey area between education, or information, and brainwashing. Much of what gets broadcast in various forms is genuine and useful, yet, much is over-sensationalized with the intent of addicting the consumer. What if we have choice, but we are being brainwashed into believing that we don't? Now I'm going in circles. It's okay, this brainwashing thing. As long as the line stays grey and flexible, rather than blood stained red. Maybe that's why I'm out here, surrounded by nothing. Washing my brain with a different kind of soap. Brain cleansing. I like oatmeal everyday. I like oatmeal everyday.

The oatmeal is easier to make this morning because of the thermos of hot water. It is still the same girl running the guesthouse, and we bring her our empty thermos and ask her for another. The first thermos was delivered last night, and seems to be part of the room fee. For the additional one, a nominal fee is charged. Hot water. It's such a simple, but welcoming thing, and it's the only thing Kat will consume this morning. She had such a lousy night that she didn't even want to get out of bed. She's started running a fever, and has a few canker sores lingering inside her mouth. Unfortunately, she won't eat much.

Our guesthouse is one of few buildings in this tiny town of Renda, which sits on the corner of two roads. The main road is the highway we have been cycling, and will continue along later. The other road leads to a town called Sakya. It is a monastery town about twenty-five kilometers south of here, and is described as one of the best sights along the route we are taking, and worthy of a visit, if at all possible. Apparently, it has had less Chinese influence than other communities along the highway, and the colouration of buildings is unique. Because it is off the main road, many of the 4X4 tours do not have it on their itineraries, though the more expensive ones do. We definitely had it in our original plan, but the last few days have been long and hard, and we are all tired. It is a consideration to skip Sakya and have a day of rest. Leatherfoot and I would still like to go, but there is no question that Kat will not. I wonder that I shouldn't stay, but Kat insists she'll be all right on her own. She just needs rest. My guess is, she'll be happy to be rid of us for the day, and now that we are up and have eaten, Leatherfoot and I are beginning to look forward to it. Even the weather looks like it might be agreeable.

As Leatherfoot and I squeeze our bikes through the small room door and into the light, we catch the coattail of the guesthouse girl disappear around the corner. We look at each other, and then down at our bike racks, and smile at the realization that we will not have to strap our packs on this morning. I take one last look back at Kat, and see that she is buried completely beneath the pile of blankets. The door, as usual, has no lock, so I leave it a slight crack open to let in a sliver of light and some fresh air. As I get started cycling, I have a "towing" flashback. Without the pack, the bike is significantly lighter, and the first few pedal strokes feel like stumbling as our leg muscles are so used to the extra load. A smile, laced with excitement, sweeps across my face. Maybe we can even get into higher gears today!

"And we're off! First gear .. second gear .. third gear…"

"Dogi, I think this road is even bumpier than the main highway!"

"No doubt. It's making minced meat out of my innards."

The extra speed of the higher gears isn't worth it. We slow back down, and settle in to second, at which speed we can endure the turbulence. Even still, I find I have to lift my butt off the seat, and suck up as much of the bouncing as possible with my legs. At least, without the pack weight, we are able to look around much more than usual, and it is a beautiful morning. The scenery is fabulous. We are pedalling up a new valley, and a river can be seen meandering along off to our left. Between the river and the road, several rural communities have started to unfold. We are getting an assortment of curious stares, blank stares, waves and smiles. The children along this stretch are a particular amusement.

"The kids are hilarious eh, Leatherfoot?"

"Yea, and no rocks flying our way."

The younger ones are all inching closer to doorways, walls, or adults, while the dogs of the area are undecided between barking and chasing, or running away with tails between their legs. It's the older kids that are funniest, however. Many of them are being sent into a frenzy at our passing. Some are running at us full tilt, screaming "ELLO ELLO ELLO" and waving frantically, while others are obviously torn between getting a closer look at us, and alerting their neighbors of the spectacle passing by. They look like they're performing some mad festival dance. All this attention brings huge smiles to our faces, and we return as many of the waves and "ELLOS" as possible. I feel somewhat like I'm on a float in a parade.

There is a break between the villages and the main town of Sakya, where we arrive in good time, and find that it is, indeed, noticeably different from other Tibetan towns. The style of building in terms of shape and size are similar, but the colouration makes it unique. The buildings of most towns are some shade of creamy white, with variations on the trim, such as gold, blue, or brown.

Some of the more rural buildings are even plain old mud coloured. The buildings here in Sakya, however, are all dark grey, and have vertical stripes of white and burgundy at comfortable intervals on the outside walls. As we cycle toward the center of town, we expect to be getting some attention from the locals, but don't find them affected by, or interested in our presence. Obviously, the tourists do come here in their buses and cars, but have no interaction with the small villages along the way.

We are looking forward to more exploring, but first our hunger must be satisfied, and we sense the opportunity for some good food. Food with some decent nutritional quality. Something other than peanuts, peanut butter, crackers, oatmeal and noodle soup, and the chocolate we found in Shigatse. Though we would love to have a more varied diet when we are camping, it just has not been possible. There simply has not been a lot of choice. Our camping food has filled the belly, but it's not a well balanced diet, and certainly, not the kind of energy intake that would be ideal for what we are doing every day. Fruit, vegetables, meat. Any, or all of these would be welcome at any time. That's why we search for a Chinese restaurant. Our good intentions to support Tibetan things as much as possible are still in tact, but definitely not exclusive, and when it comes to food, there is no comparison. The choice between a bowl of thugpa (oily Tibetan noodle soup), and a Chinese fried rice with vegetables, and maybe some meat, is an easy decision. It is a choice made out of need. If we want to stay alive, and remain at all healthy in this harsh land, we must take in as many nutrients as we can, whenever we can. We must eat Chinese food as much as possible.

There is nothing that sticks out as distinctly Chinese here in Sakya. We have come across no divided neighborhoods, or new expansion. There are, however, a couple of Chinese restaurants that blend nicely into the local environment. We find a suitable place, duck through the door, and settle in at a table. We're thankful for the rudimentary English menu, and decide between ordering two, or three fried rice dishes. The portions of the two that come are reasonable, and we must remind ourselves not to wolf down the food, so great is our hunger. I could do with even more vegetables, and less rice, but it is the best meal we've had since Shigatse. We enjoy it thoroughly, and will probably have another round later.

As we sit back from our meals, we catch the eyes of a man at an adjacent table, who then nods and says hello. By his face, we can tell he is Tibetan, though his appearance is neat, and his hair is short and well kept, which is a rarity from what we have seen so far. We engage in a conversation, and are pleasantly surprised at the fluency of his English. I would like to say that he is the first well educated Tibetan that we have met, but I feel as though this doesn't do justice to other Tibetans. Education can be a tough word to define. In western terms, it would imply a level of formal schooling. The kind of degrees one has, and letters they can stick on the end of their name, but education in other parts of the world comes in much broader forms. What most Tibetans within Tibet have is an education in everyday life and survival. They learn how to eke out their existence by maximizing what they have. They learn to waste nothing. These things are education. They are impressive skills. Without this education, there would be no survival. So, I would like to say that he is the first Tibetan we have met who is more formally educated, and as he begins to tell us about himself, we continue to ask more questions, and become engrossed in his fascinating life story.

"Where are you from originally?"

"I was born in a small Tibetan town further north, but I moved to Lhasa on my own when I was still young."

"Why did you go to Lhasa?"

"There was only farming and basic living in my town, and I heard stories about the 'big city,' so I wanted to try to go there. The adjustment was a challenge because I came from such a rural area. Eventually, as a young man, I became more comfortable, but that was when the encroachment of the Chinese became a serious problem."

He doesn't volunteer any details on this subject, but I can see the pain and fear flash across his face at the memories. I want to delve further into what that was like, but he continues his story before I get a chance.

183

"It became so bad that I was forced to flee along with many others, and I was one of the few lucky ones that managed to escape. We went west for many long weeks, and the travel was difficult. Eventually, we had to walk over the mountains, and we had little clothing and terrible footwear. Sometimes we would get some food to eat from people in small villages, but mostly, we were starving. I saw many people die from hunger and cold."

You know these sorts of things happen in the world, but when you meet someone and hear their story firsthand, it penetrates more deeply. It makes the hardships that we are enduring feel trivial. Leatherfoot and I are riveted by his tale and ask for it to continue.

"I found my refuge in the northern part of India along with the other fortunate Tibetans who made it out at the time, and there I stayed for many years. I applied myself diligently, and managed to find work and get myself a good formal education. Since then, I have had several jobs, and now I am employed by the Red Cross and have been able to work back in Tibet. This has been a great challenge and very rewarding. I love my people, and want to help them in any way I can."

I get the feeling that it is trying for him in a political sense to do his work here in Tibet. We would like to learn more, but the time has come for him to leave. We wish each other well. As he and his companions walk out the door, it strikes me as curious that we should have run into him in a Chinese restaurant. Has he accepted the Chinese presence here? Has the Chinese government accepted his presence here? Politics. Land. Aggression. Acceptance. Evolution. Revolution. One thing though, he did seem very happy and fulfilled.

○ ○ ○

Leatherfoot and I step outside to find that our bikes have been fiddled with. There doesn't seem a worry to actually have them stolen, but those curious Tibetans do love to touch and move parts around. We go back into the restaurant and ask if we can leave them inside for a few hours while we walk around the town. Thankfully, this turns out to be no problem.

The first place we walk to is the monastery. It is a huge complex, and it dominates the town. It has the look and feel of a fort, with outer walls that are three stories high. As we step through the entrance, we find ourselves in a large empty courtyard. Surrounded by the towering walls, we get a sense of foreboding, which is further fueled by the fact that there is no one else around. Not a caretaker, not a tourist, not a monk. Just Leatherfoot and myself. It doesn't feel right that such a place has no activity. Where is everybody?

We wander around the rooms, courtyards, and halls, and still we run into no one. The place is totally empty. At the top of a succession of stairs, we find access to the roof, which is boxed in by the waist high outer walls. As thick as they are high, we start walking along the top of them for long stretches, and soak in both the details of the rooftop and the encompassing views. We select the best viewpoint and plop ourselves down on the corner that overlooks the rest of the town, and the valley from where we came. The top of the walls, on which we sit, are covered in a semi-rounded layer of clay, mixed with shards of numerous sizes and shapes of rocks. It is not cushiony, but it is a fine perch nonetheless. Below us there are some animals grazing, and a bunch of people on the rocky bank of the small river. They are washing clothes, and laying them on the rocks to dry. This adds some nice colour to the otherwise earthy tones.

"Look Dogi, there are several monks robes drying down there."

"That might explain the nakedness of the monastery!"

There is a reasonable expanse of flat land here, much of it trying desperately to look green, but few buildings. Most of the town itself is built on a slope of one of the many surrounding hills. Perhaps, the river swells during another season, or the flat land is too valuable for its fertility. Well worn paths and some rock walls meander around the slope from building to building. The structures themselves are built block style. There are no angles, and the rooftops are flat, yet each one is built into the existing landscape. The whole thing gives off a wonderfully artistic feel. There is both chaos and harmony.

"Do you think you could live somewhere like this, Dogi?"

"You mean in this castle?"

"No, I mean in a small town like this in the middle of nowhere."

"I've fantasized about that kind of thing before, but realistically, I don't think I could do it. I think I've seen too much of what's outside, and I'd get bored after a while. Though it might be fun to do for a year or so. How about you?"

"I agree. At least right now I have too much wanderlust."

We leave through a new set of halls and doors, which lead us back into the middle of the huge courtyard. I look up and around once more, but the big burning ball in the sky suggests it is time to lower my head. I close my eyes and try to envision this place full of activity and life. What it once must have been, and what it might become again. Will it be living quarters for a few monks until it crumbles? A destination for tourists with money reinvested for restoration? It would be sad should it not rekindle some sort of life.

As we exit the monastery, we come across some painters who have begun work on its outer walls. This is an encouraging sign that life will someday come back to here after all. They are doing some brilliant work. This is Tibet trying to add colour to its world. Columns and beams are brightly painted, greens, blues, yellows, and reds. Intricate rhythmic designs and scenes of the Buddha tell stories. We watch them work for a while. Some draw the outlines of the scenes, while others fill in the colours. It's nice to see that they are happy as they do their work.

Sticking to the shade where possible, we round a corner and come across one older woman sitting in the middle of a wide path on top of some sort of old sack. She has a couple of large metal bowls and looks to be sifting some grains. As she chants softly, her voice echoes off of the walls in between which she rests, creating an interesting self harmony. She seems very content with her task.

We walk on, and come across a rather unexpected and somewhat disturbing scene. I'm going to call it the devil's door. The face of one of the protector characters on the door itself has become familiar from other monasteries, with its intense eyes, fang like teeth and fiery hair infested by mini-skulls, but it's what hangs from the roof of the entrance that gives us the willies. Stuffed animals! Real ones, that look like they were done by someone in kindergarten of a taxidermy school. The main feature, front and center, is a wolf. It is chunky in the body with an evil looking snarl and skinny legs pointing out in uncomfortable looking directions. Accompanying the wolf are the coon, the cat and the mystery creature all "flying" in various contorted positions. The devil's door indeed!

"Hey Leatherfoot, do you think these creatures all live around here?"

"I don't know. I mean I didn't read anything about it in the guidebook, but where else would they come from?"

"Are you still gonna sleep outside the next time we camp?"

We continue our walk around this wonderful place getting to the upper reaches of the slope where we can once again look down upon the town. Most of the rooftops have an outer wall or fence, which has been constructed by layering cow and yak patties. Actually, it's not just the rooftop walls, but other walls look like they are being built, patched and reinforced with the dung too.

"Check out the poo walls Leatherfoot. Those patties are like pre-fabricated bricks. A fine balance of grasses and mush baked in the daily midday sun kiln. They stack them so neatly."

"I'm not so sure they become permanent walls though Dogi. The buildings themselves are made out of clay bricks. I heard that they use the dung as fuel for burning. Maybe they just stack them to dry, and leave them like that as storage."

"But they don't make multiple rows. It's all stacked around the perimeter of the roof. And remember, we saw some being layered and pressed onto the outside of a wall earlier."

"Maybe it's both. I definitely think a lot of it is for fuel, but it does make a fine patching, and even building compound."

"Any which way, I think it's great. It's such a fine example of how the Tibetans use everything available to them without waste. Have you noticed that you never see any excess stuff lying around a Tibetan home. They eat everything, and they use everything. It's the tightest circle of life I've ever seen."

We wander back down the slope, zig zagging through the neat assortment of houses and buildings, and are being received kindly by the locals. They smile, nod, or wave, but generally leave us free to explore wherever we wish. I am enjoying all the scenes, but my attention continues to return to the construction, and the use of the dung patties in particular. It's fascinating. On closer inspection, I find that they are stacked both horizontally and vertically, and then topped with a final layer of grasses and all held down with rocks. I suspect they compress and bind over time.

Back onto the flat section, and winding through the donkeys, cows, yaks, goats and chickens, we find our way back to the restaurant and are pleased to find our bikes in good condition. The heat, combined with walking up and down the hills was beginning to wear us out, and the coolness inside the building is most welcoming. We order another two plates of food to eat right away, and one extra take away rice for Kat. Though our friend from the Red Cross is no longer there, the owner and one or two other patrons can speak some rudimentary English, and they tell us of a local's path. Apparently, it should be better riding than the road. This is hard to imagine. The road, though rough, was pretty direct over its twenty-five kilometers, but we're willing to give it a try. We are given some vague directions on how to find it and say "ka-lee shu."

The "local's path." As we exit the town, we can see two bridges across the small river. The one wide enough for cars is half missing, giving us an idea of how high the river might flow at other times. The other bridge, designed for foot traffic, is short and narrow, but plenty comfortable to cross on our bikes. On the other side there is a road that continues for a hundred meters downstream. We push our bikes to this road, and ride along it until it narrows and finally dwindles into a path. A path. The local's path.

"Well Leatherfoot, at this point I'm not quite sure why we let ourselves get convinced this would be a better route than the main road."

"Maybe we made the mistake of equating 'better' with 'easier.' But from what I can see, this path is definitely not going to be easier to ride than the main road, even if that is potty hole hell. Do you think we should turn back or go for it?"

"We're here. Let's see what happens!"

What ensues heading down the local's path is a full on adventurous mountain biking tour. There is nothing easy about it. It takes us along paths of varying width and texture, across creeks, around farm fields, across rock fields, through sheep, and horses, and locals and villages. A few sections get narrow enough that we come close to wipe outs. Other parts are impossible to ride through, and we have to get off and carry our bikes.

"It feels a bit strange to ride through people's properties, don't you think?"

"Yea, but they're not reacting any differently than when we were riding along the road."

"Of all the fascinating things here, that's the one I find most striking. The concept of ownership and possession have such a vastly different personality. It's so nice to have the freedom to do this."

I have always believed that all cultures have a certain percentage of people that steal and damage other people's belongings, but I wonder that it doesn't exist amongst the Tibetan part of the population. The thought is a stretch, but there is simply nothing guarded about their behavior whatsoever. The feeling of it is beautiful... as beautiful as the sights, sounds, smells and lovely smiles.

Better. Maybe the local's path is better. Not easier, but better. It's been a wonderful Tibetan cultural experience, but we see the road on the other side of the river, and, for the first time, a way to get to it without getting too wet. The exhilaration of the ride is beginning to get outweighed by the exhaustive pounding. With a bit of effort, including one last carry of the bikes, we rejoin the road. It felt as though we'd gone a long way on that local's path, but we discover, from a marker on the road, that we still have fifteen kilometers to go, and a harsh headwind to battle. It is most disheartening.

"This wind is almost as nasty as yesterday's Leatherfoot."

"Yep. Not as strong, but straight in our faces. Are you ready?"

"To inhale some dust? Are we gonna take any breaks or just go for it?"

"Let's go for it."

"I figured you'd say that. Hey, can you poke me in the ribs, that's where my adrenaline button is. I think I'm gonna need it."

Pedal Breathe Pedal Breathe
Try Not To Heave
Pedal Breathe Pedal Breathe
Wipe Sweat On Sleeve
Pedal Breathe Pedal Breathe

I take my short hits of wind in the face and let Leatherfoot draft for what it's worth, but it is mostly him out in front pushing the pace, and me trying to keep up. In truth, the first ten kilometers are kind of fun, as we are making a game out of reading the road and avoiding the biggest bumps. I am craving a break, but five kilometers left turns into four, and Leatherfoot keeps on pushing. When we finally arrive, I can't decide whether to hug him, or punch him, so I give him one of each.

What a day. Again. Every day here has been both fascinating and exhausting.

○ ○ ○

Kat is in bed bundled in clothes and blankets, a thermos of hot water beside her. The fever seems to have passed, but she has a sore throat and those canker sores. Her day had its peaceful moments, but she also had a visitor who lingered a little too long, and her story translated something like this...

I slept for a while again after you guys left, then the Tibetan girl, who runs this place, came in. She just kind of stayed. She was talking to me, in Tibetan of course, so I tried to communicate with her a little. About the only common word we could find was "Lhasa," so I showed her some pictures of Lhasa from the guidebook. Her eyes got so wide, and she pointed at the pages and said "Lhasa?" She was absolutely fascinated. I tried Kathmandu, but that didn't really register. By then, I was getting woozy again, so I went back to sleep. I'm not sure, but I think she left for a while, and then she came back again. She was just curious. Touching things, even my face and my hair. I wanted to talk to her more, but I am

190

so tired, and it got to be a bit much. It was hard to communicate that I just wanted to be left alone.

"Do you think you can eat any of this take away fried rice Kat?"

"I not sure, but I try."

"How about you Leatherfoot? Chicken flavoured noodle soup OR Oriental flavoured noodle soup?"

"Such selection Dogi, I'm finding I can't even decide."

We make the noodle soup as mushy as possible so it's easier for Kat to eat, but mostly, she only drinks broth and has little of the fried rice. Though we wish she would eat more of it, Leatherfoot and I have no trouble shoveling the rest in. As we finish telling Kat some of our day's stories, sleep takes us quickly one after another into its waiting arms.

EXPECTATIONS

"Good Morning, time to get up."

"Already? I can't move, but I do have to pee!"

"Well don't do it in the bed, Dogi! Come on Kat. How's it going?"

"MMmmMmm"

It is no longer early by the time we drag ourselves out of bed, and would have been even later were it not for Leatherfoot motivating us. We had agreed on a casual start, figuring we could all use extra rest. All the hot water we drank last night made the last few hours of sleep fitful, but the pressure was not great enough to overcome the fatigue and crawl out from under the warm blankets. I do finally get up with a little more prompting from Leatherfoot, and go out to relieve the bladder. The wind is at the same stage of awakening as us. Stirring and swirling, but not yet moving too quickly. Leatherfoot has the morning meal ready to go, and I help him serve it up.

"How's the body Leatherfoot?"

"A little stiff. I think that local's trail worked a few muscles I didn't know I had."

"I agree. A little more abuse in the hands and shoulders than usual. What do you say Kat? Are you going to eat any of this deluxe oatmeal cooked in the very finest of Tibetan boiled water?"

Leatherfoot and I manage to slowly loosen and limber up our bodies through the regular morning activities and a bit of extra stretching, but Kat still looks groggy and is moving in slow motion. She says she is feeling a little better, in terms of fever and sore throat, but that her mouth feels awful. The canker sores are out of control, and even her gums are swollen and her teeth hurt. I take a look, and it is a festering mess in there. They are all over her gums, inner cheeks and even her tongue. It's gross. She refuses to eat, citing that it is simply too painful. We push the oatmeal on her, telling her that she has to eat something... anything... even a little bit. She tries, but the look of agony on her face tells just how much it must hurt to have anything in there.

○ ○ ○

All we need to do today is get to the next town called Lhatse. According to our information, that should only be a ten kilometer ride. There, we will restock our food supplies, and try to find a ride up the next mountain pass. The extra sleep and casual morning have been nice, but the drawback is the wind, which is already up as we start to ride. Not surprisingly, it's a headwind, but it's only ten kilometers. Even Kat should have enough in the tank to deal with that. We let her set the pace. She wants to take an early break, but we implore her to make at least five kilometers. When we tell her that's passed, she ignores us and doesn't stop until six.

"Four more to go Kat. You can do it."

"Come on Kat. Yummy Chinese food awaits us."

"Hey Leatherfoot, this wind is ugly. Maybe we should go side by side out front, and at least create a barrier if not a bit of a draft."

"Sure, let's try it."

"Okay Kat, we'll try not to push the pace, but see if you can stay in behind us."

Depending on the road condition, this method works all right. As much as possible we stay side by side, but often the road forces us back into single file. Kat does her best to keep in behind.

"Where is it? Where is Lhatse?"

"It must be soon. I'm sure we've done ten kilometers."

Eleven kilometers goes by, then twelve, thirteen. We stop, re-check our information and map. Fifteen, sixteen... the wind is picking up... eighteen. We are pretty grumpy by the time we hit twenty. The guidebook, which has been a most wonderful and faithful companion over many years, and through many countries, receives a brutal verbal bashing, but maybe we're reading something wrong. Our map shows Renda at the turnoff to Sakya. Maybe this is not right. Maybe, we weren't actually in Renda last night, though we haven't gone through any other towns either. We hit twenty-three kilometers and Kat breaks down. She can't go anymore, and starts to cry. Laying her bike down, she sits at the side of the road, buries her head in her arms, and really begins to sob. We try our best to console her and convince her to push on a little further. It must be soon. It really must be. We can stop there for a long rest. In the end though, we simply have to wait. She's not responding to us at all. We don't exist in her world at the moment. There is only pain and frustration, and she must cry it out of her system. We wait.

I start thinking about the concept of expectations. Those thoughts developed in our minds at a time earlier than an event. The emotional responses depending largely upon the nature of what is being expected, and the gap between it, and what actually transpires. If an expectation is for fun or entertainment, it produces positive emotions in its own right, the opposite being true when less desirable things are being anticipated. If an expectation is neutral, like our assumption of ten kilometers, there is little emotion attached to it. It just sets up a parameter for the brain and body to adjust to. It's a framework from which you can establish your balance. If such neutral expectations are exceeded, the results can be joyous, and if they are met on par, they tend to blend into the reality. Yet, if they are not met, the result can be confusion, disappointment, frustration and even anger.

Kat doesn't say a thing when she finally does get up. She just gets back on her bike and rides. We let her get out in front before we saddle up, but we catch up soon enough. At twenty-four kilometers, a mere one kilometer past where Kat broke down, Lhatse unveils itself. That's twenty-four kilometers from Renda, or at least, from the turn-off to Sakya, which is maybe not Renda. Twenty-four, not ten.

"You know Leatherfoot, that information stuff is great, when it's right. But it sure does set up expectations."

"That's true. I haven't had a lot of expectations on this trip, so there's been little room for disappointment, but this morning was challenging."

"Maybe it's good never to expect anything. Then you can't be disappointed."

"I don't know if that would work, Dogi. Don't you think you'd miss out on the joy of anticipation?"

"Hmm, you're probably right. I guess learning to accept things, even if they come up short of what you thought, is the key eh."

We discover Lhatse to be a small town built mostly around the main road, which is paved from one end to the other. It could best be described as a truck stop town. There are mechanics, restaurants, hotels and supply stores of various sorts, and not much else. We drift across the pavement and stop at the first suitable restaurant. It's a Chinese place. We need the nourishment. We are given an English menu and order a few dishes, including a soup that we hope Kat will be able to eat. Leatherfoot starts conversing with a couple of German tourists at the table next to us who are on a 4x4 tour, and there is a local band playing dreadful sounding music just outside the entrance way.

Kat is alive enough to be perusing the Chinese side of the menu. Inspecting menus is one of her favorite pastimes. And, though spoken Chinese and Japanese are completely different, the Japanese language is written, in part, using Chinese characters. This means she can get the gist of things written in Chinese, though by no means fully understand them. What she has discovered, are some significant discrepancies in prices from the English side of the menu to the Chinese. The first one she noticed was boiled rice. For English speakers, it's two Yuan. For Chinese, it's only one Yuan. We don't like this very much. Many tourists don't mind this kind of thing, and even some travellers, but all of us are on a traveller's budget, and none of the three of us is too fond of tourist prices in the first place. For Kat, perhaps, the reason is basic thriftiness, for Leatherfoot and me, it's as much a principle issue as pinching coins.

"Hey Kat, did you figure out any more discrepancies yet?"

She has a very intent and focussed look on her face as she studies the menu. A challenge, no doubt, trying to translate between a language that she speaks half of (English), and one she can't speak at all, but can read some of (Chinese), AND, the side that was written in English is very suspect at best, as it was written by some who is Chinese! And if you had difficulty figuring out that sentence, then you can imagine how she feels, and why she has the crinkle on her face.

We point out the several differences that Kat has found to the waitress/owner, who reacts in an angry huff. I guess she's comparing us to the German tourists who dined beside us. They paid the tourist price, though I'm not sure if they paid a tip, which is something the locals don't do. I wonder if not paying a tip sounds selfish to many people who come from a tipping society. Paying a tip in a non-tipping society is, in effect, imposing your culture onto another culture. Perhaps people think that tipping is kind, which the thought is, but it may have unknown negative repercussions. It may cause embarrassment to other patrons or the owner. The owner may form expectations, lumping all foreigners together, or all white people together, and feel bitter when one leaves no tip, and another twenty percent, because one comes from a tipping culture like North America and another from one of the many European cultures that don't. What would happen in reverse? A Chinese person goes to North America. Should they tip or not? They don't in their culture, so why should they in North America? They should because that's what the locals do. Right!

The waitress is off talking to one of our neighboring customers, obviously complaining about us as she spews on and points in our direction. You can tell he doesn't really want to get involved, but eventually gets up and comes over to talk to us, speaking English surprisingly well.

"What do you have problem?"

We show him Kat's menu findings, and he looks surprised, as I doubt he's ever read the English side of the menu before. We figure out exactly what we ate, and discover that the tourist price is almost double the Chinese price. The man doesn't have much more to say, and simply goes over to the waitress, explains the obvious, and goes back to his table. She follows him and pleads with him a little more, but he brushes her off. He obviously agrees with our point of view. Not surprisingly, she brings us the bill with the tourist price total on it.

Our German neighbors have gotten back into their rocket shuttle to be driven onwards, but not before tipping the band that randomly showed up to play, and giving handouts to all the begging kids, who now wait equipped with their own EXPECTATIONS for us to leave the restaurant. Handing money out to beggars is in the same vein as paying tourist prices, and another thing we are all philosophically opposed to. We feel as though it's an unhealthy way to inject money into a system. Kids start to lose respect for their traditional work, and become nasty and aggressive with the begging. Even here, in this spiritual land. Just coming here and spending money on food and accommodations and such, injects money naturally, which will hopefully filter through the system. Giving to a local school, or something of that nature would be a better alternative.

We pay the Chinese amount of the restaurant bill and leave. The waitress is mad, but what can she do? The band has already moved on, and the kids figure out quickly that they will get no money from us after I hand out only high fives and move on.

Even though the food was good, Kat didn't eat much, and she still feels terrible. Not consuming a lot of food is obviously contributing to her feeling ill, but she says the canker sores are way too painful to eat anything. She stays with the bikes and generally passes out while Leatherfoot and I walk around the town in search of some supplies.

"Okay Leatherfoot, you go to the fruit and vegetable shop while I hit the butcher and the bakery."

"Sure Dogi, then we'll meet at the Deli."

We are craving more variety in our diet, but after checking a few places, we discover only the usual fare. After comparing shops, we decide on one place, and bargain a good price on a big pile of supplies; more soup, crackers, chocolate, peanuts, raisins, bread and toilet paper. We enjoy the bargaining process. It's fun when it's done in good spirit. The owner got a big sale, and we got a good deal. Both parties are happy.

We find Kat sitting against a wall with her head buried, once again, in her arms. She's disoriented as she looks up at us, and we tell her to just keep resting as we still have a bit to do, but we are suddenly joined by an older American traveller who has just walked over from across the street. He introduces himself, and explains that he has been doing some bus riding and mostly hitchhiking from Lhasa.

"It's been a good adventure, met lots of interesting people, and so far no major hassles. The local bus system is a bit of an enigma. First of all, it's infrequent, and secondly, they sometimes allow foreigners on board and other times not. There's the possibility of them trying to charge us a lot more too. Hitching is better. There are still some long waits, and you usually have to pay, but it's less, and somehow more fun in the back of those big trucks. Hey, did you guys see that young Japanese couple?"

"No, we didn't. Did you Kat?"

"Mm, I see them. I think they get off local bus."

"Ya, that was them. He was dressed more western style, but she was in Tibetan clothes. I bet that gets them onto the buses more easily."

After telling a few of our tales, and chatting a little more about various rumours and what might be coming further down the road, luck is wished all around, and the American traveller goes on his way. We start with a few adjustments on the lemon bike, which is having issues once again, and then proceed to repack our bags. This has attracted the attention of a young teenage boy and an older man. The man is unobtrusive enough, just watching and smiling. The boy, however, is nosey to the point that I have tripped over him several times. The first couple of times I tried to gently move him away, and accompanied the motion with a smile. Unfortunately, he hasn't gotten the hint, nor has the older man made any motion to pull him away, so I give him a firm shove and bark at him, and he leaves.

"I feel bad about doing that Leatherfoot, but what else can you do?"

"Not much Dogi. You did try nicely a few times, so don't worry about it."

Two minutes later, the boy reappears and invites us for tea. This makes me smile, laugh, shake my head and roll my eyes. If some impatient "alien" shoved me, I don't think I'd invite him to tea. They really do fascinate me, these Tibetans.

We decline the offer for tea, but do ask the old man to fill our jugs with boiling water. Since our filter broke way back when, we've been trying to stick to boiling water if we can get it, or clear running streams that appear to be coming from a higher source. He generously fills all our bottles, and we offer him a few Yuan, as we know the fuel used to boil the water is not cheap, but he refuses the money. A short time later, we finish the water from our large pop bottle, which we also use as a water container, and ask him to fill this as well. Yet, as time passes, he and the bottle do not return. We go to find him in his place, which is right next door, and ask about the bottle, but it is nowhere to be found. Perhaps, it has been sent off to another house, but from the way he's motioning, it doesn't seem like it. Of course, all of our communication during this whole affair has been non-verbal, so a misunderstanding is certainly possible, but it still seems a bit strange. Do they get a refund on the pop bottles? Why would they refuse our money for the water, and then take it for this purpose? A mystery it will remain!

○ ○ ○

The next mountain pass, Lhakpa La, is not too far away, and it is the highest of the lot at about 5200 meters (17,200 feet). We have decided that we should all hitch up and over this one. Kat is in no condition to ride it, and after the last three passes, I realize my own limits, and this kind of hardcore assent, at this stage of the trip, would be harsh. Perhaps Leatherfoot and I would make it, but we agree that it wouldn't be much fun. Also, it would probably take us two days, which would mean separation from Kat, and that isn't an option.

Leatherfoot and I leave her to continue resting, and walk around town asking various truck drivers for a ride to the summit of Lhakpa La. Surprisingly, we are not greeted too pleasantly, being generally brushed aside or ignored. It is yet another thing today that has not met our expectations. We assumed this would be the ideal place to find a ride.

"Now what Leatherfoot?"

"Well, either we stay here and keep on looking, or we ride."

"This isn't the most attractive place in the world. Why don't we ride slowly for as long as Kat can deal with it, and stop any trucks going our way. At worst, we'll set up camp at the beginning of the climb and try again tomorrow."

We return with the unfortunate news to Kat, who still seems rather oblivious to much of anything. She gets up without saying anything again, and we begin to ride at a casual pace with her in the middle. We keep hoping to hear the sound of a truck from behind, but none pass us. Six kilometers outside of Lhatse, we come to a fork in the road. The option to the right must be the beginning of the trek into the huge expanse of Western Tibet. We take the left, southern bend, and enter into what seems like a whole new world. This is the beginning of a new valley, and the ascent to Lhakpa La. We ride only a short distance, and it is mellow and beautiful. There are carpets of green in here, and it is back dropped by some huge winding brown foothills. The afternoon sun is once again producing brilliant shadows.

Not far along, we find such a nice spot for camping that we are quite happy not to have been picked up. There are great soft spots to put our tent and for Leatherfoot to make his bed. The sound of running, gurgling water accompanies the small wafts of wind that whistle the tune of the new valley. We enjoy a long mellow evening, accompanied by a great sunset fading into a sky full of stars. Even Kat stays awake for a while and joins in some conversation. What kind of crazy adventure awaits us tomorrow?

BRIE CHEESE

"GUESS WHAT DAY IT IS, DOGI?"

"I have no idea, Leatherfoot. I only know it's today, and I'm alive, and you guys are alive, and that's good."

"It's Day Sixteen."

"Of cycling across Tibet or since we arrived?"

"Day Sixteen of cycling and pushing and pulling and hitching across Tibet."

"Is that it? Only day sixteen?"

If someone told me it was day one hundred and sixteen I might actually believe them. The roller coaster of each day out here feels like ten. Knowing the day does, however, add some structure to the well blended chaos of the journey. Hot Cold Laugh Cry Brown Blue Pedal Breathe... Brie Cheese.

○ ○ ○

We get up early this morning, only to watch an empty dump truck pass by as we helplessly pack. We are camped too far off the main road to have had any chance of flagging it down. It's a let down, but on our more recent riding days, we have had the pleasure of inhaling a cloud of dust kicked up by passing trucks at least every hour or two, so we figure another truck will pass by soon enough. We finish packing, and relocate ourselves next to the road. Then the hours start to pass. Isn't that just how it goes. No trucks, in fact no vehicles pass at all. It is silent at the base of this valley, which, in a way, is kind of nice. Our anticipation subsides and gives way to utter relaxation. What a glorious spot! Who cares if a truck passes us today? Kat says she thinks it's Sunday, and that's why there are no trucks. Oh well. We could happily camp here one more night. If no suitable rides pass us by tomorrow morning, we'll simply have to ride, and push.

On this morning's breakfast menu were flatbreads, which we bought in Lhatse. Kat didn't eat any. She tried tiny bites at a time, but said it's still way too painful. The canker sores have not eased at all, and the burnt, split, swollen lip looks as though she came out on the losing end of a prize fight. Even drinking hurts, but at least she's forcing herself to do that.

With some extra free time, I go digging deeper into my pack than I have since Lhasa, and unearth a few things including an old harmonica and a can of Brie cheese. Cheese. I have been packing it for a long time. It's a traveller. Long ago, it started its journey in Canada, and has since gone to Japan, Thailand, India, Nepal and now halfway across Tibet. It is a gift from Mom, and bound to be full of her strength and determination. If there were ever a time for strength and determination, this would be it.

"What the heck is that Dogi?"

"Well, my good friend Leatherfoot, it's a can of Brie."

"Cheese? You have real cheese?"

"Yep. It's a gift from my Mom, and I've been saving it for a special occasion, and guess what?"

"This is a special occasion?"

"Don't you think? I can't think of a better picnic area. Break out the crackers!"

Dairy products are one of the many food groups we are starting to miss, along with fresh vegetables and fresh fruit. I guess yak butter could qualify as dairy, but it's just not the same as a fresh glass of milk, a bowl full of yoghurt, or... Brie cheese. Perfect. I crack and peel back the lid.

"How's it look?" asks Leatherfoot.

"Looks good. Looks like Brie cheese."

"Any mould?"

"Not at all. The can was a little dented and dinged up, but in tact, so it looks, and smells, perfectly good."

Actually, it smells so good that I stick my nose back for a second whiff and inhale deeply, and pass it over to Leatherfoot who does the same. Kat is looking both longingly and apprehensively. She's hungry. She hasn't consumed much, other than water, for days. I cut the cheese!

A Tibetan boy has suddenly appeared, just wandering down the road. Where did he come from? He stands, stares at us, and taps his thumbs together, but says nothing. As we have nowhere to go in any hurry, we'd like him to join us. The "lunch crowd" Tibetans have been so welcoming and generous to us so often, we'd like to share some hospitality and food in return, like crackers and nuts and... well... maybe not the Brie cheese. By waving, we invite him to sit and join us, but he doesn't react at all to our motions. He continues to stare in a somewhat dumbfounded manner. There is no fear or anxiety, no excitement, no noticeable emotion at all. It's as if we are a television in a shopping mall window, and he has stopped for a brief viewing. As suddenly as he appeared, he is off again, wandering down the road. Here now, there now. It strikes me as beautiful. Is that simplicity the ultimate way to be? The ideal human condition? Why do we take photos? Why do I write? The past, the future, the complexities, the analysis, the discussions. The boy stops, turns, and stares one last time. Is it all going somewhere, or is there really nowhere to go? Here now, there now. That's all.

"How is it Kat?"

She has a queer look on her face as she sucks, more so than chews, the small piece of cheese she has put in her mouth. Leatherfoot and I haven't tried it yet. We're enjoying watching Kat's reaction.

"It's creamy. I think I can eat it. It's really good."

It's funny. Now that it's right there to be eaten, I feel like delaying a little longer. Though I'm craving it, I am enjoying the anticipation. Slowly, I spread my first piece onto a cracker covering it uniformly. Then, I watch as Leatherfoot puts his first piece in, and a smile creeps across his face. I close my eyes, stick it under my nose, and shove the whole cracker in. I am not let down. It's creamy, and flavourful and delicious. It's hard to savour rather than gobble, but Leatherfoot and I pace ourselves with Kat, who can only put small pieces in and slowly suck on them. There is no talking, though we exchange a lot of looks, and all have big smiles on our faces. I eat my last piece without a cracker to savour the flavour on its own. And, as the last of it slides down my throat, I get to thinking about the Tibetan diet. Barley, a bit of rice, yak butter, and some meat is the extent of it. I find it truly amazing that they can not only exist on this basic fare they consume, but look quite vibrant and healthy. At least the majority of those that we have come across are strong looking human beings that are weathered, but not under-nourished. Of course, genetically speaking, they must be used to this, but still it seems so little energy to ingest compared with what they must put out, and what the environment takes from them. Is their strong spirituality actually a source of energy? Can it actually manifest itself physically this way? Certainly their calmness, and their pace and wasteless ways translate to a minimum of wasted energy. The thought makes me realize how spoiled we are in wealthier countries. How diverse our food supply is, and how much we can afford to waste. But where are our spirits?

With not much to do but hang out, I've had a chance to skim over what I've written so far, and have discovered that I'm missing a story worthy of sharing. It's about KIDS! Mean kids. It's a funny combination of words to write, it really is. I love kids. We all do. Kids have been a huge highlight throughout all of my travels, and Kat and Leatherfoot share the same sentiments, but there are some horrible kids in this country. Though there are a hundred times as many wonderful ones, I'm sure. Just as there are always a handful of evil kids, or adults in any country, city, town, or neighborhood. This particular story of evil kids is another episode of rock throwing, which happened a few days ago…

The three of us are riding together as we approach a school and it's yard full of kids. Half a dozen of the older boys are congregated out in the middle of the road staring in our direction. We don't think much of it, until we begin to get bombarded with stones. What a shocking feeling. We are absolutely flabbergasted. Somewhere in the middle of the Tibetan plateau, and we are under attack from a bunch of school kids. What is going on here Buddha? Fortunately, their initial assault has come up several meters short, though they are prodding each other to come closer and continue chucking from their endless supply of weapons. We are forced to stop and assess the situation. A kid or three from a distant side perch is one thing, but this is a full fledged hold up. What to do? What to do?

"Hey Leatherfoot, let's get the little shits!"

"Sure Dogi, what's your plan?"

"Okay. It goes like this. We load up on our own stones and chase'em down screaming. Once they've backed off enough, Kat rides by, then we retrieve our bikes, replenish our stone supply, throw and ride!"

"I like it. Are you ready Kat? Let's go…"

ARRGGARRGGYEAHAAA!

Not being a big fan of the fine "arts" of warfare, I am quite impressed with the results of our strategy. We induce a mass panicked retreat, without actually hitting anyone. The youngest don't stop running, while those older boys stop at a safe distance. Kat is able to ride by easily, and Leatherfoot and I are now standing in the spot formerly occupied by our assailants. We turn towards them with a new handful of rocks and some evil stares.

"So do you feel like you're in an old western Leatherfoot?"

"Yea, though I'm having a hard time looking mean and not laughing!"

"WHO'S EVIL NOW YOU LITTLE BUGGERS!?!"

Though this is semi-serious business, we go back and retrieve our bikes laughing. Prepared with a new handful of stones, we walk them as far as we had been before, and stop in line with them for a punctuation stare. Keeping their distance, we don't need to throw anymore, and jump on our bikes and ride off quickly. We can hear a few rocks landing behind us, but we don't get hit. Mean old kids! Mean old aliens right back at them!

○ ○ ○

There are some canals where we are waiting. Narrow and meandering, they will likely provide irrigation in the valley below. We're filthy. I don't think any of us has done more than wash hands and face since that shower in Shigatse about a week ago, and even the hand and face washing is infrequent at best. It's not a stinky, musty kind of dirty. I'm sure we sweat as we ride, but it's so dry here that this moisture never hangs around. It's more of a gritty, dusty, caked on kind of filth.

Though the water that flows through these canals is mountain fed, and thus frigid, the sun is getting warm enough that I can strip at least my upper half, lie on my stomach and dunk my head. I have to psyche myself up, as I know it'll be freezing, but it feels unbelievably great. After the first dunk, subsequent dunks are not so bad, and then I even wash my pits. Oh yeah. This is exciting. To feel clean and refreshed.

Kat and Leatherfoot watch. They are skeptical, and after all of my screaming, don't necessarily believe my rave reviews.

"You want me to wash your hair?" asks Kat.

"I just did."

"I mean with shampoo."

"Shampoo? Sure, if you want."

So the water is bitingly cold, and I am resting on uneven, rocky ground, but I feel like I'm in a spa. Not that I've ever been in a spa, but this must be how it feels! There is fresh clean air, flowing water, sunshine, and shampoo!

"OUCH. Come on Kat, take it easy."

"Oh don't be such a big baby!"

I don't think Kat would retain a job at a spa for very long. She's not exactly gentle. My hair is a long, tangled mess. Not quite dread locks yet, but well on the way. Kat doesn't care much for dread locks. She works through, and rips out, as many knots and tangles as she can. When she is through, my scalp feels somewhat raw, but invigorated. Something gives me the sense that she took some pleasure in causing me pain. Leatherfoot enters the spa area next, and Kat gives him a thorough, but far more gentle sounding wash.

"Okay Kat, your turn."

"It really does feel good!"

She's not totally convinced that this is a good idea, particularly being at the mercy of my hands, but with more prompting from Leatherfoot, she relents. Her hair doesn't tangle anyway, and I try hard to be more soothing than abrasive. Fortunately, no trucks pass us while all this is going on.

206

Still no trucks, and it has gotten deadly hot. The high point of the now familiar daily temperature roller coaster. The mornings are beautiful, midday scorches, the late afternoon into evening lovely once again, and the nights are cold. As is often the case, there are no shade options and we must get creative. We arrange the three bikes leaning against one another in a "U" shape and drape the tarp over the top. Though a bit squishy, it's an effective shelter, and the wind is minimal enough in here that we can play cards. Leatherfoot wins the first game by a hair, and Kat runs away with the second. What's going on here? The clean hair must be affecting my brain functioning.

"One more game?"

"Sure, why not. It's looking like we might be here for one more night after all."

'Whose deal is it?"

It's so nice to hang out together with all of us feeling somewhat refreshed. We actually have some time to review a bit of the journey, and some of the craziness that has befallen us thus far. Long ago Lhasa, Leatherfoot's lemon, big passes, towing, cold lakes, kids, dogs, ice cream, trucks… "TRUCK! TRUCK! TRUCK! Shit, run, go, flag him down, stand in the middle of the road!"

The truck stops, and out pops a rather stern looking Chinese man. With little in the way of greeting, he does a quick assessment of us, our bikes, and our stuff and demands fifty Yuan each. Supply and demand are hard at work and we have no bargaining power. At least, he leaves us feeling as if we don't. It's already pretty full in the back, and he doesn't appear to care too much whether we come or not. Fifty Yuan each. It feels like a steep price, but not as steep as the hill we need to get up and over. We don't even try to bargain. We pay, and scramble to disassemble our shelter. Though we are moving as fast as we can, the driver looks impatient. Most of the passengers look indifferent, and not too keen to make space for us, though a couple of them do lend a hand lifting in the bikes. We climb up and squeeze in where we can, bracing ourselves as well as possible.

BANG BA BOOM BOOM PATTER BING BANG BOOM BA BOOM OOOFF! It's jarring, and loud, and the wind whips our freshly washed hair into a frenzied mess, but it is beautiful. The landscape is huge and alone. There are no other visible signs of humanity out here other than this rumbling monster, and the road that it grapples along. If there were ever an antitheses to places like Tokyo or New York City, this would be it. The pounding back here is relentless and unpredictable. Certainly not per kilometer, but per minute, it's almost as exhausting as riding. Some of the passengers have places to sit on the boxes and sacks, but we must search just to have places to put our feet and a reasonable place to hang on. Shifting body position once in a while is imperative to avoid ripping or cramping one set of muscles. The legs absorb as much of the shock as possible, but the innards feel like the inside of a bartender's shaker. We thought the bikes had been set in securely, but they have jarred themselves lose in no time. They are taking a beating, but trying to secure them any better at this point in the ride is impossible. All we can do is hope that the damage is minimal, and repairable and HANG ON AND ENJOY THE RIDE!

We're not really sure how far we're being taken, but it's happening fast. Having gone up a long way already, we're now gently rolling up and down. The breathing is noticeably difficult as we must be around 5200 meters (17,000 feet). Have we gone past the apex of the pass? We certainly haven't stopped to add any prayer flags to a stone pile, but then again, it is a Chinese driver. We were hoping to be dropped off at the top of the pass, but it definitely feels like we're descending more steadily. All we can do is wait until he decides to stop. Heading down, the rumbling isn't quite as loud, and we get a chance to have a conversation with the one other foreigner on board, though we still have to yell.

"HOW FAR ARE YOU GOING?"

"ALL THE WAY TO TINGRI. HEY, ARE YOU GUYS GOING UP TO MOUNT EVEREST BASE CAMP?"

"YEA, WE WANT TO."

"THERE'S A NASTY CHECK POINT ON THE ROAD GOING UP THERE! YOU WON'T EVEN GET THROUGH WITH YOUR ALIEN TRAVEL PERMITS."

"WE'RE NOT GOING TO RIDE. WE'RE GOING AS FAR

AS TINGRI TOO, AND WANT TO STORE OUR BIKES
THERE AND TREK UP AND BACK."

"NICE."

We have suddenly stopped in the middle of a small town and
been instructed to get off. We are about to do so, but this other
traveller seems to be protesting, saying he paid his fifty Yuan to
get to Tingri, and this little town is apparently not Tingri. He
asks us to stay on with him. We're a bit confused at this point, as
an argument between the stern Chinese man and this traveller is
escalating. Apparently, there is a check point coming up shortly,
and the Chinese man doesn't want to have any aliens on board
when he goes through. The traveller says this is bullshit as we have
our passports and alien travel permits. Each able to speak the rudi-
ments of the other's language, this is all going on in a convoluted
mix of Chinese and English. The truth is, we'd be happy to get
out here. We've taken enough of a pounding, as have our bikes.
Getting up the pass was all we really needed from the truck. The
other traveller is imploring us to stay on board in order to stage
a protest against this guy. It's a tough situation. Fellow travellers
are like family. Many times over the years on the road, I have
helped other travellers in need, and been helped generously just as
often. It's one of those unspoken cultural things. For us, it makes
this situation awkward and confusing. We want to help him, but
we also want to get off and start cycling. In addition, there is the
question of the fifty Yuan, which, although we had no idea, was
supposed to be the fare all the way to Tingri. That is, apparently,
still quite a distance away.

We wait on the truck while the argument continues at a stalemate for a while. It stops, and then it starts again. The Chinese
man paces around having agitated conversations with some men
from the town. He sits, obviously stewing. I feel a bit sorry for
him too. In one sense he is doing us all a favour by taking us
along, and he probably has good reason to be wary of the Chinese
authorities as related to foreign passengers, yet for the other traveller, being dropped off here would be horribly awkward. Eventually,
the Chinese man gets impatient enough to offer us a refund of
ten Yuan each if we get off here. This strikes us as reasonable,

and by this point we just want to get on with it, so we disembark. Strangely, however, he ignores the other traveller, lets him stay on the truck, and drives off to what fate we'll never know.

Suddenly, as the dust from the leaving truck settles, we find ourselves surrounded by hell children from scum town. What a decrepit little place we've landed. The kids are all over us, touching, poking, fiddling with our bikes, our packs and our bodies. It's not the usual innocent Tibetan curiosity. They are aggressive, and for the first time since the Asshole, we are worried about things being taken.

"Kat, you just keep an eye on things while Leatherfoot and I get these packs on. How are the bikes Leatherfoot?"

"I think yours and Kat's are okay, but I'm not so sure about mine. Let's get her loaded and out of here first."

Trying to get bags onto bikes is a mental endurance test. Doing bike checks and maintenance in these surroundings is an impossibility. The only immediately noticeable bike damage is a very bent back rim on Leatherfoot's Lemon. It's so bad that he can't even ride it. In fact, it's getting caught on the brake pads so hard that it won't even push through, but we have to get out of here. The frenzy around us has become unbearable. I liken it to being feasted upon by mosquitoes, except that I don't feel right about swatting them. When Kat's bike is loaded, we tell her just to go, and when we get our two bags secured, Leatherfoot tells me to go ahead also. He'll be all right. He says he'll deal with it. As I round the first bend, I look back to see him jogging while half pushing and half carrying his Lemon. He is being pursued by a drawn out string of kids. I stop and wait, hoping the sight of me will discourage the last of the stragglers. When he finally creates separation, and the last boy gives up, the hilarity of the scene strikes me. Poor Leatherfoot finally catches up to me completely winded.

"What the heck was that place?"

"I have no idea. I couldn't even tell if they were Tibetan or Chinese, but I think they were a mix of both. That was a seriously strange aberration of energy."

"Definitely weird. Where's Kat?"

"I don't know. I hope she didn't ride too far."

Fortunately, it only takes one more bend in the road to

completely lose sight of scum town, and Kat awaits us patiently at the bottom of the next hill. With the state of Leatherfoot's Lemon, we decide not to travel too far, though we do want to get a comfortable distance beyond that horrible place we just escaped. We walk together, Leatherfoot and I taking turns lifting the back of his bike and pushing it on its front tire alone. Before we see any signs of the checkpoint that apparently awaits us, we find another appealing campsite. With the exception of our first night on the road, a little patience has brought us exceptional camping locations. Once again, we are blessed with soft sand, spectacular scenery, and hopefully, security and solitude. This particular area is an ocean of fine wind rippled sand. Two sculpted mounds of slightly harder dirt act like islands behind which we can set our tent and our gear. Generally hidden from the road, we hope it will also provide shelter from the wind, though it is, at the moment, quite calm. There is a very small river flowing by, but it is a couple of hundred meters down the slope. That's enough to make it a tiring walk, but we're thankful for the fresh water supply. I love this part. When we are at rest, the weather is calm, and the light is soft, the surroundings are enchanting. A distant ridge line has a layering of rock and sand that is unique to my eyes. From this distance, it looks like many large, thin shards of hard milk chocolate jammed vertically into soft chocolate ice cream. In reality, these shards of rock, or hard dirt, are massive, and the way the row of them sticks out of the sandy base is impressive.

"Water's here. I see you guys already have the tent up. Shall I cook dinner?"

Kat is passed out, and Leatherfoot patiently works his rim, while "chef Dogi" prepares yet another gourmet meal! I wish you could see the light here. Somehow, no matter how much chaos the day brings, this evening light and the way in which it dances, brings peace back to everything. What a day it's been once again! From Brie cheese, to hair washing, the roller coaster truck ride, the thin air of 5200 meters (17,200 feet) above sea level, protests, hell children, bent rims and now this, another brilliant camping spot. A return to peace and beauty at its finest. Welcome to just another day cycling and hitching and pushing across Tibet!

SOMEWHERE and NOWHERE

IT'S THE MIDDLE OF THE DAY, AND WE'RE IN THE TENT, OR SHOULD I say the oven? It is today's version of shelter from the big burning ball. Where in the hell is the wind that was pushing our bikes all over the place just a short time ago? There are the choices then. Roast Human or Fried Human? Take your pick. Ahh, there's the breeze again, that helps a little.

I guess we are somewhere, but really we're nowhere. What is the difference anyway? I suppose I could say we're between this name and that name on a map, like, let me see… Shegar and Tingri, but it's still nowhere. Do I sound bitter? Maybe. I'm whacked out. This is it. Perhaps the middle of the day, roasting in a cramped tent, located nowhere, is not the ideal time for me to write, but I can't nap and we've already eaten. I have to do something. Maybe it is a good time to write. Maybe I'll learn something.

There's not a lot to tell about the morning. We got off late as Leatherfoot needed more time to straighten out that rim. He worked on it patiently until dark last night, and another hour this morning. In the end, he did an impressive job as it runs smoothly enough not to touch any brake pads. We had some anxiety going on regarding the check point. Rationalize the concept as much as you like, those expectations, be they positive or negative, are tough to resist. As we approached, we could see there wasn't a lot to it, though the heart still began to flutter. Out to the side of the road came one Chinese official who stared intently at our approach, yet as we neared him, he simply waved us through, turned and walked away. We didn't even have to stop and show our passports, or our Alien Travel Permit. After that, riding was more of the same.

Gravel road and wind, with Leatherfoot and I breaking the wind as best we can for Kat, biting off the usual five kilometer sections.

Water. The lack of a functional filter has made our search for sources of water its own little sub-adventure. Of course, in towns, the bottled version is an option, but it's expensive. Instead, in any guesthouses we've stayed at, we ask for more than one thermos of boiled water. We drink a lot of the warm liquid, but also let much of it cool so that we can refill our various water containers, and make sure we leave hydrated and full. It is out on the road, in the middle of this nowhere I write about, that water can be a challenge to find. We do pass streams, canals, or small rivers, but they are usually not in a state to be drunk out of directly, though there have been one or two exceptions to this. On one occasion in particular, we were very fortunate. Being dangerously low at the time, we were in dire need when suddenly, pouring down the mountainside, was this raging stream. It was fresh, pure, bubbling bliss. No filter? No worries. This stuff was virgin mountain run-off, and we drank to our hearts content! The reality is, however, hours and even whole days of riding with no towns, and no fresh mountain streams, so what do we do?

Road crews. When there is no other humanity for hours at a time, we inevitably run into a road crew. A small group of workers who have set up a temporary residence somewhere in the nowhere who actually do road maintenance. I know by my descriptions that it must seem this road never gets maintained, but it actually does. The signs of an area being worked on are the piles of gravel that are spaced out along the side of the road, dumped by trucks. From this point on, however, there is no mechanical grater, in fact, no machines at all. The distribution of the piles of gravel is all done my manual labour. The road crews use shovels and rakes to fill in the potholes. This must be hard and lonely work.

On a couple of occasions, we have seen the crews out working, though they are often on an extended break in the middle of the day, to escape the sun no doubt, and this is usually when we are consuming a lot of our liquid, and thus, beginning to get low. We ride in yelling "Hello" until someone comes out to greet us and, by showing them our nearly empty bottles, ask for a refill. Ideally

213

we top up before we are out, as otherwise the boiling water distorts our plastic bottles too much, which is not desirable to us, but has created some amusement for them. They are generally friendly, and have been generous in what they give us. Sometimes it has been free, and other times a nominal fee has been charged. Thank goodness for these people, as otherwise we'd have some serious issues with a non-functional water filter. Humans helping humans in need.

Broken crackers, peanuts, raisins, peanut butter and some dried fruit eaten out of a Frisbee. That was lunch. The wind has definitely picked up again. That's nice in terms of staying a little cooler here in the tent, but it's going the "WRONG WAY." We will be riding into it once again. Oh well. New choices. Sit here and do nothing, or get off our backs and put our back sides back on our bike seats, and pedal. From nowhere to nowhere else, or maybe, if we're lucky, to somewhere with a name... like Tingri. That's where we want to get to today. Tingri. It sounds cute doesn't it? Tingri. I guess I have to be the voice of motivation. Kat won't move unless prompted, prodded, and pulled, and Leatherfoot is actually napping. Okay, let's go.

"LET'S GO! COME ON KAT, TIME TO GET UP, KEEP MOVING... EWEWEE COME ON LEATHERFOOT, let's say Hi to that wind, pack the tent, eat some more dirt, get a more filthy shirt, and maybe Tingri will have some girls with whom you can flirt! Look at those GORGEOUS mountains, brown, red, sandy, rocky, pointy, rounded, sharp, chasmed, troughed, jagged and smooth. Let's move, let's move!"

"Okay Dogi, give me five more minutes."

"Mm, maybe ten minutes more ne Leatherfoot."

We get repacked and loaded and back onto the road, which stretches out in front of us forever. From nowhere to nowhere, though the wind must be coming from somewhere, and that's where we need to go. To wherever the wind is coming from. I'm feeling intimidated again. The grandeur and the elements are far harsher than any school yard bully I can ever remember. We talk about ditching the bikes. Literally, putting them in the ditch and leaving them there for whoever, and simply hitching back to

Kathmandu. It's not the first time we've had the conversation, and probably won't be the last. It is an option. We could bail out, but somehow, we don't. Pride? Determination? Stubbornness? I don't know. A little of each I suppose.

We're worried about Kat. She really hasn't eaten much for the last few days. Well, her eating has been minimal all trip really. The canker sores and burnt lip show no signs of healing, and given our pace and location, there is little hope that they will before Kathmandu. I try not to worry or let it affect me, but I love her a lot, so it is impossible not to. As much as I am concerned, however, I also feel a lot of pride in the fact that she's still here, persevering. I knew of her physical talents, her athletic abilities, but I wasn't sure how she'd deal with the mental stress. She's tough in every respect. You learn a lot about each other, and especially about yourself, when you're in an environment like this that breaks you down mentally and physically every day. It exposes your roots, your core. I don't think I've looked at myself in a mirror since Lhasa, but in ways I can see myself with greater clarity than ever before. There is a lot of good there, but I have unearthed a few evil roots too. Sarcasm, negativity, arrogance, a need for gratitude or payback for things given. This is crazy. Where do these things come from? How did they get planted? How did they grow? Is it just human? Innate? Learned? A product of my time and societal surroundings? It's good to see it. I can dig and hack and cut away at it while I am aware of it. They're like weeds, these kinds of personality traits. I think you have to remove the root to really get rid of it. Just cutting the top off and burying the root won't do it.

Not that we have any firm "expectations," but we figure Tingri is about twenty kilometers from here. The last ten kilometers have been very slow. The wind is gustier and more punishing than usual today, and Kat is simply going on fumes. She's dead tired and we're on another break when, suddenly, a dump truck appears going in our direction. Leatherfoot and I quickly jump up and flag it down, hoping, for Kat's sake, to hitch a ride to Tingri. The truck does stop, and as the dust cloud is quickly blown away by the wind, the driver and his companion hop out. They come across as very friendly, though I can see, and smell, that they are drinking some beer. The homebrew they call Chang. They are Tibetan, and the driver, who is the younger of the two, is in his mid-twenties. His friend is about ten years older. They seem to understand that we only want to go as far as Tingri, but look a bit confused and point to our bikes. We show them Kat's cracked, swollen lip and point at her, making some coughing noises and such, trying to get the point across that she is ill. He then takes us to the back of the truck, where we can see that it is jammed full of stuff. We could probably crawl on top and hang onto something, but getting any bikes up there is not promising. It's not looking good. We decide the priority is getting Kat there, even without us. We can ride, but she really is worn out and needs a longer rest to recover some strength. I'm not so sure she'll be able to make it to Tingri by bike today. We begin to plead our case, separating her bike from ours, and motioning that Leatherfoot and I will ride if they can only take Kat along. They have a short discussion and agree, telling us to remove the pack from the bike. Getting it up on top of the load is a bit of an effort, but they manage it and secure it well enough. Kat's relief is obvious as she climbs up into the cab and settles in between the two of them.

With the wind blowing directly in our faces, it takes a long time for the dust to settle as the truck drives off. Even with our faces buried in our shirts, the grit gets up the nose and into the mouth.

"How does today's dirt taste Leatherfoot?"

"A little grainier than usual. Are you ready to ride?"

"Let's go!"

Leatherfoot and I are definitely faster without Kat, though we are still slower than usual, as today's wind really is wreaking havoc. I do my best to avoid the section of soft mushy gravel at the edge of the road, only to be slapped in the face and whammed on the side by a left jab, right upper cut from the wind, and pushed into it anyway. There, I waver and wallow until I pull myself back out, only to encounter a hard bump, followed by three potholes and a section of washboard. Sometimes I scream, or grunt, and some-times I laugh. I got myself here. This is voluntary. Pedal, pedal, pedal. Around and around and around. Just like the prayer wheels. Spin, spin, spin... SNAP!!

216

"SHIT!"

"WHAT NOW LEATHERFOOT?"

"MY CHAIN SNAPPED!"

"WHAT?"

"MY CHAIN. IT SNAPPED. IT'S BROKEN. I CAN'T RIDE."

"AHH. THE LEMON STRIKES AGAIN!"

The wind is so ferocious that we must yell to hear one another. We find the chain, and pick it up off of the ground. It's caked full of dirt, and a link has definitely snapped. It cannot be repaired. We do have a spare chain, but the thought of changing it, in what has become a full on dust storm, doesn't seem feasible. It's all a little overwhelming. Kat is gone, we're still somewhere, but nowhere, and with the usual horrible timing, Leatherfoot's Lemon breaks again. Suddenly, I'm feeling a little weak, woozy and chilled. Before I can even attempt to think what the best thing to do is, I need to drink some water and put on another layer. Leatherfoot does the same, and digs out some dried fruit, which helps settle the shakes.

"MAYBE FIFTEEN K'S TO TINGRI DOGI, WHAT DO YOU THINK?"

"WHAT ABOUT THE SPARE CHAIN?"

"I DON'T EVEN KNOW WHOSE BAG IT'S IN. IT MIGHT EVEN BE IN KAT'S, BUT I DON'T THINK WE CAN CHANGE IT IN THIS STORM."

"DO WE HAVE ANOTHER CHOICE THEN? LET'S JUST KEEP GOING. I'LL JOG WITH YOUR BIKE FOR A WHILE AND YOU RIDE MINE, THEN WE'LL SWITCH."

I half jog, half walk a few hundred meters pushing the Lemon. Then we switch, and I simply concentrate on keeping as much energy as possible for my next turn. We know we are moving, but not much around us is changing. I take a second turn, a third, a fourth...

"THIS IS OKAY, BUT TOO SLOW. IT'S GONNA GET DARK LONG BEFORE WE GET TO TINGRI. DO YOU WANNA TOW?"

"NOT REALLY, NO. BUT I WILL."

This is a crazy scene. We're still nowhere, but Tingri must be only about ten kilometers away. We rig up the all too familiar towing system. I look at it and shake my head. I can't believe we're doing this again.

"All aboard, the Dogi Express is about to depart!"

Maybe. I start out much like a massive, loaded steam engine might. All my weight on my right foot. All my weight on my left foot. I start adding up the weight of myself, my bike, my pack, Leatherfoot (who is noticeably heavier than Kat), his bike, his pack, and a headwind on a sloppy gravel road, then I decide I don't even want to know the physics of what kind of load there is on my thighs right now. All I can say is, they feel as though they want to bust. This is even worse than the last time, but I battle as best I can, and manage to do one kilometer before I stop and look up to a most staggering sky. The wind, the clouds and the setting sun are having one hell of a party. Purple shafts piercing layer upon layer of orange waves, dancing with dust particles, and all changing so rapidly. It's spectacular. I'm in awe, while at the same time my legs, my lungs, and my heart are threatening to explode.

Leatherfoot digs in and does his kilometer, while I get a turn at being towed. I must admit that I thought this would be fun, and perhaps even relaxing, but that is totally not the case. I think Kat tried to tell us this long ago, but we didn't really listen. The truth is, you have to focus and pay attention even more than when you are riding. It's random, and unpredictable, and requires a lot of fine tuned braking in order to keep the tow rope as taut as possible. Keeping the cycle in balance requires one hundred percent attention. I do one more kilometer, and then Leatherfoot does one more while the sky continues to party. I start my next kilometer, and do about four pedal strokes before I realize this is it. This is the end. I can't do it anymore. My leg muscles have flat out quit, and I can feel huge stress on the joint network of my knees. This kind of pain will lead to permanent damage, and I won't do it. Besides, I've started sneezing and shivering, and it's getting dark. There are at least five kilometers to go, and the wind will not let up. It's too much. Too bloody much. I can't do it. I can't.

Pitching the tent is the final adventure in another long and frenetic day. As we pull it out of the bag, the wind immediately takes charge of it. At first, it flutters madly and I hold on for dear life as Leatherfoot tries to feed the poles through the holes. Then, as we try to expand it, the wind says "Hey great, a sail," and I feel like I am windsurfing across the desert. We manage to hold it down enough that I can crawl in and spread out to act as an anchor, while Leatherfoot finds a few decent sized rocks to put on the corners. It is not until we get our bags and both of us inside, however, that we trust it will not blow away. Once in, we take a few deep breaths and laugh. There is no point in crying.

"And, for dinner tonight in our fine establishment... dried fruit!"

"Oh, you are a great chef Dogi! How about the drink menu?"

"Well, you are in for a special treat tonight, Leatherfoot. Not only do we have an exceptional vintage of Yak Butter Tea, but it has aged enough hours now to be perfectly cold!"

The look on poor Leatherfoot's face is priceless. We cannot be fussy with what the road crews give us. We'd prefer plain water, but if it's Yak Butter Tea, then that's what we drink. If we have both on hand, we leave the water for Leatherfoot, and Kat and I drink the tea, but at the moment, we have only half a bottle of the cold tea left. It is gross. I think you'd have to be literally dying of thirst to enjoy a sip of cold Yak Butter Tea. It's much worse than when it's hot. You have to take one gulp, and then wait for the feeling of nausea to settle, but we manage to stomach enough of it, while listening to the wind howl outside. Now that we are snug in our bags and tent, it is a fun sound to listen to. What a crazy day. How many times have I said that on this trip? What a crazy day!

"Hey Dogi, how are you feeling? About Kat I mean?"

"Of course I'm worried about her, alone in Tingri with no idea where we are. She'll be all right though. She can take care of herself. Hopefully she found a nice warm bed to sleep in. Hey Leatherfoot, what was your highlight of the day?"

"Oh my Dogi. I barely remember where we were this morning. Probably that incredible sunset, even though we were in the middle of that towing nonsense, but let me think about it some more."

The next thing I hear from Leatherfoot is the heavy breathing of sound sleep.

TINGRI TINGRI TINGRI

"GOOD MORNING LEATHERFOOT. I GUESS YOUR HIGHLIGHT OF THE day was closing your eyes and going to sleep last night."

"I think you're right Dogi. Hey, the wind is gone. It sounds calm outside."

Indeed, as we unfold ourselves from the tent, we discover it to be a calm, beautiful, peaceful morning. The winds that raged for hours last night have not even left a trace of our footsteps in the sand. The serenity lifts our spirits tremendously. We figure that we are close enough to Tingri that we will eat and fix the bike chain later when we are there. In fact, we don't even need to rush into fixing the bike chain, as we are planning on storing the bikes in Tingri for a while as we hike up to Mount Everest Base Camp. Hiking should be a nice change, but first things first. We begin by walking, and pushing the Lemon until we hit pavement, from where we begin to tow once again. We find that towing on paved road is far more tolerable than the gravel. Quite suddenly, the peak of Mount Everest comes into view on our left. That, amongst a band of other snow capped peaks. This lifts our spirits even further, and not a few minutes later we arrive at the outskirts of Tingri.

"KAT KAAAT KAAT"

Tingri is not huge. The main strip is perhaps a couple of hundred meters long. There are a few side roads and the rest of the village meanders off to the left, but Kat must be somewhere here along this main road. I think the guidebook says something about three or four guesthouses.

"KAAAT KAAA HEY!"

Seeing no signs of her at the first couple of places, we are very

220

relieved to finally find her bike parked out front of the last place along the road. She shuffles out of her room looking sleepy, but at least she is safe and sound. We thought she'd at least be surprised, if not distressed, about our odd arrival time, but as we recount our story, she doesn't appear shocked at all. She said she knew the winds were worse than usual last night, and figured we simply gave up, or broke a bike again. Her own story of yesterday evening is brief and uneventful. She says the chang drinking truck boys were very nice, and they dropped her off here at this guesthouse. She checked out two other guesthouses as well, but found this to be the best. Her dinner in the guesthouse restaurant was a bowl of mushy rice soup, which was the first food she has enjoyed since the Brie cheese. She stayed awake long enough to enjoy the spectacular sunset, while waiting for us. Once it got dark and cold, however, she sojourned to her room, and since then, wrapped in sleeping bag and under wool blankets, she's been sleeping. She says it may have been the best rest she's had in a long while.

The room Kat got for us is as basic as most have been. There are three sagging cots on the ground, two small tables, no windows, and one door. The door has no lock. That all said, it is clean enough, and Leatherfoot and I are happy to plop down on our beds for a rest and drink some of the chai Kat has ordered from the guesthouse restaurant. Chai. What a welcome change this is from hot water, or Yak Butter Tea. It's sweet and milky, and comforting on the tummy.

As the room is dark and chilly, we have left the door half open to let in a little light and warmth. What the open door has also brought, however, is a visitor. It's a middle aged Tibetan woman. She stands just inside the entrance and stares at us. We smile and wave at her, but she just stares back. She doesn't come right in, but neither does she leave for several minutes on end. I have the urge to make funny faces, or throw things at Kat and Leatherfoot to see if I can make her laugh, but she turns and walks away before I succumb to the feeling.

"Shall we do a little town exploration?"

"Good idea Leatherfoot. How about you Kat, are you coming?"

"No, I think I stay and rest more. It helps. I start to feel a little more better."

Our immediate impression of Tingri is positive. I don't think there is much here from a touristy point of view, but the majority of locals are used to foreigners, as all of the 4x4s and tourist buses pass this way, and likely stop for at least a meal. It is also largely Tibetan, though there are a handful of Chinese restaurants and shops along the main road. The view southward, past the end of town, looks way across a huge flat valley to the snowy peaks beyond. Presumably, this is the direction we will be heading as we trek to Mount Everest Base Camp in a couple of days.

Mount Everest. Or in the Chinese translation of the Tibetan name, Qomolangma. It's one of those places that I've known the name of, long before I'd ever heard of places like Tibet or Nepal. It's one of those mysterious words known from childhood. You know it's a real place, and yet, it has a fairytale like quality to it. Especially when you call it Qomolangma. At 8850 meters (29,000 feet) above mean sea level, it is the highest piece of land on earth.

"Do you want to climb it Dogi?"

"What? Qomolangma? No. Definitely not. That's crazy stuff man. This bike trip of ours is turning out to be crazy enough, but the top of Qomolangma? No way. I wouldn't make it anyway. I'm not that strong, and my fingers and toes would fall off halfway up! I don't see the point for myself. How about you?"

"I'm with you. I like climbing mountains, but that's beyond my desires. I really do want to get up to Base Camp though."

Our guidebook gives us some information on trekking from Tingri to Base Camp. It's sixty kilometers each way, which makes it three to four days, or six to eight return. Leatherfoot and I have both done enough backcountry hiking to be confident about finding our way, yet our only map of the route is the basic one in the guidebook. The lack of a good topographical map means we are considering hiring a guide, and possibly also some beasts of burden, to shoulder some of our load. The idea of pack animals sounds fun, but it is definitely a foreign concept to us, having always trekked carrying our own packs in the past. Leatherfoot and I set out to do some general research regarding more route information, and the guide and animal options. There are no tourist facilities here. This is Tingri, Tibet. There are no signed travel agencies or tour agents. There is only the "main man." After asking around various shops and restaurants, we are continually pointed in his direction. I guess he's the only one in this small town that takes care of these things, and, unfortunately, he is an arrogant schmuk.

The "main man." He does speak some English, and informs us that we have three options. We can hire a guide only, and pay for his service and his food, and carry our own packs. We can bring along a donkey to carry all of our things, but that would also require an extra person to care for the animal. Donkeys are, apparently, stubborn creatures, and without an experienced handler, they run the risk of bolting. The third option, which sounds kind of fun, is yaks to carry our packs. The problem here is the fact that yaks don't like to be alone, so we would need to take two, and a handler, and the guide, and even more animal food. Naturally, each option increases proportionately in price.

We return to our room only to find three kids hanging out just inside our doorway. We assume Kat is inside, or maybe they're just staring at our stuff. As one of them notices our approach, he signals the other two and they scurry. At our height, we are probably quite intimidating when vertical.

"Hey Kat. Did you have a nice rest?"

"Kind of... until the kids came. They don't do anything, but it's hard to relax. They just stand and stare."

"How long were they there for?

"Ten, maybe fifteen minutes."

"Oh well. Are you hungry? Shall we have some lunch?"

O O O

Leatherfoot and I go back out into Tingri a second time in the afternoon. This time, we wander much further off the main road towards the southern end of the town. Other than just a general walk about, we poke our heads into a few supply shops to consider the food options for trekking. At first, we find nothing beyond the usual fare, until we make one excellent new discovery. Chinese Army Cookies! This is no joke. Try to picture a super compressed short bread cookie, the size of a chocolate bar, stuffed in a single plastic wrapper! They are dense and shockingly weighty for their size. Being reasonably priced, we buy one to try. Short bread indeed! Except without much sugar or butter, and ten times the density, but it's reasonably tasty. It does suck the moisture out of the mouth, though not nearly to the extent of tsampa, and the weight to size to energy ratio for trekking seems ideal. At the very least, it will be a change from nuts and crackers.

The more we explore Tingri, the more appealing it is to us. Beyond the main road, there are no signs of anything Chinese. The roadways, pathways, and alleys are a rough combination of stone and hard dirt, with a smattering of larger rocks and boulders, and several muck puddles. They are plied only by foot and cart. Motorized vehicles do not come off the main highway. The houses are what we have become accustomed to, being square or rectangular with whitewash walls, blue and brownish red trim and some decorative stripes. The roofs are flat, as usual, and rimmed with the short walls. The corners of most buildings have a bouquet of tattered prayer flags sticking out of them. Everywhere are piles and stacks of dried or drying shaped mud bricks and cow patties. Once you add in the chickens, cows, yaks, dogs, children and other locals, you have a scene that is purely Tibetan. The sounds come only from the wind, the animals, and the voices of the people, and the air is tainted only by dust kicked up by the breeze, if anything at all.

As we reach the southern end of the town, we can see across a huge flat expanse of land. The dominant colour, as always, is brown, but the tiny grasses and scrub brush are trying their hardest to make an appearance. The grazing sheep and bovines, however, don't make their lives any easier. Mixed into the landscape are some irrigation canals, and fields of fist sized stones that add a dappling of white. Way in the background, the foothills obscure the lower halves of the mountains, but the mighty peaks in their majestic coats of white and grey reach out to the bold blue sky. From this distance, they are inviting.

Most of the rest of the afternoon has been spent enjoying the coolness of our room. For the sake of air circulation, we have left the door only a slight crack open, which we were hoping would also leave us our privacy for a while. Yet, as we awaken from short naps, and are resting and talking, we suddenly find ourselves not alone. Once again, we have a visitor. This time, it is a middle aged Tibetan man standing inside our doorway. He just opened the door and came in, and now stands and stares at us blankly. Can you imagine this? Someone just comes into your guesthouse room uninvited and stays! As usual, there is no threat of violence or even theft. He is obviously here purely out of curiosity. We give him a couple of minutes, but somehow none of us are in the mood for a visitor at the moment.

"Hello... Ta-shi-de-le... I know, I know, us aliens are pretty interesting, but you've had a good long look around, so it's time to move along."

"He's not listening Dogi!"

"Imagine that. How rude that he doesn't understand any English... just kidding Kat... I do wish we'd learned more Tibetan, but we've just been so exhausted at the end of every day... any other removal suggestions?"

We all give our best efforts, in terms of hand signals and acting, to communicate our wish to have him leave, but it appears as though this is only entertaining him further. "What are these aliens doing? Some kind of dance?" We let him be for a while longer. He'll probably leave soon. As I stare back at him, I wonder what's going on in his head. His expression is so neutral, so blank. Having travelled in many foreign countries, and even lived in a few, I know well the feelings of curiosity and fascination that come with witnessing and experiencing a different culture. It goes both ways. Traveller and local alike share new emotions and learn new things. You can usually tell by the eyes and the body language, the reactions and opinions of one another. Often there is amusement, sometimes fear, but this character, like other Tibetans before him, shows nothing. It's as if there is no emotion, no opinion, no judgement, no thought. Just blank. Staring.

We've had a lot of interaction with locals on the trip. When we are the visitors, such as at the monasteries or the lunch breaks, the people are often jovial and animated. Such has also been the case with some that have visited us, such as the two men who we played Frisbee and cards with beside the lake, but the overwhelming majority of those who have visited us have been more like the guy at our door now. That look of complete neutrality.

Visitors. Most of them have been while we've been camping. That seems much more understandable than hotel room visitors. We are camped on their lands after all. Hmm, actually, I still never have gotten a sense of who might own these huge expanses of nowhere. They still feel like they are not owned, yet I'm sure the Chinese government would say that they "own" it. I doubt the Tibetans agree with that. Just land then. It's not anybody's possession. It's free.

That's a lovely thought isn't it? No possessions. Quite an ideal really. It probably does exist, at least to certain degrees, in some small sub-cultures in the world. And, it probably existed even more in past times when there was greater need for sharing. Western thought is so far removed from this idea, and continuing in that direction. Everything is a possession. Things can't just be things anymore, they have to belong to something else. I think the structure of language itself perpetuates this thought process. English, and probably many other European languages, are extremely possessive in their nature. We make heavy use of possessive pronouns like my, your, his, her, their, etc. There are few things left that don't belong to somebody, and our status is measured by how much we have. We share less and less. I know the Japanese are a little different. They still have possession and ownership, but they do seem to be more communal with a lot of things compared to many westerners. I believe this is a function of a less possessive language structure. Objects are referred to more neutrally. Naturally there is a chicken and egg debate that could go on between language and thought, but in the end they breed and feed each other.

The Tibetan culture seems like the least possessive of any that I have ever come across, which would explain their poking and prodding of "our" stuff and sticking their heads into "our" tent and inviting themselves into "our" hotel room. It's funny now that I write about it. The side of me that sees the value in patience and wants to open my mind to the vast cultural network that

226

encompasses our earth comes out. Tolerance, peace, kindness, and sharing as opposed to "GET YOUR GRUBBY FINGERS THE HELL OUT OF MY STUFF!" which has escaped my mouth more than once on this trip.

I know I can philosophize all I want, but all three of us would really like this character out of "our" room. He's been here too long. We'd like our privacy and he's invading that.

"I can't believe this guy is still here."

"I hear you, Leatherfoot. Shall we remove him?"

Leatherfoot and I get up and walk towards him, figuring this in itself might coax him into leaving, but he just watches us as we approach. It would appear that the only way to get him to leave will be physical removal. Not violent, but physical. We grab him by the shoulders and turn him around. He doesn't resist at all as we push him gently out the door and beyond.

O O O

We just finished dinner in our little guesthouse restaurant, and we had a feast. The Tibetan family that runs the place is wonderful. They serve mostly Tibetan food, but with a slightly greater variety, and though it is oily, it's not too oily. We drank a whole thermos of chai, and have ordered a second to bring back to the room. We are trying to eat and drink a lot to regain and store some energy before going trekking, but I think tonight, we ate a bit too much and all had to waddle across the courtyard back to here. I'm feeling quite bloated, and a little woozy. Actually, it's not the first time I've felt woozy today. I think yesterday took its toll. I should be tired, yet somehow I'm not ready to sleep.

So here we are
Candlelight and playing Cards
Three saggy beds
Three saggy heads
Tingri
Tibet
Somewhere but
Nowhere but

Somewhere high up
On a plateau
Far away from any sea

TOTAL BODY SHUTDOWN

I FEEL LIKE CRAP. I WOKE UP THAT WAY, AND I STILL FEEL THAT way. Food is completely unappealing. I don't want to move. All I can do is lie here in bed, drink hot water or tea, and get up to go pee. And that last part has been a big ordeal. I have to go from lying to sitting, and wait for the head rush to settle, then hold on to something after I stand up. Walking as far as the toilet winds me. When I get back to bed, I simply collapse onto it and wiggle back under these heavy wool blankets.

Leatherfoot and Kat went shopping, and to do more research. We want to leave on our Base Camp trek tomorrow, but there are still things to do and decisions to make. What we have accomplished so far is finding a good place to store our bikes, and reworked our packs so that they will fit on our backs again. Oh, I hear them coming.

"Hey Dogi. Are you feeling any better?"

"No, not really. Did you guys buy any food yet?"

"No. How much do you think we should buy?"

"Enough for a week."

"You and Leatherfoot are right Dogi, that 'main man' guy is a big grump. I kind of don't want to make deal with him."

Leatherfoot and Kat are having a hard time making decisions. What food to buy, how much to buy. Trekking guide or not? Maybe... should we... maybe not? It's the second time already that they've been back to consult me. The issues are the cost, and the fact that the "main man" continues to be a jerk, versus the idea that the path may be challenging to find, and we'd have to carry our own stuff. Now the "main man" wouldn't actually be our guide. He's just the control guy, and the one who likely keeps the better half of the cash. So, the actual guide could be nice... or not. Who's to know. We feel like we can carry our own packs. Well, I felt like that until today anyway. Just now, I'm not so sure, but I'll probably feel well enough tomorrow. Then again, travelling with a yak might be its own adventure. That said, they too are rumoured to be stubborn and unpredictable pack animals.

I didn't realize until today that I was the main decision maker in the group. Kat, for all her talents, has never been much for making decisions, but I was hoping Leatherfoot would deal with it. Maybe he can, but he's just always viewed it as a Dogi adventure, and been happy to come along for the ride any which way. I don't feel like these are hard decisions to make, but it does all feel confusing and I'm in no condition to weigh them right now. I told Leatherfoot and Kat that they should just go ahead and decide everything, and not come and consult me anymore. I can't even listen right now. Maybe one or two sentences and then it sounds like "blah blah blah." Just decide, please. Whatever it is I'll deal with it.

These blankets are so warm, but so heavy... they are weighing on my bladder... I don't want to get up... it's so bright outside... I need to drink, but this tea is just flowing through me so fast... my head hurts... my teeth hurt... okay, I have to get up... a bucket in here would be nice...

No visitors today, but Tingri is happening outside the door. Trucks are shaking the ground as they roll in and out... dogs are yelping... cows are mooing... arguments, kids, laughter... mmmmm... I'm bored and still feel like crap... mmmmm... I can't sleep and my body is getting stiff... mmmmm... I'm such a lousy sick person... such a big baby... I want to do something, like write, but my brain is empty... mmmmm... I'm all empty... mmmmm... I'm an old rag doll... mmmmm...

OH! A flying ant has just landed in my drinking vessel. It's having a chai bath. Hello ant. It's splashing it's wings around in desperation. The sides are too slick to get a grip. It's current plight reminds me a little too much of my own. It sensed something sweet and went for it. Being a creature of instinct, it no doubt gave no forethought to its actions, yet I'm sure is experiencing shock and panic as it struggles to remove itself from the drink. It has had a taste of the sweet liquid, but is left to wonder… how the hell did I get myself here? It's a good question. How the hell DID I get myself here? From one paragraph in a guidebook to a sick, sick Dogi on a bed in a room in a place called Tingri, holding onto sanity by watching a flying ant struggle helplessly.

I am so happy when Kat and Leatherfoot finally came back. As much as they were driving me nuts this morning, I love them doubly for going out and buying everything and making all the decisions. We will take no guides, no donkey, and no yaks. We can carry our own stuff, and find our way. Tonight, early to bed. Tomorrow morning, the hike to Qomolangma Base Camp begins!

○ ○ ○

"KNOCK KNOCK KNOCK"

It's dark, and late in the evening. We are already in bed, though not yet asleep. Whoever it is, it's nice of them to knock at least, but who would be knocking? Two Tibetan men come in. We don't recognize them, but they say they have heard about us trekking to Base Camp, and proceed to offer themselves as guides. They come across as sincere and friendly, and their offer sounds significantly better than the "main man." We confer.

It's tempting, but we're already packed and set, and our decision has been made. We pass on their offer. I must admit that I was leaning towards taking it because of my weakened condition, but, after telling Leatherfoot and Kat to decide, I was certainly not going to second guess them. We are all on a slim budget, but Leatherfoot in particular is tight on cash, which, in the end, swayed the decision in that direction in the first place. For all he's done for us, Kat and I must respect that too.

Dogi's Journal Of Tibet

Part III
The Trek

THE TREK TO BASE CAMP BEGINS

So, a new phase of the journey begins. A short respite from the bicycling, though not from the environment. The small town of Tingri sits at 4300 meters (14,200 feet) above sea level, and on our way to Base Camp, which is at 5300 meters (17,500 feet), we will need to go along more dry open plains, wind funneling valleys, and over one big mountain pass. Being back on our feet, with packs on our backs, feels much more familiar, at least to Leatherfoot and myself, though not as much for Kat. She has partaken in some shorter hikes with me in the past, but not one of this distance and magnitude. Along with us are the tent, three sleeping bags, the tarp, cooking gear, dried food and Chinese Army cookies. We loaded up on this last item. Informationally, we have only the guidebook, and its brief descriptions of the route and its basic map. For strong hikers, the return trip is estimated at six days. For strong hikers, or hikers that are feeling strong...

Not good. This is not a good start for me at all. It was a hot and cold feverish night, and I didn't really sleep. Conscious and unconscious dreams mixed in dark blends. I sit up on my bed when

Leatherfoot says it's time to get up. Breathing is laborious, and my body aches from lying in bed for most of the last thirty hours or more. I have developed cankers on my tongue and gums. As I stand, I am dizzy, but it settles. The food that Leatherfoot serves up is the same as it has been for most of the trip. Oatmeal. I force myself to eat some, though it is painful on my mouth, and unappealing to my gut, but I am going to Base Camp. I am determined. Will I ever have this opportunity again? I must try. I can do it. I'll feel better once we get going.

Not twenty paces into our journey, we come upon a sight for which we must stop. There is another foreign cyclist who has just pedaled into town. We pause for a brief chat, and discover that he is Canadian, but living in Nagano, Japan. He and his travel companion managed to bring their nice mountain bikes along from Japan. Having taken the shorter and flatter route from Lhasa to Shigatse, they have had a relatively smooth sounding trip. No major issues other than the days of wind pounding and, of course, the odd rock assault from kids. He looked pretty well equipped and healthy. It is an uplifting random encounter. We would like to stay and talk to him more, and meet his partner who has not yet shown up, but we have a long day ahead of us and must be moving on.

Leaving the far end of Tingri, we are walking across a huge flat plain. Our general direction is south as we are aiming straight for the band of distant snowy peaks. Qomolangma is no longer in view from here. Step by step, we follow a network of horse and buggy tracks, and trails through little villages, past locals and animals, across sand, gravel, dirt, rocks, and over creeks. With each footstep, the larger snow capped peaks begin to disappear behind the closer foothills.

Breaks are frequent, mostly on my account now. Kat, though certainly not healthy, seems to have gotten past the worst of her ailments, and appears stronger and more alive than in any recent times. Leatherfoot is fine. Wait, that's not completely true. Actually, he has a case of the shits, which has also caused an emergency break or two. Myself, I'm wobbly. I feel as though I'm stumbling rather than walking. We are not moving that fast, but I feel like I never have enough air.

The horse and cart. Away from the main highway, and even on it, this is the main mode of transportation used here, other than walking. The animals and carts alike look as hard worked as the people who live here. The horses are never big, but lean. Some look very healthy, others that we have seen look worn out. As with everything else here, all have a thick layer of dust on them. The carts are as basic as can be. Two wheels topped with a box of wood, with a simple but functional harness system to the animal. There are no frills here. No fancy paint jobs or details. They are built to work, and patched and repatched to keep on working as long as possible.

Three horse and carts have passed us, but they have all been going in the opposite direction. The Tibetans riding them have all given us big waves and smiles. Just as we are joking about how nice it would be to hitch a ride, two of them rattle up from behind us and stop. Without even asking, they invite us to load up and go for a ride! Kat and I load into the first one, and Leatherfoot and all of our packs go into the second. For the first time all day, I feel alive and well. The driver waits until we are settled, gives the pony a yell and a whip and off we lurch.

"Hey Kat... is this cool or what!?!"

"I love it! Look at Leatherfoot back there. He has a huge smile on his face!"

We go bouncing along the main path for a while. It is rough, and the cart is rocking, weaving and shaking all over the place. For the first time all day, I can take in more details of the scenery. Tingri has faded, but there are smatterings of buildings here and there. Close to where the waterways lazily snake their way across this nearly flat valley, there are thin carpets of green. Mostly, however, it is the usual expanse of brown, and fields of small white boulders reflecting in the morning light. The rough cart track makes for a pretty noisy ride, so we can't say much beyond the usual small talk to the driver, but his grin is as wide as ours. I guess he's happy that we are having so much fun.

"HEY LEATHERFOOT, HOW'S IT GOIN BACK THERE?"

237

"THIS IS AWESOME! HOW FAR DO YOU THINK THEY ARE GOING TO TAKE US?"

We have to scream to hear each other, but the conversation ends as we are suddenly crossing the small river we've been running along. Now, we're really wobbling all over the place, and water is spraying all around us. This must be the most fun I've had since Sand Skreeing. These are the kinds of reasons you travel like this. This is Randomland adventure at its finest!

Our ride, though exhilarating, is not too long in the end. Shortly after the river crossing, we arrive at a set of structures, which is presumably their home. We disembark, and wonder whether there will be a fee for the ride, but the drivers simply give us a wave and a smile. We're still packing some Dalai Lama pictures, so we give them one each. Once again, the photo of their exiled spiritual leader is touched repeatedly to the head before being tucked up under the hat.

The buzz generated from the ride lasts for some time, but a certain kind of nausea creeps in after we have walked for a while. It's amazing how the mind and body can suppress ill health for a while. I'm sure that the increasing heat of the day is not helping, and we are also getting hungry. Craving a break in the shade, we head for a single hut that we can see in the distance. We hope to shelter outside along a rock wall, but the usual dilemma of the straight up sun is upon us. It is so vertical that there are no shadows. We find that there is no one around. The door to the hut is latched from the outside, but not locked. To just walk into someone else's place still feels somewhat awkward, but I am beyond caring. Once again, I NEED shade. Besides, the Tibetans have no qualms about coming well into our "private space," and when in Tibet…

The gratification of the cool air is immediate. I take some deep breaths and let my body temperature settle. As our eyes adjust to the dim light, we see that there isn't much in here. It's definitely not intended for living in. We surmise that it's a grain storage and processing shed, but it's mostly empty now. Sometimes people use the expressions "end of a cycle" or "beginning of a cycle," but I think cycles don't ever end. They might change in nature with each revolution, but the flow is continuous. Being spring in Tibet, they are at a point in the cycle where they are nearing the end of their stored food supplies from last growing season, and are in the early stages of growing new crops. This is the point in time where a well balanced cycle shows its merit. Was enough food grown? Was it harvested without waste? Was it stored and processed well? I get the impression that the balancing of cycles goes deeper than just spiritual dogma here. It is a physical necessity. Slight imbalances could be the difference between life and death. There is so little room for waste. With these thoughts spinning through my head, I make space next to the last few sacks of grain and lie down to rest. Kat sits and rests too, while Leatherfoot prepares a little food.

After eating, I drift in and out of a light sleep, until the door opens and a Tibetan man comes in. We can also see a boy standing outside the doorway. We are nervous, figuring they might be shocked, or angry or scared, but there is no panic. They seem perfectly at ease with our presence. Good. I need more rest and go back to napping on the dusty floor.

Kat and Leatherfoot finally tell me I have to get up. It's time to go, but suddenly, we find ourselves in a state of confusion. As we are about to walk away, the man stops us and begins to motion what looks like a horsey whipping action. Maybe he's offering us a ride as far as Lunja, the next, and last town along the trek to Base Camp. So, we've left the hut and come to the side of the small river near the horse and cart, but we wait... and we wait. We go through the sign language a couple of more times, and there does seem to be understanding, but no action. Both the father and son are just kind of coming and going, and looking at us once in a while. They seem unusually agitated.

"M o n e y"

"Money?"

Why the young boy took so long to say this we don't know. Maybe, he just remembered the word, or maybe, they were nervous to ask or fretted about whether or not to charge us. He could have said "Yuan" or showed us a coin or a bill, but perhaps they have neither. Of course, after the first free ride, it never crossed our minds to offer, but then, they were on their way and took us only a short distance. This will be a special trip, and much further. It makes perfect sense. Once the money thing is out in the open, everyone is able to relax, and we have a short bargaining process which is done in good faith. Finally, we are on our way.

Much like myself and many other things in this land, the poor horse that they have looks to be bordering on death. And this is before the three of us and our packs and the driver all crowd on board the cart. We're all quite happy to be getting a ride, but we really are feeling sorry for the horse who, beyond dragging our weight, is also battling a head wind, and getting its butt whipped frequently by the driver, who happens to have a big smile on his face. The ride is long and bumpy. For the first while it is fun, and we are able to enjoy the small river crossings and the passing scenery, but it begins to wear on us after a while. The shaking and bouncing is hard on the innards. I'm afraid to ask Leatherfoot how his bowels are faring. It is the horse that has it the most difficult, however. There is no room for self pity when watching another creature struggle like this. Fortunately, it survives the ordeal. We give him an extra little pat on the head and say thanks as he turns to head for home.

We are now in the small village of Lunja. The driver has dropped us off at a guesthouse where we have ordered some thugpa. As we eat the oily "treat," we listen to the wind pick up more and more in its ferocity. It was our original intention to walk for an hour or two further, and then camp, but there is no need to fight the elements when they are that strong, and we have the option of a sheltered room and a bed to stay in. We have decided to stay put for the evening.

SPIN WOBBLE STUMBLE

WE SLEPT OKAY IN OUR LITTLE ROOM, BUT I HAVE WOKEN UP to a mouth with even more canker sores than yesterday. Eating the flatbread and some boiled eggs we ordered from the guesthouse has been trying, but I know I need to get some food in to be able to continue hiking today.

As usual, it's nice to get an early start in the morning because it is cool and windless. Nevertheless, because of my weakened state, we still have to rest frequently. Kat is feeling even better today. After a whole trip of suffering, she finally seems to be on the mend. There are no more headaches, and the canker sores are finally fading enough that she can eat regularly. Only her lower lip remains an ugly swollen cracked mess, but that isn't likely to heal until we get off this desert plateau. Leatherfoot is okay, though he is still peeing out of the wrong orifice.

We are on the eastern side of the valley now. There have been some foothills and cliff to our left as we walk, keeping us largely in the shade. We are passing only the odd nomad shepherd, and though there are no more villages, we still find the path easily enough. The snowy peaks that we have been walking towards have completely hidden themselves behind the now close foothills. I'm doing my best to keep up, but it's a struggle. I just feel so damn weak. Leatherfoot says we're making good progress, but for me the morning is turning into a blur.

A few hundred meters to our right, there are two tattered looking nomad tents and a series of rock walls around them. They are set up next to a river, that is not huge, but flowing quickly, signaling the ending of this massive plain and the beginning of a valley incline. This nomad camp is the first sign of anything constructed by humans since leaving Lunja behind. It looks interesting, and we would like to check it out, but that represents too much extra effort for me right now. We agree that we will have a look on the return trip, if it works out. With a few more paces, we see that the river bubbles and splashes down from the valley which curves up to our left. Leatherfoot and I consult the map, and figure this is the way we need to go. We round a corner, such that we are heading in a more south-easterly direction, and walk up stream as the water flows to our right. This represents the beginning of the assent of the mountain pass, and it has greeted us along with the wind and high sun all at the same time. We walk about three hundred meters up the slope, before I need to take a rest. Kat and Leatherfoot wait patiently while I recover from spinning, take a few deep breaths and continue. Everest Base Camp. I can do this. Three hundred more steps, and I waver again and need another rest. Walk three hundred... REST... walk two hundred... REST... two hundred... REST... one hundred... REST... spin wobble stumble... MUST STOP.

We see a small broken down rock wall that looks ideal as a sheltered tent spot. It sits next to the river about twenty meters below the path, down a sandy, rocky embankment. I'm not sure what sick demon temporarily possesses me. Maybe it's a delirious Sand Skreeing flashback, or just the fact that I love to run down hills, but I launch off the path and descend the slope at a full clip. It's stupid, but fun. It takes me about two full minutes to catch my breath from this seven second sprint, and usurps whatever minimal energy my legs may have had left. That really was foolish.

After two days, we're not nearly as far along as we'd hoped, but for me to have any chance of continuing, I need rest. After spending much of the afternoon in and out of fitful naps, any consideration of making more headway today is given up. Camp chores are happening around me, and it's frustrating not to be able to help, but I have nothing to contribute but sorrow and pain. Kat and Leatherfoot put up the tent, rebuild the rock wall a little, get water and cook. It's nice to see that Kat has regained enough strength to help out, and fortunately for both of us, Leatherfoot continues to stay reasonably strong and healthy.

Over the little rock wall that our tent hides behind, we think we can see the top portion of Qomolangma in the distance, but from this angle we are not sure. In any case, whatever mountain it is, it's absolutely breathtaking, as is the rest of the scenery around here. The tone of the land is a little different along the edges of the river. The patches of grass and shrubs that can't eke out an existence anywhere else have a fighting chance here. A nearly full moon is losing ground to the sun, and across the way, at the edge where valley meets plain, I can see a small herd of black sheep. They provide more contrast than their cousins to the grey and white boulder strewn ground. There is still some light, but I am craving sleep. Tomorrow will be another day. Hopefully, we can make it all the way to Base Camp.

NOMAD TENT

QOMOLANGMA BASE CAMP. IMAGINE SITTING ON THE STEPS OF the world's highest monastery staring up at the massive chunk of mountain known as Everest, or Qomolangma! The echoes of prayers being chanted in the background, the faint whispers of voices on the wind of those who have stood on top, and those who have taken their final rest. Imagination is all I have left now. It's finished. That part of my dream is over. At least on this trip, I will see no more than the distant peak, and wait for a return invitation to come my way.

I slept horribly last night. Horribly. In fact, I don't think I even slept at all. It was freezing cold, and I simply couldn't warm up. Sometimes the shaking was voluntary, but mostly, my body just did it on its own. As planned, we woke up early. Not having gone as far as hoped yesterday, we wanted to get a good start, and at least get over the main pass if not all the way to Rongphu Monastery. The sun is already up, but the shadow line is well on the opposite bank of the river.

"Well, Dogi, you don't look so good."

"I don't feel so good, Leatherfoot. I wanna go on… but…"

"I think we must go back, Dogi. I don't mind. I think you are too sick."

"I agree with Kat, Dogi. I know how badly you must want to go, but I think it would be foolish of you. As weak as you are right now, it would take us at least two more days to get there. This is how people die, Dogi. It's your decision, but I think you should go back to Tingri."

"You guys are right. What about you Leatherfoot? Are you okay to go forward on your own?"

"I'm going to try it. Though I am a little nervous, I'm pretty sure I can find my way. I really want to go. Of all the things to see and do in Tibet, this is the one that is most important to me. I have to try."

We split our gear as sensibly as possible. Kat and I keep the tent, but Leatherfoot keeps the tent fly and the tarp. Big hugs are given all around, and we watch Leatherfoot trot off confidently. It's a strange feeling. Of all the times we have temporarily split company, this one feels the most uncomfortable. Though he is an experienced hiker, we're definitely still concerned about him. He's now travelling alone, with no more than a guidebook map, over a 5250 meter (17,300 foot) mountain pass, in a completely foreign land and less than hospitable environment. But he'll be all right. Somehow, we just kind of know he'll be all right.

Kat and I lay on the river bank long enough to let the morning sun come and warm us up. I have a good long cry. Never in my life can I remember feeling so thoroughly beaten and defeated. Too weak to go forward. Frustrated. Maybe this is what it feels like to get very old or have a significant disability. You just can't. Period. There is no more choice. Even will power has an eventual limit.

Crying is good. It washes away a lot of the frustration and makes room for acceptance. It's okay, Mount Everest Base Camp is not that important. Certainly not more important than staying alive and trying to regain some semblance of health. I feel fortunate that Kat doesn't care so much about Base Camp. She's not so goal oriented, and I think she's actually happy to do less walking and more resting. Her health continues to improve, but she is by no means up to full strength. Besides, I cannot really be left alone in this condition. So, there we have it. The sick taking care of the sicker.

The sun having finally penetrated enough to warm up the core of my body, I feel ready to start walking. The decision to head back has also lifted a weight off my mind. We throw the packs back up on our backs, and begin to return down the hill we'd climbed yesterday. I am so lightheaded that we have to move very slowly, but the sun feels good, and I am actually able to enjoy the Himalayan scenery. The white peaks, and the gently flowing rivers...

We are approaching the nomad camp we passed yesterday, and decide to stop by for a visit and a rest. We leave the path and follow along the river, and arrive to no signs of life. If there were any nomads here, they have taken their animals beyond anywhere we can see, to graze. There are two tents, one larger than the other, and an extensive network of one meter high rock walls that really intrigue me. They create several enclosures with small entrance ways. Built mostly with rounded river rock and few wedges, the stability of them amazes me. A lot of diligence and patience has been put into their construction.

Kat has set herself up along the bank of the river. She stays fully bundled up in several layers of clothes, but prefers to lay in the sun. The only sound to be heard is that of the gurgling water passing by. It is a fine place for a nap. Myself, I have ducked into the larger of the two nomad tents. Much like many of the people here, it is probably not as old as it looks. Built triangularly, it is centered on three posts, and the material is some sort of heavy cloth, like canvas, but has been patched and repatched about a hundred times. It is stretched out by a series of tattered old ropes, which are held taut by rocks. The top is actually open, presumably to let out smoke. So what would nomadic people keep inside a weather beaten old shelter that is at least half a day's walk from the nearest small village? For a start, there is a pile of sheepskin blankets, that are grubby, but soft and warm. Otherwise, a random selection of tattered old clothes, two and a half pairs of worn out shoes, a couple of big iron pots, a few cups, a fire pit, and a decent sized pile of dried dung paddies.

Shelter. The ability to stay cool enough when the elements make it too hot, and warm enough when they make it too cool. Simple. Basic. Functional. Though I know there is a time of rain here, most Tibetan structures seem to be built more to protect against the effects of sun and wind, rather than falling water. The drainage in the flat roofs must be sufficient to deal with the moisture levels, and perhaps nomad camps like this are not used much during the wet months. The hard, dried out dung patties attract my curiosity, but

246

of all the inventory in here, it's the two and a half pairs of shoes that I like the most. When I say two and a half, there is actually only one pair that match, and three other singles, though two of the three make good companions. It's telling of the worth of things to the people out here. Just because one shoe is broken down beyond functionality, doesn't mean the other half of the pair is garbage. It's still a shoe. It still has the ability to provide some protection and comfort for a foot. There exists the stored energy of several days of footsteps in the shoe. All energy is used, none is wasted.

It's so funky in here. I can lie back and stare up through the crack and see the blue sky, but I am completely sheltered from the sun and the wind. Though my feet do need to rest on top of the dung pile, I can completely stretch out. Oh! I've just been joined by a little birdie who flew in through the crack. Hello birdie! He's fluttering around and checking out this and that... gone... oh, back again. He's a little braver this time, having landed on the hook that holds the kettle above the fire. Is he trying to sing me a song, or just complaining at the lack of crumbs? I doubt birdies have it much easier than the people out here. Trees are scarce when present at all, and I haven't noticed many bugs all trip. Where do you live little birdie, and what do you eat? A meager diet of tsampa grains on a good day! Op, he's gone.

Drifting in and out of fitful sleep, it takes me a moment to distinguish between dream and reality, as a Tibetan nomad has just entered the tent. At first, he is a little shocked by my presence, but after checking that the tea pot and dung pile are in order, he's settled in to a big smile, and we have exchanged greetings. I really like this about the Tibetan people, the sincerity in an initial meeting without the formality. There is no awkwardness, at least not on his part. I make a questioning gesture about whether or not I should leave, but he makes it clear that I am welcome to stay. Picking up a piece of dung, he begins to rip it into smaller chunks. He then stirs up the fire remains, piles the poo bits carefully, and lights it up. It's quite smoky, particularly at first, but as it catches and the draft establishes its flow, it burns surprisingly well, and doesn't smell nearly as bad as you might expect. The teapot, filled with river water, is hung above the fire. Though his hair is severely matted, it still has the braids and colourful jewellery in it that most Tibetan men have. His clothes are not in much better condition than the fabric of this tent, and his shoes are in slightly better condition than the leftovers in here. Though he is not a large man, he looks healthy and strong, and I would describe him as good looking. While managing the fire and waiting for the water to heat up, he has been pulling tsampa out of a little side pouch and eating it, though I can't tell if he's been mixing it with butter or not. He's also produced a bone, on which he is gnawing. It could be yak, but judging by the size, I'd guess it's lamb. Either way, there is little, if any meat left on it. There must be nutrient value in the marrow, and once again that is not wasted. As much energy as possible stays in the cycle. The water didn't boil, but it's hot enough, and he's made some tea and offered me a cup. As a bonus, he's having it without yak butter, and I must say it tastes much better.

With as little formality on departure as on greeting, he wanders off, and I am left to feel fortunate for such a beautiful experience. That was as pure and unspoiled a scene as you could possibly imagine. Having dung warmed tea with a nomad! As sick as I am, I still absolutely relished in it. Life is amazing. As horribly harsh and bitter as this place and this journey have been at times, the priceless few moments like these make it all worth while.

O O O

The afternoon has worn on and turned into early evening, and Kat has joined me in the tent. She says she had a long and wonderful nap beside the river, and didn't even know about my nomad friend who came and went. It was our original intention to get back to the village of Lunja for tonight, but it is too late for that now, so we have decided to stay here. Leatherfoot will be a few days, so we are in no real hurry to get back to Tingri. This tent is slightly bigger than our own, and with a bit of shifting about, we have even fit our packs in here with us. It should be a comfortable place to sleep. I hope nobody else comes for the night!

"Where do you think Leatherfoot is Dogi?"

"It wouldn't surprise me if he made it all the way to Rongphu. I hope so. I know he's been looking forward to seeing that monastery as much as the big mountain itself. It would certainly be a warmer place to sleep than a high mountain pass. Any which way, it looks like the weather is staying clear for him."

Well now, this really sucks! We were already snug in our sleeping bags, settled in for the night when, suddenly, two men have shown up. They are definitely too wealthy looking to be nomads. The way they are dressed, they seem like Chinese businessmen, which makes them as out of place here as we are. In this case there has been no greeting, formal or otherwise. Though I wouldn't describe them as unkind, they have made it quite clear that they are staying in this tent and we have to leave. It's a strange situation. A part of me wants to argue, but maybe they have somehow prearranged this with the regular users of this camp. Seeing no point in making any hassle, Kat and I gather our things and simply shift ourselves over to the smaller tent. It's considerably smaller, but without our packs, we can each lie on a side. I can't quite stretch out, but it's close enough.

"What was your highlight of the day Kat?"

"The nap next to the river. I just float. It feels nice."

"Mine was sharing tea with the nomad. Sometimes I crave the ability to speak every language, but then not being able to talk, and communicating in other ways, has its own special quality to it."

"Yea. I like to be with locals, but I hope we can stay here tonight."

○ ○ ○

"Well Hello. Ta-shi de-lek."

"Ta-shi de-lek."

"Well Kat, it looks like we won't be able to stay here either."

Barely settled in once again, a young boy has appeared. Not quite scared, he definitely looked rather surprised by our presence as he opened the tent flap and peered in. As Kat and I crawl out of the tent, we see that it's edging into twilight, and it's gotten cold. Strangely, after a relatively calm day, a late evening wind has started to howl. At this point, we're not in the state or mood to travel far, so we decide to pitch our tent right here between the two nomad tents and at least retain some shelter from the rock walls.

249

I'm starting to feel a lot like the night Leatherfoot and I got stuck out before Tingri. The tent is flapping all over the place as soon as we pull it out of the bag. Meanwhile, the boy has disappeared, but here he comes again with his father and their big flock of sheep. Now, wrestling with our tent, we have a huge herd of antsy sheep coming our way. It's one of those moments that's probably hilarious, but it certainly doesn't feel like it at the time.

As we see the father and son herding the sheep, we understand the reason for the enclosed portions of the rock walls. For a fluttering moment, I wonder how they will close the entrances once they are all in, but my attention is immediately jerked back to the task at hand. I just want to get this tent set up, and get into my sleeping bag for the third and hopefully final time. With the process well under way, the father tells his boy to finish up while he comes over to us. At first, I think he is going to help us get this raging pink and green monster under control, but he actually motions for us to put it away, and points back at the small nomad tent. There is a long moment of hesitation. If we sleep in the nomad tent, where are they going to sleep? The floor area in there can't be much bigger than our own. He's not a big man, and the boy is quite small, but does he mean to stuff all four of us in there?

Well, isn't this cuddly and cozy. Here we are. Kat, myself, and a pile of sheepskins are squished on one side of the tent. The boy, and his father and more sheepskins on the other. Between us is a burning pile of dung, which is making the place a bit smoky, but nice and warm. It is the son who diligently and skillfully started the fire, and heated the water for the tea while his father was out checking on the sheep. You can feel the father's pride in his boy, checking first to make sure that it is okay to serve us some tea. We use our own cup, and gratefully accept some of the warm liquid, which, pleasantly, is again served without any yak butter. As we sip away and breath the mixed smell of raw wool and dung smoke, we watch them go about their evening routine in the cramped quarters. Their meal consists of a few mouthfuls of tsampa, and since then, the father has been going through a boiling, shaking, and mashing process that has taken me a while to figure out. Of course, he's brewing Chang, their homemade version of beer. Taking his last sip of tea, he has filtered it through a cloth into his cup and offered it our way. Losing my Yak Butter Tea virginity not too long ago, I am wary as I take a small sip, but find it to be surprisingly tasty. He offers some to me a second time, but today has taught me how precious all of their things are to them out here, and I decline. This is obviously his privilege, and I don't want to deny him another drop.

It has been the most special evening of the whole trip, and perhaps one of the most special of my life. When we first came into this smaller tent, we wished strongly that we'd be left alone for the night, and rarely if ever have I been happier that a wish did not come true. We have been spellbound throughout. The boy, who is perhaps ten years old, has been staring at us a lot, and he has the most beautiful smile. He's obviously just as fascinated by us as we are by them. The father has continued to go about his business. He's gone out a couple of times to check on the sheep, and otherwise he's been shaking up more chang and making sure the fire keeps burning. Late into the evening, he unexpectedly, and sheepishly, requests a little money from us. Perhaps the chang built up his courage to ask. The fee being nominal as it was, we happily paid, and any awkward feelings soon dissipated. It is an evening I will not soon forget.

FARTALOT and BABA

WE AWAKEN TO THE SMELL OF ANOTHER DUNG FIRE BEING LIT, and the continuation of the drama on primitive living. And, in reverse, the show on how modern travellers live. We get the impression the father has had contact with trekkers in the past, but the son is wide eyed as we stuff our fluffy sleeping bags into their small sacks, and even more astonished as he watches Kat reef on the compression straps, halving the size of the bundle once again. As more tea is prepared, we accept another small cup. Breakfast for them is more tsampa, and a piece of animal bone on which to gnaw. Vegetarians the Tibetans most definitely are not. Kat unwraps another of the Chinese Army cookies. I have too many cankers in my mouth to eat them. We really have nothing left which isn't crunchy, and thus, painful to chew. Cooking up noodle soup is an option, but I decide not to eat, opting to wait until Lunja.

When we finally do poke our heads out the door, the sun is just up, and we notice that we are a mere two meters away from the whole herd of sheep. No wonder they sounded so noisy all night. They are various themes of black and white. Some have curly hair, and others are quite shaggy. Some have curled horns, some have swirled horns, and some have no horns at all. They are endearing. The boy, who is comfortable with us now, flashes his big smile as we admire the animals. This is their life. This is his schooling. He will hang out with his father and learn to herd and care for sheep. As he walks long distances with the grazing animals each day, he will also learn to spin wool, a common sight among the nomadic Tibetans. Most of his meals will be tsampa, and when he is old enough, he will begin to make and drink chang. This will be his life. In one sense it sounds hard, and yet, at the same time, it sounds easy. His comforts may be minimal in comparison to many other humans, yet he may never really be aware that this is the case. There will be no plastic toys, no teenage fashion pressures, no decisions on which university to attend and what to study, no television, no computer, no cell phone. He will have almost no material possessions, and neither the joys of them, or the stresses that come along with feeling like you need them, and trying to earn enough money to buy them all. What he will have, is good clean water to drink, fresh, unpolluted air to breathe, and the simplicity of always knowing what he should do when he wakes up tomorrow.

We are happy when the boy agrees to have his picture taken with us. I will never see him again, but I feel as though I have made a friend. After the photo, he looks at his dad and, nodding towards Kat, inquires if she is Chinese. Surprisingly, he answers correctly that she is actually Japanese. We wonder how it was that he could tell. We try to express our gratitude to them as deeply as possible and head on our way.

"TU-JAY-CHAY... KA-LEE SHU"

○ ○ ○

Feeling energized from our special encounter, we manage the first kilometer or two back to Lunja at an okay pace, but suddenly, my energy is all but gone again. I am so frustrated and irritable. Kat is walking out in front of me now. She must have tired of my whining. After all this time in Tibet, she is really starting to feel better, but she knows how it feels to be where I am. In a way she feels sorry for me, but there is also a strong sense of spite. She told me that she thinks we didn't give her enough respect when she was so sick and worn out. Apparently, there were times when she really thought we might kill her. She also decided to tell me that she doesn't want to take care of me when I'm old and incapacitated, citing that I'm too grumpy when I'm sick. I tell her not to worry, I'll probably never make it to being old. Right now, I'm not so convinced I'll make it back to Lunja, or Tingri.

Kat has stopped, and I almost bumped into her as I have been walking with my head down and my eyes half closed, just concentrating on putting one foot in front of the other. I look up to see what she has been staring at. It's a fat white pony and a three legged dog following a lone Tibetan man. I give my head a little shake just to make sure it is not the onset of true delirium, but there they are. It really is a fat white pony and a three legged dog. What a peculiar sight! The dog looks as though he's been without that leg for a long time. He's secure in his hobble as he comes over and gives us a cursory sniff. The pony, for all its girth, looks a little weathered and worn. Then again, what out here doesn't. It looks happy to take a break, and goes in search of some scant grasses to munch on. The man walks up to us with a smile. He can see that I am not well. It's obvious. We go through some small talk, sign language and gestures, and figure out that he is offering me the services of his pony for thirty Yuan. Thirty Yuan! Though I do feel like death, I think this is too much. Stubbornly, I pass on his offer and off they go, the man, the pony and the three legged dog.

Kat gives me a good long look. We are both highly frugal, and have this ongoing joke about who is actually cheaper than who. I say nothing, and start walking again bolstered by my stubborn pride. Only a few hundred meters pass, however, before I realize that stubborn pride is no better than will power when you are this down and out. Once again, I have stopped, taken off my pack and plopped down on it with my head buried in my arms. I feel like crying again, but opt instead for laughter. Kat laughs with me. No, she's probably laughing at me.

"I guess you wish you take the pony ride."

"Hmm... yea... but thirty Yuan was too much."

"Cheapo!"

"Yea it's true, I'm almost as cheap as you."

"Hey look!"

The three legged dog is not with them this time, but suddenly, the man and the pony are coming back our way again. He smiles at us, and presents a new offer. I counter, and we bargain for a while, both with a little smile on our faces. We agree on a price, but remain at a small stalemate regarding Kat's pack. I want it loaded on the pony too, and he doesn't. We have a silence, while he takes a good long look at the beast. Finally he gives in. The pony will carry me and both packs back to Lunja for ten Yuan.

He straps our two packs down and helps me mount my little steed. When I am settled, he has a brief word with the pony, and then turns and walks off in the opposite direction from where we want to go! I can't believe he just left us here with me sitting on his pony. On top of this, after all the bargaining, he didn't even collect his money.

"Hey! Excuse me! Um, we want to go that way..."

So here I am. Sitting on a fat white pony in the middle of a huge expanse of the Tibetan plateau! Kat looks up at me. She looks back to where the man is already a distant speck, and then looks back at me once more and shrugs her shoulders.

"How do you feel up there?"

"Well, I feel a little confused, but pretty good really. This is obviously a mellow horse, but I'm not sure I'll know how to guide him."

"Her. I think it's a her."

"Okay, her. Maybe the man told her where to go. Come on girl."

I nudge the pony to see what will happen. I'm pretty sure the animal's instinct will make her follow the man and the dog, but I am wrong, and she starts walking back towards Lunja. I guess all is well.

I have been on horses perhaps a dozen times since childhood. It's often enough to feel somewhat at ease, but not overly confident. What helps is that this mare, though wide, is neither large nor intimidating. In fact, she's quite docile. At first, I keep my feet in the stirrups which have been lengthened fully, but are still way too short for my legs. After getting the rhythm of her gait, however, I remove them and let them dangle. There is no risk of her rearing, or bolting. Soon, I am settled in quite happily, realizing how cool it is to be riding a fat white pony across a huge, flat, rocky plain with mountains all around me. Much more so than on the bikes or on foot, I am able to take in my surroundings. Maybe we should have ridden horses across Tibet. They don't get flat tires, broken wheel bearings, or snapped chains, although...

255

"She's pooping again! That's the third time already."

"Does it stink, Kat?"

"Not really. It's kind of funny to watch. I wonder if you can burn this poop too? Ahh, now she farted again. She is farting many times."

"Yea, she sure does fart a lot. I can feel the vibrations from up here!"

"Fartalot. Hey that's a good name Dogi. Let's call her Fartalot."

Fartalot obviously knows exactly where she's going. Her pace is perfect for a packless Kat to follow leisurely on foot. All the farting and pooping is somewhat distracting from the gorgeous scenery, but it's awfully funny. Much like the pony cart ride a few days ago, being perched up here has temporarily suspended my misery. This is fun!

As we see Lunja approaching, we begin to wonder how this is all going to end. Since that initial nudge to get her going, I have not given Fartalot any instruction. Will she keep walking until I tell her to stop? Will she plod right past Lunja, and continue on to Tingri? No, she turns right down "main street," and right again, and finally comes to a stop in front of a house. Now what? I ask Fartalot, but she doesn't even neigh in return. She just stands, as patiently as ever, and waits. Just as I am about to ask Kat to hold the reigns, while I attempt to dismount, a young man pops out of the house. I don't think he came out for us. He just happened to be on his way out, and, not surprisingly, he looks at us somewhat queerly, before helping me dismount and removing our packs. Then he motions for us to wait as he leads Fartalot away.

Not a minute later, a lady, who we figure to be the young man's mother, comes out. After studying us briefly and intently, she points at the house, makes a sign for sleep, and holds up five fingers. At this point, as if it has been previously ordained, we nod our heads and follow her unquestioningly through the small entranceway. It takes our eyes a moment to adjust from the bright sun to this dim light, before we can see that this ground level has very little in it. The shift in air temperature is as radical and immediate as the change in light, and we inhale the cool air deeply. Our hostess leads the way up some steep stairs to the second floor, which is when we realize that we have not wandered into a guesthouse, but rather a family home. At first, we walk through a room and catch a glimpse of a large weaving loom. Amongst other things, like boxes, baskets and boots, there are several large balls of yarn dangling from the ceiling in a corner. All that pulling and twirling of wool, that we have seen so many people do, ends up in a place like this for the next stage in the long process from animal's coat to human's. One small window sheds light on the work of the young woman weaving on the loom. She looks to be about our age, which is to say in her twenties. As we continue, we come into a big room where the light is also dim, except for where it streams through the few windows. It is rimmed with one continuous bunk, that looks to be for sitting, counter, and bed space. There is what I would normally describe as a free standing wood burning stove, but I suppose "dung burning" stove might be more appropriate. On top of it, there is a pot of water and a bunch of potatoes. Other than toilet facilities, this room functions as everything else. It is the kitchen, the living room and the bedroom all in one. A space has been cleared for us along the bench near the stove and one of the windows.

O O O

bang BANG... three seconds
bang BANG... three seconds
bang BANG

I'm beginning to feel suicidal. Well, maybe not that bad, but *INSANITY* is reaching its sharp thin claws deeper into the base of my brain. Though this banging noise comes from that traditional hand weaving loom, which has been very fascinating to watch in operation, it is causing my headache to grow substantially. That, and this three year old boy that is ripping around all over the place, screaming and yelling as three year old boys do, joined now and again by a little screaming from his younger brother. Add in that the family has gathered for a meal, and between the laughing and giggling, there is a whole lot of open mouthed slurping, chewing and swallowing going on. Kat slurps away too. It is agony to hear the sounds of a meal being enjoyed when you can't eat! AHHH!!!

I'm coming and going now. I'm pretty sure I have a fever. Hot, cold, hot, cold, and very, very dizzy. As close to death as I feel, I must say that I am still fascinated by this place. It's like having a front row seat for a documentary on traditional Tibetan life. It is the grandma of the scene who we find most interesting. We have taken to calling her Baba, which is a Japanese colloquial for grandma. Baba has been rocking something under her arm for a very long time. Between the banging of the loom, we can hear a sloshing sound, as though from a thick liquid. At first, we thought she was making butter, but now, we guess it's cheese. We're not sure of the family structure, but we get the impression that the girl working the loom is Baba's daughter-in-law. It's not overt, but there is a strange kind of tension there. For most of the time we've been here, which is a few hours, she has been weaving on the loom. It is amazing to see first hand how much time and effort goes into making one of the dense, heavy fabrics that they use to make their clothes and aprons. The time pays off, however, in the incredibly durable quality of the garments. Their clothes are made so well, that they probably last for ages, even in this hard wearing environment.

The men on the scene, like the one that showed us in, have been coming and going. Again, it's mostly guesswork by the inquisitive Kat, but she thinks the father of the boys, and husband of the girl working the loom, is the man with the three legged dog, which would make him Baba's older son. The young man who met us at the entrance to the house is thought to be Baba's younger son. Presumably, they are doing work outside. Tending to the animals, gathering fuel for the stove, building and repairing structures. The basics. Everyone is putting their energy into the basics. Food and body protection. Except the younger kids. They are free to play, and laugh, and scream and cry. The older of the two boys, who is the greater terror, has a very reggae looking hairdo. At the moment, he is engaged in a little wrestling match with his younger sibling.

258

Kat has just returned from a walk around this little village and seems to have had a really good time. First, she tells me the story of three teenaged girls who came up to her wearing their usual Tibetan clothes and began speaking to her. Once they clued in that she couldn't understand, they were making motions as if to ask if she had any lipstick! Most of the rest of her tale revolves around animals. She says that goats are funny, and sheep are okay, but stupid. Yaks are definitely cool, and cows are just cows, though cows in Nepal are, apparently, cuter than the ones here. She doesn't mind "shit" anymore because it's everywhere and it's used for fuel. She was really going on and on about "shit," and she wants to try making a fire with it and cooking on it. Also impressive to her is the total use of animal materials. Milk, hair, skin, meat, bones, and "shit."

"What about dogs, Kat?"

"I think they should be recycled too, and maybe I can sleep on their fur."

As Kat settles back in, Baba brings us some Yak Butter Tea. Kat has quickly grown quite fond of Baba, and thinks she's smart. We have explained our journey to her, and she seems to have understood it, recognizing all the names, including Kathmandu. She certainly has been well in tune to our needs since we've arrived. Kat is, however, less impressed with the daughter-in-law, particularly since she grabbed her ear to check out the piercing. Baba has now had a closer inspection of the two of us, starting with Kat's ugly, swollen, cracked lip. She produces a dollop of yak butter and smears it on. With the younger son on his way out again, she takes some his way and smears it on his face too. Then, Kat insists I show her my mouth full of canker sores. These things are horrible. Have you ever accidentally eaten a super spicy killer chili? Experienced the kind of burn that, despite your best efforts with ice, water, rice, yoghurt, or "whatever," just won't subside? That's what it's like trying to eat with these canker sores, and they are worse than ever. They are all over my tongue and gums, lips, the roof of my mouth, everywhere. The only thing I've eaten in the last two days is one small bowl of noodle soup and three Chinese chocolate wafers. Each of those dining affairs has been more painful than you care to imagine. It burns like hell. Now I know why Kat resisted eating so fiercely all those times. But I need to eat. I'm starving. Baba has given both Kat and I a couple of potatoes, and she looked at me as if to say I should eat them. As they are small enough to fit, Kat shoves a whole one into her mouth. Her eyes light up, and a big smile creeps across her face.

"This is best potato I ever eat."

"Really? You think I can eat one?"

"You can mush it up and then try. I think you like it."

It's still painful, but I manage to get both down, and my stomach is singing their praises. In fact, my stomach has overruled my mouth and told me to eat more of them. I don't know if I should ask Baba's permission or not, but she's gone back to her work, and I don't want to disturb her, so I take three more of the spuds. Food is good.

○ ○ ○

Thankfully, the loom has stopped, at least for a while, though I'm hoping for the rest of the day. I thought about going out for my own walk, but I've been unable to move since we got here. Even standing up has given me severe head rushes. The daughter-in-law, who a short time ago came by and gave us each one more potato, is now helping Baba with things. Baba has been working a churn for the last little while, and we were wondering whether she was making butter or chang, but, as we have since seen her pour it into a thermos, we realize she must have been mixing Yak Butter Tea. After we first had it, I thought it was just brewed tea with a dollop of yak butter in it, but we've always been served it as a finished product. I think she added some milk and some salt too. I must say, it does make a difference to drink it fresh and hot, though I still won't go so far as to call it good. After being here for long enough, however, I can understand why it is good for you.

Kat's second favorite person in the house has just reaffirmed his good standing by swinging by and offering us more potatoes. I think Kat likes the second son because he's handsome, and has particularly beautiful hair. He wears it long and plaited, with the red tassels. It may also be the cleanest and well kept hair we've seen on anyone since leaving Lhasa. I wonder how often most rural Tibetans get a chance to wash their hair, or their bodies, for that matter? Do they attempt to brush it between washings, or simply leave it braided until the next cleaning? What, if anything besides water, do they use to wash? Bathing is not a privilege we've been able to enjoy ourselves, nor have we ever seen the activity happening with any of the locals. With the lack of moisture, however, body odor doesn't seem to be a big issue. Then again, maybe I've just gotten used to it.

WOW. The documentary continues. So much better than TV, we get not only the sights and sounds, but the smells, tastes, and feelings too. Somehow I thought a Tibetan household would be peaceful and serene, but in the last little while we've witnessed the extremes of human emotion going on. Laughter, crying, hot, cold, hunger, yelling, giving shit, getting shit, all within a few hours. The scene going on at the moment is particularly intense, as two men, who I don't think are part of the family, have come in. One of them has been crying and wailing for about ten minutes, while the other one, and Baba and the rest of the family all try to console him. It is the first time I have seen this level of anguish amongst the Tibetan people. As with so many times before, we wish desperately to be able to understand more, but there is no chance of us learning beyond the basics of the language at this point. The man is being offered tea and food, but he just keeps going off on one rant after another. If he's noticed us at all, it hasn't tempered his mood either. Finally, they have him sitting, and his outbursts are becoming fewer and further between.

Though we stay seated in our place slightly away from the rest of the family, we are included in their evening meal. It is a bowl of tsampa with Yak Butter Tea poured over it. Baba, you're brilliant! It's so much better than the dry version, or even dry washed down with a sip of tea. The powdered grains have a chance to soak up the liquid, making it taste somewhat like porridge, and I can eat it without a lot of pain. It was our intention to supplement this with a bowl of mushy noodle soup, but Kat slipped on the serving and dumped it on the floor. Oops, sorry Baba.

After the late evening meal, the hub hub of the day finally settles. Without any electricity, there is only the soft glow from a few candles, and these are soon extinguished as people take their places around perimeter bunks for the night. From a nomad tent, to a fat white pony to a bunk in Baba's house. What a day!

FIGHTS

WE ARE AWOKEN BY A LOUD VOICE. IS IT THE SAME YOUNG MAN who was creating all the fuss yesterday? It seems as though we're not the only ones he's decided to be an alarm for. The rest of the family comes out of their slumber along with us. No, the daughter-in-law must have been up already. She just showed up carrying a big load of water. The house has no running water, and ferrying it in, and up the stairs is no easy task. She is a strong young woman. Baba re-stokes the fire, and water is heated and food prepared. Once again, we are offered tsampa with Yak Butter Tea. It is beyond me how the Tibetans can eat the tsampa dry. Dry old bread is bad enough for sucking the moisture out of your mouth, but raw flour? It feels like your mouth wants to implode. Like the inside of your cheeks are being sucked down your throat. Each time I've tried the tsampa raw, I've had to drink quickly and substantially, even if the only thing available was Yak Butter Tea. So, eating it already soaking in the tea has come across like a fantastic new invention.

"Hey Kat, another bowl of tsampa Yak Butter Tea cereal. How is it today?"

"It's, okay. It still tastes like Yak Butter Tea."

"Yea, too bad it's not more sweet, but I'm happy I can slide it past the mouth mines with less pain than anything else I've eaten in days, and my stomach is thankful."

O O O

We get ourselves ready to go right after breakfast. Sorting out the bill creates a small amount of confusion. There is the ten Yuan charged for night's stay, but she is asking for twelve, which she

263

explains is for the food we have eaten. As we still haven't paid for the services of Fartalot, we add in that extra ten, which she can't understand. I get on my imaginary horse, offering up my best galloping and neighing sounds until comprehension sinks in, and we all have a little chuckle. The whole family has shown us a lot of kindness. Baba, in particular, has been caring, and as a final gesture she has once again smeared Kat's face and lips with yak butter to protect them during today's walk. Kat says she feels even better today. All of the extra rest has done her a world of good. There have been no headaches for days, and her canker sores are all but gone. Only that lip is still an ugly festering mess. Myself, on the other hand, I am still spinning and wobbling... and whining. Kat has just informed me I'm doing a lot of whining today. Even more than yesterday, apparently. She has decided that she doesn't want to spend the rest of her life with me anymore because I whine too much when I get sick. For the first time all trip, we have a fight. Probably the only reason we haven't had more fights, or at least disagreements, is because Kat has never had enough energy for it... until now. Me, on the other hand, I will fight even when I'm knocking on death's door, which I feel like I am. The current issue is a river that is laying across our path. Kat wants to walk around it, and I want to walk through it because I don't want to take one more step than absolutely necessary. When we've had enough of the argument, and still come to no compromise, we simply go our separate ways. She walks off to the left to search out a better route, while I take off my boots and socks, and wade through the knee deep water. It's not wide, nor is it flowing too quickly, but is it ever cold. There is such a fine line between walking slowly enough, so as not to lose your balance, and quickly enough, so as not to freeze your feet.

The plains here are so open and flat that we never fully lose sight of one another, and it's not too much later when we reunite again. We exchange one of those "I hate you right now, but I don't really hate you" stares that couples have, but there is no more conversation. She walks out in front, and I try to keep up. The rest of the walk back draws on way too long for both of us. I am moving excruciatingly slowly, even for Kat, who likes a slow pace.

264

It's just left foot, right foot, left foot, right foot. There are no pony rides today. For me, it simply becomes a battle of trying to stay conscious, and not fall flat on my face before Tingri. My world is wavering. In fact, on several occasions of rest, all I do is lie flat on my back desperately wanting to sleep, but Kat wakes me up each time, with no great affection, and tells me we have to keep moving. Though she doesn't like me very much right now, she knows that she must still take care of me out here. There is no one else.

Many hours pass before we finally hit the main road in Tingri. I just want to get a room and lie on a cot, but Kat wants to eat and thinks I should eat too. This time I don't argue. She's probably right. I should try to eat something, and then I can sleep for as long as I want.

We head for the Chinese restaurant where we had eaten once before we left on our trek. The owner had been kind, and the food quite tasty. As we settle at our table, we notice a skittish puppy. He was here last time too, and is obviously the local leftovers scrounger. Vacuuming fallen food scraps is fine, but Kat and I don't care much for begging dogs and, remembering this from last time, the owner is kind enough to issue the puppy out the door. Kat looks over the menu and orders, while I rest with my head on the table until the food comes. As I look up, I can see that the puppy is cautiously making his way back in under the door hang. His eyes are expectant, but he makes no noise and keeps a short distance. The owner makes a motion to shoo him away again, but I tell him not to worry about it. This is his adopted home, and I should respect that.

Amongst other things, Kat has ordered a tofu dish. Tofu. I got exposed to it often enough in Japan, but have never gotten beyond thinking of it as tasteless mush. Today, however, it is absolute heaven. I can actually eat it without excruciating pain, and compared to mushy packaged noodle soup, it is a taste delight! I've probably never sucked on it the way I have to now, and I've certainly never been nearly as hungry as this when I've eaten it before, but I like this tofu. Kat likes it too, but I can't eat the other food she's ordered, so she lets me eat as much of it as I can. One cube after the next, my stomach begs me not to stop. Hunger is a powerful thing.

The only other patrons in the restaurant are sitting at the large round table in the corner. A mix of Chinese and Tibetan men, they are a most incongruous sight, and with most of them drinking heavily, they are loud and obnoxious. One Chinese man in particular appears to be showing off in front of his new friends. It is obvious that the owner is not too pleased with their behavior, but with the amount of money that they are spending, he will be tolerant. Kat, of course, is not impressed with them either, but she has her back to them, and has a talent for ignoring bothersome things going on around her. I am downright irritated, though I don't even have enough energy left to whine to Kat about them.

'SMASH!!!'

"Dogi, what was that?"

"That asshole just smashed a beer bottle over the puppy's head!"

There is glass all over the ground, and the mangy young dog scuttles for the exit with its tail between its legs and a severely bloodied head. I am flabbergasted. Though I do empathize with being bothered by a begging dog, and I can understand them being thrown out of a restaurant, or even given a mild boot once in a while, smashing a beer bottle on its head and then laughing heartily about it is unacceptable. Without thought, I launch off my chair, walk over to the round table, and, hovering over it, scream…

"WHAT IS YOUR FUCKING PROBLEM YOU ASSHOLE. WHAT THE FUCK ARE YOU THINKING. YOU JUST DON'T DO SHIT LIKE THAT! YOU IDIOT! YOU WANT ME TO SMASH A BOTTLE ON YOUR HEAD, YOU DICK!"

The human body and spirit are an amazing thing. Never in my whole life have I been so depleted of energy, but somehow, I had enough fight left in me to absolutely lay in to this idiot, regardless of the consequences. Had he decided to retaliate physically in any way, I wouldn't have lasted a second, but fortunately, he didn't. The lot of them, though they presumably didn't understand a word of my eloquent speech, were dumbfounded into a temporary silence. Even the perpetrator of the smash had a look of some remorse on his face.

We leave the restaurant, and fueled by my residual anger, I manage the walk back to the hotel well enough. We check in to the same place, and are even given the same room. In no time at all, we are both passed out on our cots.

DOG EAT DOG

It has been two days since we left Baba's house, Leatherfoot is already back, and I am sitting at the side of the main road in Tingri, town of wonders. I am leaned against a rock wall, and await that one gracious truck that may bring us up the final pass of our journey at over 5100 meters (16,800 feet). Lalung La. It has a nice name, doesn't it.

There is a dog... and there was a dog. They are both in a ditch less than ten meters away from me, and the one that still is, gnaws ravenously on the remnants of flesh of the one that is no more. The dead dog looks as though he lost a confrontation with a truck. Perhaps he was delirious after having a beer bottle smashed over his head. The one that lives, and eats his former neighbor, is still a puppy, though he already looks somewhat psychotic. He is in heavy competition for the fleshy bits with swarms of flies. The insects alternate between feasting on the rotting flesh and buzzing around the puppy's eyes and nose just to irritate him. Cycles. Death providing opportunity for life, but not without a fight.

In the background, along the road from where we came several days ago, the browns and the greys mix nicely with the blues of the sky and the white fluffy floating clouds. Across the road to my right are a few colourful shop fronts, and behind them, the huge backdrop of the Himalayas, including the tip of Qomolangma. It is gorgeous, and I soak it into my being as deeply as I can, but I am human, and invariably my attention is drawn back to the scene of "dog eat dog." It is appalling, and mesmerizing. I've always found it fascinating how we humans are so drawn to happenings that are horrific and hideous. One look, or listen, to the daily news is proof enough of the kinds of things that we are attracted to.

The dog eat dog scene is framed by a pile of trash, old sheep and goat horns, and urine stains. The puppy yelps and growls as he fends off flies and tugs at tendons. The minutes tick by, but no trucks pass.

O O O

Our first evening back in Tingri, we pulled ourselves out of the warmth of our guesthouse restaurant and returned to our dark and frigid room with a thermos of chai. For perhaps the next fourteen hours I was back to the basic routine of sleep, drink, and pee, in whichever order the need arose. With a dirt parking lot right outside our room door, I fortunately didn't have to woozle too far in the dark to have a wizzle. Just a minor awareness of any breeze was good enough.

The morning brought us only as far as our guesthouse restaurant once again. We trundled to the far corner where we could lounge, and even nap on the bunks. Ordering tsampa and chai, we made ourselves a "Baba Deluxe!" The mushy tsampa cereal with the sweet milky chai was a massive improvement on the mixture with Yak Butter Tea. It was the most canker sore friendly meal I'd had in days.

After so many hours of being horizontal, or only walking a few paces here and there, our bodies were starting to get stiff and achy, and we decided a late morning walk was in order. We wandered around Greater Tingri to some of the areas that we'd not yet been, and amongst other scenes, came upon a small festival. Though disorganized looking, it was colourful and joyous. It had a familiar quality to Kat, who said it reminded her, in ways, of the kinds of festivals she grew up with in Japan. And, though we were unable to figure out what it was about, it was a pleasure just to watch people having a good time. For me, it was a small lift to my struggling spirit. The whole walk did feel good to give the body some movement and stretching, but we plopped down back in our usual corner of the guesthouse restaurant once again, with myself in particular, feeling exhausted. From this wonderful vantage point, however, we were able to watch the continuation of the "documentary on life in Tibet." Such has it felt to me since the nomad tent episode a few days ago. Strangely, I think being so sick has made me more aware of my surroundings. I guess I've slowed down to the extent that I can't do much besides watch life go by.

Between thermoses of chai and various other goodies, we watched the actors come and go from our stage. To begin with, there is the family that runs this guesthouse and restaurant. We have spent a lot of time observing the coming and going of food and water, laundry and all of the other things that comprise their daily cycles of life. We have gotten to know them quite well, thanks, in large part, to the one young boy who speaks English well. He had the opportunity to move to India for a few years where he learned the language, and now manages to use it more frequently with the slowly increasing tourists that pass through. Though the rest of the staff speak absolutely no English, we have developed a good relationship with them simply by hanging out and asking questions of the young man.

It was during a peaceful moment when the young man was chatting with us, that there was a sudden commotion outside, followed by the first of a bus load of exuberant, camera toting French tourists that came ducking through the curtain. In minutes, the restaurant was packed. Even the remaining space in our little corner of the lounge was needed. It felt like a sudden whirlwind on an otherwise calm day. Having freshly arrived in Tibet from the Nepali border, they were fascinated by everything, and eager to take photos of all of it. The family, the food, the walls, even we became subjects of their film. The whole family and staff got hopping. Everyone got a bowl of thugpa, and several plates full of momos were brought out for sharing. I enjoyed watching their faces and listening to their comments while they ate. I haven't been able to eat any of the thugpa or momos due to the cankers, but Kat says they are a little better than average, though she's been in Tibet for weeks. Some of the tourists genuinely seemed to like their soups, and ate the whole bowls, while others were less than enthused, and left the majority. The momos did get mostly eaten with variable facial expression and commentary. Then, as abruptly as it had arrived, the whirlwind ended. I was thankful for this, as the swirling energy, and trying to understand and use some of my rusty French, was making me dizzy. With the last tourist and the guide out the door, the only residual energy left was the mass of messy of dishes.

○ ○ ○

At the side of the road...

The dog is still chewing on the dog. He has since lost a couple of chunks to another, larger dog, who came along and dragged a portion elsewhere, though he defended the main carcass admirably. Still no traffic has passed by. Well, that's not true. There have been no trucks, though I did just watch a terrorized calf go ripping down the middle of the road at full speed with yet another tooth bearing mongrel in hot pursuit.

○ ○ ○

Just as the calm had settled over the restaurant once again, a second unexpected storm blew in. Rather than a playful whirlwind, this one was much more like an ominous cloud and threatening thunderstorm. It was as if a gust of arrogance preceded the first Chinese soldier through the door hang, and the thickness of it was almost palpable by the time they had all filed in. In truth, they were mostly kids. Almost all of the military personnel we've seen so far have been teenagers or in their early twenties at most. I wonder how they must feel being stationed in such a remote and barren outpost. Beyond their military exercises, there is not a lot out here to entertain young men of that age.

There were as many of them, or even more than the French tour group. Once again, we were joined at our table by a few. We thought about leaving, but I still had no energy to move, and it was so much more pleasant in there than in our dank room. We also got the sense that the Tibetan family were happy to have us there. The army brats were still loud, obnoxious, and demanding, but somehow more measured in their behavior than they may have been without us present. We always get the impression that the soldiers here in Tibet don't know what to make of us "aliens." They certainly don't feel the need to treat us with respect, but they seem careful not to disrespect or hassle us either. Some look at us with curiosity, but most simply ignore us.

I'm sure any group of this size is a welcome business opportunity, but there was an obvious discomfort for the Tibetan family. They were being barked at. This appears to be the Chinese way, at least in this region. Generalizing about anything Chinese would be a mistake. China is such a vast and ancient culture, with an endless amount of ethnic variation. Yet, from my observations on this trip, the Chinese people here have been fairly blunt and abrupt, even in dealing with each other. Tack on young, male, and military, and the barking becomes more vicious. This is not the Tibetan way. Tibetans, from what we have witnessed, are calm and attentive. Many of them may not be broad in understanding, as theirs is a simple life, but they are kind and humble. It does not mix well. And though I prefer the gentler approach of the Tibetans, I would not wish to pass negative judgement on the Chinese way. If I were to go into an area of China where this was the norm, I would accept it and expect to adapt. What makes Tibet intriguing, and saddening, is that the Chinese are doing exactly the opposite. They are imposing their culture onto the pre-existing Tibetan one. But then, humans have been doing this for as long as we have existed. It is the nature of things, be they bacterial or human, that cultures want to grow.

The food served to the soldiers was mostly the same as the tourists, as there are not many other options, though they ordered individually rather than collectively, which meant a lot more mad shuffling by the staff to try and keep up. Between the slurping of the noodles, the barking of the orders, and the decibel level of the general banter, the noise level was also significantly higher. And though the tourists were not exactly neat, it was nothing compared to the mess left by the army kids. On their departure, the tables, dishes, and floor were left in a state of complete chaos. The sigh of relief from all the Tibetans, when they finally left, was easily noticed. Slowly going about their cleanup, we got the sense that they felt trodden on and abused. If I'd had more energy, I'd have gotten up to help, but the whole event made me just want to close my eyes and pass out again for a while.

○ ○ ○

I've been here at the side of the road for a good hour, and only one truck has passed. It was going the other way. The dog is still eating the dog. I don't think there's any meat left, so he's working the tendons and crushing the bones. He has not taken a moment's break, and is oblivious to the other fifteen dogs that have shown up in a mass of yelping, snarling, barking, biting and drooling. It looks like a serious gang war. The Growlies from the east end of town are having issues with the Raunchy Rabids from the west. It's an all out street fight in the middle of the road. Why not, it's not like there's any traffic.

○ ○ ○

There was one more scene yesterday involving an army boy. It was staged in the middle of the dirt parking lot of our guest house. There were a few boys around, off duty by the looks of it, and one young girl. She was a Chinese prostitute, and whatever it was that this one boy did, or didn't do, she was letting him have it. She was right up in his face, jamming her finger into his chest and bawling him out. How I would have loved to understand what was being said there. The boy was trying to argue back, but she wasn't giving him any space to defend himself. The remainder of the boys looked unsure as to how to react, standing there mostly wide eyed and tight lipped. The local Tibetans, on the other hand, were having a good giggle at the whole situation. What a world. A country's government gives guns and such to a mass of teenagers, and sends them into a land where they are not welcome and tells them to "occupy" it. To make sure these boys don't get too bored, and have something to spend their wages on, girls are found to do things that they'd likely rather not do, but somehow are left with little option but to do them to survive.

○ ○ ○

Kat has just come to the side of the road to relieve me. She's not impressed with my choice of location. The dog eat dog scene holds no attraction for her. Fortunately, the street fight has ended and the canine gangs have gone their separate ways for a while, though

Kat is keenly aware that the rabid creatures could come back at any time, and she does fear them. We load her up with a small pile of rocks. She'll deal with it. She always deals with it.

She washed her body yesterday. It was the first time she peeled off all of her clothes in longer than she cares to remember. She noticed a lot of wrinkles, and realized just how much body weight she must have lost in the last few weeks. A wrinkled body, burnt lips, she says she looks and feels like an old lady. Farting, burping, she doesn't care about any of it anymore. She feels so far remove from society at this point that nothing much matters. Just avoiding a dog attack at the moment, that's all that matters.

Kat tells me an interesting tidbit just before I leave her to the mercy of the flea wagons. When she and Leatherfoot were walking around the town this morning, they saw two other bikes in a shop that she was sure belonged to the Dutch couple from Noodle Soup Pass.

"So it seems they bailed out at this point."

"I don't remember for sure, but maybe that was their plan."

"Really? And give up the endless downhill ride that's gonna start from the top of the next pass? That should be the best part of the riding."

"I hope so."

"I'm just happy we won't be finding her dead at the side of the road in the next few days. See ya."

I leave Kat to her shift of trying to hitch us a ride. As I wander back into the hotel parking area, I find Leatherfoot, who arrived back late last night, doing some tuning up on the bikes. He's ready to replace that broken chain, and I stay to help him. Fortunately, we did buy that one extra chain in Lhasa. It was a borderline decision at the time. There would have been no replacement here. The changing of the chain goes smoothly enough, and we tighten and lubricate as best we can. Having all the gears function at once is impossible, so we set them to make sure the lowest range runs smoothly. It is rare to go beyond the first few gears anyway.

Leatherfoot. It was so nice to see him arrive back safely last night. Kat and I were talking about him a lot late in the evening. We thought there was a slim chance he might be back, but, truthfully, didn't expect him until today. When he finally did arrive, we were already in bed and it was dark. So happy to see him alive and well, we anxiously listened to his tale...

The day I left you guys was great. I found the way easily enough, and the weather and scenery were spectacular. Here and there I saw some nomads, and they pointed me in the right direction. I walked pretty long into the afternoon, and then wrapped up and went to sleep early, and awoke again just before sunrise. It was bloody cold, but I was so excited to get there and see the monastery, and then get up to Base Camp. It's funny, since the day the idea of coming to Tibet to do this was suggested, and I did a little reading, I wanted to see and stay at Rongphu monastery. The highest monastery in the world!

Eventually, the trail came out onto the road that comes up from Shegar, and from here it wasn't too far to the monastery. But when I got there, it was a totally different experience than I'd fantasized about. The setting, of course, is spectacular, but the aura around the place was not positive and friendly at all. Many of the monks were even on the rude side. I took a place there to sleep anyway, and it was early enough, and the weather nice enough, that I hiked the rest of the way up to Base Camp that afternoon. I expected to be in awe, but had mixed emotions. Once again, the overall scenery was incredible, and it's nice to have seen and been so close to the great mountain, but the amount of human leftover junk from all the expeditions is shockingly disgusting.

I went Base Camp once more early in the morning. I figured I was there, so I wanted the opportunity to see sunrise in the company of Qomolangma. That was a definite highlight. The shock of the garbage was no longer unexpected, and I simply basked in the glow of the early morning light. I even walked up further than the day before, but not too far. It was my original plan to stay at the monastery for another night, but there wasn't a lot of joy there. Everyone else in the area was on a tour, and zipping in and out. I could start to understand why the monks here were less pleasant than usual. I met one group that I got along with, and was hoping for a ride back to Tingri, as they had ample space for me, but after humming and hawing, they decided they didn't want to risk the check point on the way back out. I had such mixed emotions at this point that I thought it best to just start hiking again, so I slung my backpack on, and headed down the road and onto the trail. I enjoyed that night more than anything else. That feeling of peace and good spirit, that I assumed would be there at the monastery, was there when I was alone again in my little enclave sheltered at the side of the trail. It was like so many of the nights we've had on this trip, with a theatrical sunset and all encompassing silence.

I got lost the next morning. Well, not really lost, but I went a direction that I didn't intend to, and had to backtrack for quite a while. That was harsh because I wanted to make it all the way back here by the end of the day. Oh well, I guess I did anyway.

Leatherfoot looked exhausted and somewhat frazzled when he arrived back in the dark yesterday. Though generally losing elevation, he must have walked at least thirty kilometers, and, with his wrong turn, probably even more. Factor in a wind that was as nasty as usual, and the last couple of hours in the dark, and it is no wonder that his story began in a jumpy, convoluted fashion, but we soaked in every last detail with great interest. After finishing his story, a wave of tiredness washed over him, and he suddenly got a dose of the shakes. Kat got him to drink some tea and eat a bit of food, after which he managed to calm down. Though he was exhausted, he said he wasn't yet ready to sleep, and insisted on hearing our tales of the last few days. We told him of the magical night in the nomad tent, Fartalot and the three legged dog, and Baba's house, as well as our most recent entertainment here in Tingri. When all was told, Leatherfoot said he thought our adventure was far more interesting than his, but he certainly doesn't regret having gone up to Base Camp. Finally, a calmness fell over him, and the sleep which I'm sure his body was begging him for soon followed.

Leatherfoot awoke this morning not feeling well at all. The rushed pace of his hike was no doubt very taxing on him. There was a bit of nausea, but it came mostly in the form of a relapse of diarrhea. We are encouraging him to rest as much as possible before we truck out of here. I am feeling somewhat better today. Not good by any stretch, but better. There was one other traveller who was through yesterday on a 4WD tour. Coming from the Nepali end, it was only his second day in Tibet. His enthusiasm was infectious, and, once started, he couldn't get enough of our tale, reacting with shock and fascination. He said we should write a book about it one day. Having along an extensive medical kit, he gave me some vitamin C and some other tablets to suck on, that he said would ease the cankers in my mouth. His other suggestion was a dilution of tea tree oil in warm water, that I've been swishing around faithfully ever since. Whether those remedies, the discovery of tsampa and chai to get some nutrients in, the rest, or the combination of all, there has been some definite improvement. Perhaps my cycle of sickness has run its course. Hopefully, Leatherfoot has just hit a bump in the road, as otherwise his strength and resolve have been unfailing.

O O O

The afternoon has worn well into evening. Fortunately, we were able to check back into our same room, where we are hanging out contemplating a game of cards. We sat for two long shifts each, but there simply were no trucks today, or at least none suitable to take the three of us to Lalung La Pass. That's okay. The extra day of rest didn't hurt any of us, and Tingri was as captivating as usual. Tomorrow we will get back on our bikes and ride.

Dogi's Journal Of Tibet

Part IV
Cycling to Kathmandu

A MONK and a DRUNK

THIS MORNING, ALL THREE OF US AGREE THAT IT FEELS FINE TO be getting back on the bikes. Leatherfoot has mostly recovered with the extra night of rest. Kat feels better by the day, and I continue to improve as well. Even my canker sores have receded to the point that I can eat more food again. Having spent enough time here, this guesthouse has taken on a homey feeling. We will miss the family, but the Tibetan people are, in their goodbyes, as they are in their hellos. There is sincerity, but nothing in the way of emotion. I really wonder how much their thoughts travel into the past or the future. The present appears to occupy the greatest percentage of their minds. In contrast, our minds are bent slightly towards the future. There are thoughts of still trying to hitch up the pass, and of the long downhill ride that awaits us on the other side of the Himalayas.

We leave Tingri on a paved stretch of road, and as we ride it, Qomolangma and its surrounding peaks rise further and further above the foothills that had them obscured from town itself. Though we have just gotten started, we stop for a few minutes as it is our best view of the mountain yet, at least for Kat and myself. Lucky to have such clear weather, we appreciate its picturesque boldness. Qomolangma. Just a few days ago, Leatherfoot was somewhere way up there. All three of us feel elated.

Elation soon takes a blow, however, as it's not long before the road inevitably turns into gravel again. The sad part about the gravel is that you can no longer keep your head up as easily to appreciate the view while riding. It's back to that game of avoiding pot holes and absorbing washboard bumps. Back to our five kilometer chunks between rests.

○ ○ ○

The riding goes well throughout the morning, along a road that has been flat and straight. Kat might be on her best pace of the whole trip. We still take our regular breaks, but keep them shorter than they have been in the past. It is when we are on an extended break, and deciding whether we should eat lunch or do another five or ten kilometers, that the first truck of the day passes us. Though we are feeling good at the moment, we know that the wind is bound to make its presence felt soon, and climbing the pass may be too much for us. If possible, we will still try to hitch a ride. We attempt to flag it down, but it doesn't even slow down, leaving us nothing but a dust shower. Soon afterwards, a second truck passes with much the same result.

"It's starting to look like we really might have to ride Lalung La after all."

"Come on Dogi. That's not like you. Keep the faith!"

"Listen, I think next truck is coming."

"I don't see it Kat. Oh wait, yea, there it is. Okay, everyone put on their best smiles. This could be our last chance."

Knowing our chances are dwindling, we make a more concerted attempt than usual at getting this truck to stop, and fortunately, it does. Amazingly, out jumps the same driver that gave us a lift up the last pass. Now that he has stopped, we can recognize the truck, and he obviously recognizes us. He must have been back and forth again, on what is perhaps, his usual run of supplies. We try to make it clear that we want to be dropped at the summit of the pass, and he tells us a price that is steep, but not outrageous. Being less full than last time, we try bargaining, but he won't have any of it. He knows that at this point, we'll probably pay.

We try our best to secure the bikes in such a way that they will not take too much abuse, though we know some damage will be inevitable on this kind of a road. There is room enough this time to find a sack, or an old tire to sit on, so we won't have to stand for the whole ride. Our only company in the back is a monk…

282

and a drunk. The monk has his hat on quite crooked, and a pair of glasses and a set of teeth worn to match. He doesn't say much, but he sits, and bounces and sways with the road with a big grin on his face. The drunk is still drinking. I feel like he was here the last time we rode this truck too. He takes a swig and attempts to talk to us, genuinely wondering why we don't respond. After a few more sips, he chats with the monk, who nods and generally looks to go along with whatever he's saying. One more shot of the liquor, and he settles into some singing and eventually a conversation with himself. The monk just keeps on smiling.

We eat up a few more kilometers of flat road, and then begin to climb up this massive valley. The view expands, and we stand for a while and stare in awe. It feels good to be moving so quickly. There are no feelings of regret about hitching, rather than riding. This is best for all at this point in the trip. We are ready to start going downhill.

Hoping to be at the top in short order, Tibet has had other thoughts. It does not let things happen easily. The first flat tire was actually a nice short break, giving us a chance to stretch and use the outdoor facilities. The second flat tire, however, proved to be complicated. It was something I hadn't paid much attention to before, but the tires on this truck, and probably most like it, are in rough condition. I'm sure plying this road grinds them down quickly, and they are expensive to replace. As I watch the truck driver struggle with the repair, I realize it's a hard life here in Tibet, even for many of the Chinese people. Though I don't for a moment condone what his government has done, in forcefully taking over this land, I see here an honest and hard working man who is trying to make a life for himself. He is not evil. Much like myself being of European decent in a country like Canada, what our ancestors did to the native north American populations is horrendous, and though I would love to find a more harmonious way going forward, what happened in the past is not my fault. I wonder that there can't be a future in Tibet, where the Tibetans and Chinese can coexist more harmoniously, rather than live as the conqueror and the suppressed. A place where the Tibetans can live under autonomous rule of the Dalai Lama, the Chinese military leaves, and the Chinese people who have already established a life here are allowed to stay and live cooperatively within the system. It is a pleasant thought.

We have stopped for a third time, and the top is still nowhere in sight. This stop, according to the monk, is for food. There is a long, narrow, ramshackle looking building clinging to this flat spot in the middle of nowhere. I can't believe there is someone living way the heck up this pass. We must be nearing 5000 meters by now. We jump off the truck, and follow the monk and the driver and his partner towards the building, scattering the free ranging chickens, though not as far as when the truck first pulled in. The drunk, who had passed out at the last tire repair stop, was shaken awake by the monk, and drags himself along too. We enter the cool dark building, and sit at one long table. There is no menu here, no ordering, no choice. It's thugpa.

"I think this might be the oiliest thugpa we've had all trip."

"The noodles are pretty pasty too."

"I think it is not so bad. You two should not complain and just eat. Did you try boiled egg yet? It's really yummy."

"We're not complaining Kat, and we should eat it, because we still need all the nutrients we can get."

"And you're right Kat, the egg is delicious. I could eat more of these."

The remainder of the ride to the top of the pass goes without further interruption, and we are deposited here at over 5100 meters (16,800 feet). The noise of the truck is swallowed almost immediately by the wind as it pulls away. It's so gusty up here that it causes me to stumble a few times before I get used to it. Seeking some form of shelter, we first walk up to an unusual structure. Odd, in that we can't figure out what it is, and why it's here. Made of rock and clay bricks, the base is square and about thigh height, while the top, which is slightly recessed, is conical and reaches to above my height. Naturally, it is cracked, weathered and crumbling. Walking around some more, I feel so alive and free. As well as this bizarre mini tower, there are a couple of bundles of prayer flags up here, more wind battered than any we've seen previously. They are shredded, faded, and tangled providing a descriptive foreground to the distant snowy peaks, including that of Qomolangma. It seems like so long ago that we flew over this band of mountains, staring down and fantasizing about riding a bicycle through here. A little more than one month later, and here we stand, some sharp contrast between the fantasy and the reality. It's funny the aspects that fantasy either cannot contrive, or conveniently leaves out. As I look around, I see a distant plane fly overhead. I wonder what the people in there are fantasizing about. The great Tibetan plateau. It will be left behind us now. The peaks that surround us are like a gateway to a new world, entered into by a road that will take us down, down, down.

This is apparently the second longest downhill stretch of road in the world, though I have read somewhere else that it may be the longest. Either way, it should be a fun ride, though to ride it, we will need to once again do a few bike repairs. Shockingly, Leatherfoot's came out unscathed, while mine needs some minor adjusting on a bent back rim. It is Kat's, however, that took the worst of the damage this time. Her rim is also bent, as well as the gear system getting buggered up. It's an interesting place to make bike repairs. With the wind as strong and loud as it is, we must virtually yell to hear each other. We go over each bike, and I hold while Leatherfoot adjusts spokes and such. He's most definitely the group bike repair expert by this point in time.

A touch of sadness starts to creep in. Though there are still a few days of riding left before Kathmandu, and though there have been so many times along the way that one or more of us may have thought "get me the hell out of this misery," we now look at each other with mixed emotions, but there is an overall feeling of great pride. We've been through a lot together, and here we are. Still alive, and still with each other and our bikes. We go through the journey in snippets; Lhasa, the Sera monastery monks, Sand Skreeing, flat tires, the broken bike, swimming in the frigid lake, *towing*, Prego Prego, the German tour group, Gyangze, Shigatse, a night on the roof of a grain mill, Sagya, Tingri, the nomad tent, Baba, Qomolangma...

"This wind is starting to penetrate through all my layers."

"Yea, I'm getting cold too."

285

"It's downhill time! I've been looking forward to this. It's gonna be fun."

We have a big group hug, one final look back to where we came from, and then saddle up and ride onwards. Downhill, but up wind. I guess Mother Nature isn't ready to ease up on us just yet. It seems she wishes to blow us back up onto the plateau, so hard is the wind funneling up this new valley and blasting us in the face and chest. It's shocking how much we have to pedal to keep moving on this grade of a downhill. It has the quality of an amusement park roller coaster, the gusts of wind mixed with the curves in the road, and the potholes creating unpredictable twists and turns. It's hard to go with the flow, when the flow is so erratic.

Suddenly, we come upon a small village. It surprises us, once again, that it exists so high up in altitude. As if life isn't difficult enough down on the plateau, it is hard to imagine how a village survives in such a location. Though there are enough buildings, and they are obviously inhabited, we don't see any people. Likely, they are hiding from this wind, and as the afternoon is already wearing on, we decide not to linger here, thinking we must soon find a place to camp. Riding not too far past the village, we see the leftovers of an old stone building with two walls still reasonably in tact. Upon closer inspection, we decide they would provide good shelter from the wind, so we pull in for the night.

The drawback to our campsite is the lack of a water source in the immediate area. Though our water bottles are still half full, we have nothing with which to boil our noodle soup, and we are starving. We realize that not stopping at that little village and sourcing some water out was a mistake. Leatherfoot has gone to search for the river, or creek that we were hoping was over the distant rise, but he's been gone for so long that we are beginning to worry about him. Kat and I have already ventured out twice looking for him, repeatedly yelling his name, but we cannot find him, and it is beginning to get dark.

What seems like an hour passes before he finally comes back looking quite exhausted.

"What happened Leatherfoot?"

"First I tried the creek bed over that way, but it was dry and I couldn't see any other options, so I walked all the way back to the village to fill up!"

"My friend, you are the greatest!"

Kat cooks the noodle soup tonight. After an entire trip of early bed times, she finally has the energy to stay up and watch the light show and help with camp chores. It's nice to see her smiling.

GRAVITY versus WIND

Round twenty-eight in the cycling across Tibet series. Coming from the north, a new and mighty opponent for WIND today. GRAVITY! Governor of physics, deep and encompassing reach, and friend of the wheel, running water, and thoroughly exhausted cyclists. Lay your bets on the table folks. GRAVITY versus WIND!

O O O

We went to bed last night with grins on our faces, and awaken with "expectations" of a glorious downhill ride all day long. The second longest downhill stretch of road in the world, and we're at the top of it on bicycles. What could be more appealing than that !?! What a blast! No pedalling. A whole day of coasting downhill, all the way to the Nepali border and beyond! Today we will say "Bye bye" to Tibet.

Having gotten used to nights and mornings being frigid, but calm, we are somewhat surprised that the wind whistled loud tunes all night and has greeted us with ferocity as we crawl out of the tent this morning. Our little corner of crumbling rock wall affords us enough protection to get through breakfast and packing, but the second we step out from behind it, the full force of the wind smacks into us. How quickly one forgets how foolish these kinds of expectations are to possess. It is so strong, that just getting going on the bikes on this first flat section is a chore. It's heads down, first gear and full energy output just to negotiate it.

Such becomes our plight all morning long. We are endlessly whipped, pummeled and bashed. There is no consistency in direction or force of the wind, though it is never behind us. Front left, front right, or straight in the face. Strong, stronger, or really strong, there is no respite. Much as the river is tumbling and bouncing off the banks of the ravine down which it flows, the wind funnels up this valley, careening off the cliffs and hills, creating blasts, swirls and eddies. The river kicking up clouds of spray in its wake, the wind clouds of dust. Even on the steepest downhill sections of road, momentum is tough to gain. On shallows, flats and the short up-hills, of which there are many more than "expected," it is furious pedalling, with granny paced advancement. This wears heavily on the psyche, as much as the body, and we have not gotten nearly as far along as hoped by the time we are hungry again and stop for lunch.

The spot at which we have stopped is incredible. We perch ourselves out on a massive boulder, which presents a fine view further down the valley, but the wind exposure forces us down to a more sheltered spot to eat our food. The river below, which didn't even hold enough water to fill our bottles last night, increases its volume and pace with each passing kilometer, fed by snowmelt, through waterfalls and creeks. The road has been following the general meandering of the river. In places, it has been intense, cut into steep banks with no room to spare on either side. A mistake to one side would have you joining the river way down below. On occasion, there have even been large rock overhangs or small tunnels under which we have cycled, often dripping with moisture. All the water is nice. After weeks of so little, there are the beginning signs of plant life. Sprinklings of green. Fortunately, however, this is a dry season. The melt waters from the mighty mountains above are adding quickly to the river system, but there has been no rain here for a while. I can only imagine how treacherous this stretch of road would become in times of heavy precipitation. Washouts must be numerous.

"Are you okay Dogi?"

"So so Leatherfoot. I guess I still don't have a lot of strength, but I'll be all right."

"How about you Kat?"

"I feel good today. It is difficult to ride in the wind, but finally I am not sick anymore. You look good like always Leatherfoot."

Even in our sheltered spot, a sudden wisp of wind finds us, and gives us a little shove, signaling that it must be time to move along and continue riding again.

We pay little attention to distance anymore, being content to simply ride and take breaks, both to rest and enjoy the scenes. There is the odd farming village, a waterfall that drops down half a cliff, bounces off a jutting rock platform and sprays droplets of water in all directions, a bird that soars on the currents above, a sharp "S" curve in the river gurgling and foaming water into a tumultuous roar, or simply the road ahead as we catch snippets of it snaking along the steep banks we are about to ride.

"What happened to Kat?"

"I don't know. I haven't seen her since our last rest stop, but she's been right with us all day long."

"I hope she didn't wipe out. That last part of the road was pretty hairy."

Somehow Kat had fallen behind further than we'd realized. We were careful not to let this happen all trip, but a combination of feeling confidence in her improved health, and simply trying to keep our own bikes on the road, made us lose track of her, such that we've lost contact. Leatherfoot and I wait for two minutes, and the worry builds. Then it's five minutes, and ten, but still she isn't coming.

"Oh Leatherfoot, this is not cool. I'm gonna start back up the hill."

"You sure you don't want me to go?"

"No, I'm all right. I'll go."

Amazingly, with the wind full in my back, going uphill it is not that bad. I ride hard until the first bend, stop and look, but still I don't see any signs of her. Head down once more, I dig in for the next stretch, and still there is nothing. Trying to stay calm, but feeling worried, I consider dropping my bike and walking, but decide to ride to the next bend. I have my head down again, but after a minute, I think I hear a faint whisper and am surprised when I look up that she is almost right in front of me.

"Kat! Are you okay? What happened?"

"Yea, I'm okay now. I lost my bag. My black bum bag. It has my passport and money and other stuff."

"It looks like you found it again though. How far back did you have to go?"

Well I don't know it happen at first. I think I hear a funny noise, but with the road and wind and everything, I just ignore. But then I stop for a short break and turn around and it is gone. I leave my bike and walk back up the hill. Then there is a Tibetan man. He is standing on a small cliff above me and wants to tell me something, but I don't understand him. I try to ask him about my bag, but he doesn't understand me either. So I keep walking and go back where I think I hear the noise, but I still don't find it. Then I start to get worried. Suddenly a 4WD stops beside me. It is strange because he just pass me a few minutes before. There are two men and the driver speaks a little English. He asks me what I am looking for. He has my bag! I am so happy and say thank you so many times. Thank you, thank you I say. But the man is not so nice. He won't give me my bag, and asks for ten dollars for a reward. I am very shocked. I tell them I have no Chinese money because you have it, but I think they look through my bag and see some of the money. I can't believe it! Anyway, I start to cry. I don't really feel like need to cry, but it's a good girl's trick. The other man is nice, and it looks like he starts to worry and he tells the driver to give me the bag. I think the mean man doesn't want to, and they talk to each other and I just keep crying. Finally it works and he gives me the bag! Then he says not to look at his license or tell the police because he didn't take anything from the bag. He just looked through it. I am so happy when they drive away.

Leatherfoot is happy to see us again, and Kat tells her story a second time as she checks more thoroughly that everything is still in her bag. Strapping it on extra carefully, we check and tighten down the rest of our gear, before we move on to another one of the more hectic stretches of road, where the consequences of a broken brake cable would be a long flight down the gorge into the river below. These sections are exhilarating, and we stick to the middle of the road as much as possible, hoping there will be no oncoming traffic. Keeping Kat in the middle, we negotiate it without incident, and get onto a flatter section once again. We lose touch with the river for a short while, but join it once again at a bridge where it runs less violently not far below. It makes a good place for a break, and Leatherfoot scrambles down the bank and refills our water bottles. At this point in time, I am beginning to feel horrible again. The fact that I haven't eaten a lot in the past week, coupled with today's sizeable gap between expectations and reality, has me feeling bitter as the day wears along and I get weaker. I tuck in under the bridge, taking shelter from the wind and the sun, and close my eyes trying to settle my feelings. Frustration. That's what it is. It is so frustrating to feel weak for so long. Kat knows. She's dealt with it for most of the trip, though she really looks strong today. She and Leatherfoot know that consoling me will do little to help, but they do both graciously offer to take some of my weight. Stubbornly, however, I refuse to give up any of my burden. I cry enough tears to wash away some of the pain and strengthen my resolve. Then, saying nothing and looking at no one, I just get up, get back on my bike, stick my nose up at the wind, and ride on.

Our next stop is the town of Nyelam, the last town before Zhangmu and the border to Nepal thirty kilometers away. It is meant to be another break, as it is not yet too late in the day, but I give the other two no choice as I say "WE ARE STAYING HERE TONIGHT." On the edge of passing out, I can't go any further. Tomorrow is another day. Perhaps, I will feel stronger again. Perhaps, the wind will abate. Wind. It was wind versus gravity today, and out of ten rounds I'd give gravity only one, and perhaps a draw on one or two others. The overwhelming winner was wind. Riding was a blast today, in fact many blasts. Blasts of moving air. Gravity didn't stand a chance. It was blown out of the water, off the road and presumably buried somewhere up in the north pole, or at least the great Tibetan plateau!

We find a guesthouse along the main street and are given a huge second floor room. The building is old and decrepit, but gives the impression that it must have once been something grand. Other than the fact that it is big enough to sleep eight or ten, this room is much like the others we've stayed in. It is dark and cold with the usual saggy cots, and an added musty smell, but I am so happy simply to lie down and rest again.

○ ○ ○

Having recovered a little, we head out to explore the small town, and are eventually drawn into a small Chinese restaurant. Unfortunately, we can only order scantily as we are in a bit of a money dilemma. The price of hitchhiking on the truck, and this unexpected stay here have depleted the funds we thought would get us to the border. The restaurant has few customers at the moment, but among them is a good looking Tibetan man sitting on his own. We start talking to him, and discover that he currently lives in Paris and was once a tour guide here, but on this occasion is only a visitor. He shows great interest in us and our journey, asking question after question and listening intently. His comprehension of English is remarkably good. Suddenly, a beer arrives in front of us, complimentary of him. I'm not so sure that beer is what my body needs, but I take a few sips and find it refreshing. Feeling comfortable with him now, we ask if he would change twenty dollars to Yuan for us, which we figure should be enough to get us to the border. At this point, we don't even care that much if it's a good exchange rate, and simply hand over the bill after he agrees. Surprisingly, he gives us significantly more than twenty dollars worth of Yuan and says, "You three look as though you've had enough struggles, and you shouldn't need to bear any more over the next couple of days until you get to Nepal. Once, I was very poor, but these days I have plenty of money, so it is no big deal. I am happy and impressed that you have traveled and seen my culture in such an up close and unique way." Thanking him repeatedly for his generosity, we immediately order more to eat.

Every day here in Tibet amazes me. The events are a continuous teeter totter. There are such pronounced swings in mood and occur-

293

rence. The hill goes down, the wind goes up. One man, a current tour operator, tries to profit on finding Kat's lost bag. Another man, and former tour operator, is generous enough to help us out freely with a little extra.

We tour around the rest of Nyelam, but find nothing more of great allure. Or, perhaps, I am too exhausted to notice anything entertaining. With darkness setting in, we head back to our room. We are all tired enough to want to go to bed early, but have enough energy for a round of cards. It is surprisingly quiet here. Not even the dogs are howling yet. The only unpleasant thing about our current situation is the trek down to the main floor to get to the toilet. The toilet itself is one of the both gender, no wall types. All excreted matter oozes through the same holes in the outer wall of the building, and onto a concrete slope. From there, it mixes with various other bits of trash and slowly slides its way down to the river below. It is a gross sight and foul smell, but it's okay. This is basic living. It's not hidden from view, or treated with chemicals. Food in, shit out. It is the cycle of life on full display.

GREEN IS BEAUTIFUL

KAT HAS TO POO. SHE HATES THE TOILET, BUT THERE IS NOT REALLY another option except, perhaps, to pinch. No, apparently pinching is not an option, off she goes with a big crinkle of disgust on her face.

Since it was only yesterday this time, we awaken with no expectations. Today will be what it will be. What we have so far, however, is no wind. It is a calm and beautiful morning, and I'm feeling a little livelier once again. Judging by yesterday's ride, I'm not so sure we actually left the plateau behind at Lalung La after all. Of course, we have descended since the pass, but Nyelam is still more than 3700 meters (12,200 feet). There were definitely more ups between the downs than expected. Today, however, it starts down and doesn't stop. The plateau is surely being left behind. The road itself is a hairy, bumpy, winding mountain bike paradise/hell. It's hard on the body with the relentless vibrations and jarring. The choices are to take the shock in the backside, or the thighs, but either way, the innards are being shaken like a martini. Whatever the physical punishment though, it sure is fun. The key is trying to stay in control. Trying to find that balance between letting the speed go, and pulling on the brakes to slow down. It's an intense game, with the eyes working desperately to negotiate potholes and bumps. We are thankful as we round every bend that there are no oncoming trucks. I wouldn't want to react quickly to anything.

The scenery changes rapidly as we descend. There is a moisture in the air that our lungs have not felt in five weeks. Each breath is deeper than the last. The surroundings are getting greener and greener. The smell of the vegetation is invigorating after such a long time without it. Spectacular waterfalls become a dime a dozen, as they plummet into the raging river canyon below, feeding its insatiable thirst. Oh, to be a droplet of water. What a ride that would be! We are moving fast. For perhaps the first time all trip, faster than we want to. We take frequent breaks to enjoy the surroundings to the fullest. The road itself is a part of the incredible scene. It is often carved into the middle of a cliff. There is no guard rail here to protect from the hundred meter or more drops into the canyon below. This is the wildest stretch of road I've ever been on, and I can think of no vehicle better than a mountain bike, though a better quality mountain bike would make me feel more secure.

Easing into the first flat section we've seen in a while, we come upon a curious sight, in a massive pile of snow. Other than on the distant mountain tops, and that brief flurry in Lhasa, it is the first snow we have seen all trip. It is thick and hard, almost like a chunk of glacier, and it stretches along the side of the road for a hundred meters.

"How do you think that thing got here Dogi?"

"Good question. It is bizarre. Do you think there is so little light in this particular cleft of the valley that it just hasn't melted yet?"

"Maybe, it crashed down from somewhere far above."

"Or, chunks of snow get lodged in this sharp bend in the river."

Leatherfoot and I can come up with no logical explanation, though there certainly must be one. Kat adds no opinions, though she does like the shape, and the patterns of dirt and debris mixed into the snow.

The next section of road is as hectic as ever. It is a combination of wicked switchbacks, and a narrow part, with cliff going up immediately to our left and down immediately to our right for a long stretch. After a while, we decide to give up on the idea of waiting for a flat pullout for a lunch spot, and sit, instead, on the edge of the road with our feet dangling. The cliff we are looking over drops way, way down to the torrent of water below. It is a grand picnic location, though definitely not for those with any fear of heights. We throw rocks down, but can't even see when they hit the ground, or the water. They just get swallowed by the depths.

"What's for lunch today?"

"Well, Kat and I went shopping in Nyelam yesterday while you were passed out, Dogi, and found this lovely can of mystery meat."

"Open it up. I'll get the crackers."

"Oh, Leatherfoot. It looks a little bit scary. I can't even tell if it's fish or something else. Do you think you can take out the stove and heat it up?"

"Sure, Kat, why not."

The funny part is, as questionable as it looks and smells, it still gets split equally into three pieces. Crackers, help yourself, but no one is to get less than their fare share of this "delicacy," and the residual oil in the can is all soaked up with crushed crackers.

○ ○ ○

Green, green, GREEN! It's so exciting. All the lush and moist bushes, trees, and plants. Green is such a beautiful colour. Perhaps, in other seasons, there are more things green on the Tibetan plateau, but we saw so precious little during our sojourn there. We inhale the moist air deeply as we continue to negotiate the chaotic road. Sand Skreeing was exhilarating, and the pony cart ride fabulous, but descending this road on a mountain bike is epic. I could easily take a lift back up to Nyelam and do it again. I'm grinning so much, that my cheeks are getting sore!

At long last, we arrive at the border town, which, on the Tibetan side, is called Zhangmu. I can't see anything of geographic significance that would put a political border here. It is a town built along either side of the winding descent that doesn't seem to end any time soon. On the natural side, there are a few streams dropping through the carved rock that are dazzling. The water is singing and dancing its way down to the main river. Maybe, they are the reason a town has sprung up here. The humanity is the kind of mixed energy found in many border towns. There is a pronounced mix of things Tibetan, Chinese and Nepali. It's hard not to chuckle at the pompous air of the Chinese "officials" that are around. Though convoluted, it seems peaceful enough for a border town. We have no desire to stick around for long, but thanks to our wonderful friend from Nyelam, we have a little extra Yuan. Exchanging it into Nepali funds is an option, but we decide, instead, to go shopping. Not in need of anything in particular, we buy a handful of various snacks and head for the border.

"Hey everybody, last chance to show off that Alien Travel Permit. What do you think? Will they ask for it, or should I just hand it over?"

"I doubt they'll ask for it, Dogi!"

"Don't give it to them, Dogi. I want to keep it as a souvenir."

"Okay Kat. Hey, let's go, it's our turn."

The border guards are suitably miserable, and take a long glance at our passports. There is some other paperwork to be filled out and signed, but they do not ask for the Alien Travel Permit. It has not left my money belt since it was deposited there in Shigatse. As the gate lifts, I have a flashback all the way to that day on the living room couch where I first read it was possible to ride a bike across Tibet. We walk our bikes through, and the gate drops. Wow. That's it. That's the end of Tibet. We still have a couple of days of riding to get to Kathmandu, but it's bye bye Tibet.

"How do you feel, Dogi?"

"Kind of mixed, I guess. It was something I'd looked forward to for so long, and now it's almost over. And, it was so different from what I expected. Hellish much of the time, but there are so many brilliant memories mixed in. It's okay though. I'm happy to leave. How about you Leatherfoot?"

"I pretty much agree with you. It's been an incredible trip, but I'm ready to move on. Kat?"

"I thought I would be sad to leave Tibet, but actually I feel quite happy. I think I'm just not sick anymore, and that makes me happy. But the journey is not over yet. Look at this road! I wonder how far away the Nepali part of the border is."

Switchbacks. I remember those. The ones that went on forever, after the night we slept in the middle of the first pass. Here they are again, zig zagging out of sight, except this time, we are going the fun way. Down, down, down, with full power on the brakes to negotiate the tight corners. This neutral zone between Tibet and Nepal goes on and on and on. It is by far the largest patch of land between borders that I have ever seen, and the road is rough. I guess neither government is in a hurry to volunteer to maintain it. It's even steeper, and more bumpy and jarring, than what we've been riding since Nyelam. There is no chance for a lapse in concentration for fear of a nasty spill on the road, or over a cliff, and the forearm muscles, of all things, are getting tired from constantly pulling on the brakes. That said, it is far more tolerable and enjoyable than being wind blasted on the plateau, or climbing some grueling hill. It is pleasurable pain.

I go into a slight wobble after a big bump, and manage to stop just before my pack is about to jam into the side of my back wheel. It worked its way loose from under the strapping, from all the bouncing around. In my exuberance to keep going, I do a quick fix, but it becomes insecure in no time again. With the other two out in front, I try once more, hoping it'll get me to the Nepali border, but it works itself free again. The third time, I lay the bike down, and take the time to look around me. I don't need to rush. It's not unbearably hot here. There is no howling wind. There are no rabid dogs. It's green, and it's beautiful. I could sit here for a while, but I know the feeling that must be creeping in down below. I shouldn't make them wait more than necessary. Relaxed and focussed, I reef the pack down solidly again, enjoy one last solitary look around and resume the adventure of switchbacks.

"Hey, sorry I'm late. My pack came loose a few times."

"That was so, so, sooo fun!"

"Ah, Kat, that's so, so, sooo nice to hear."

Kat, Leatherfoot, and I are all beaming as we lean our bikes outside the Nepali immigration shack and file in. The men working in the little structure are smiley, and friendly and speak English well. They get a kick out of us, as filthy and disheveled as we must look. Filling out the paperwork, and paying the requisite fees, without the addition of "presents" for a change, we are welcomed into Nepal. Why can't all border crossings be this warm and fuzzy?

"Welcome to Nepal."

"It's good to be back alive."

"I read there are some hot springs in Tatopani."

"Really? Well, let's go then!"

Now that we're in Nepal, we have the feeling that we are home free, but it is not long after we start riding that Leatherfoot's Lemon strikes again. This time it is a brake cable that he has snapped. After a moment of stunned silence, we see a gleam in his eyes, and a smile crack over his face and we all break out in laughter. A broken brake cable. That's no big deal. It's not like he stripped a wheel at the beginning of a mountain pass, or snapped a chain in the middle of a wind storm (and had to drink cold Yak Butter Tea). It's okay. He's got another brake, and Tatopani, our destination for the day, is not far off. AND, as a huge bonus, we are on a paved road! Oh wait, maybe that's not such a good thing all of a sudden. A paved road means more speed, and with less braking power.

We continue, coasting at the highest speeds we've felt all trip, when suddenly, it starts to rain. Nice. It's warm rain too. It feels good on the face and the skin, and the plants look even more lush and green, but we have to slow down a little as the road is getting slick. A few minutes after the rain starts, Kat and I find ourselves coasting into the upper part of the small town, which is when we realize that we have left Leatherfoot so far behind that we can't see him anymore. We wait for a minute, but the rain is getting harder, so we decide to find a guesthouse in front of where one of us can wait for him.

We find a place easily enough, and manage to get under shelter just before getting soaked, in what has become a downpour. We wait for a while longer, but still, he does not come. It's hard to know what to do. He's probably fine, maybe changing his brake cable after all. Most likely though he's just been going slow because of only having one brake on this steep road. I don't fancy going out into this rain, and riding back up the hill, but...

"OH, Kat, there he is... LEATHERFOOT, LEATHERFOOT... OVER HERE!"

He can't miss us, really. It's another one street town, mostly built on the lower slope, and we're about halfway down on the left. Poor Leatherfoot is drenched by the time he arrives, but he has a big grin on his face.

"It was a little tense with only the one brake functioning, especially when it started to rain, so I had to go really slow so as not to lose control. It feels pretty nice to be wet though!"

We leave Leatherfoot outside to drip dry, while we sort out a room. The young boy managing the place is tremendously friendly, and helps to bring our gear in to a room where we are stunned by the spectacular view. We have a balcony looking out over the river gorge, and it is so... well... green. Brown is nice, especially when so well balanced with blue, but green! Now there is a colour. It is so alive here. Alive in a more tangible way. SMELL the rain, and the wood and the plants, SEE and HEAR creatures of the forest!

Tatopani. That means "hot water," or "hot springs" in Nepali, and in no time at all, we are on our way. This is very exciting. We are filthy. Layer after layer of caked on dirt. The anticipation builds as we take the short walk back up the road to the hot springs area. Along the way, the drizzle eases off, and then ceases. Upon arrival, it is different than we'd imagined, though not disappointing. Having lived in Japan, we had grown used to the idea of deep soaking pools, yet here, the hot water is running into town through big pipes coming out of the cliff above, dumping generous quantities of water into a shallow concrete pool below. There are a few locals bathing, and washing some clothes and they give us a short look of curiosity, then a friendly smile and otherwise leave us alone. Some clothes that haven't been taken off since Tingri are peeled off, and we expose three skeletons. Actually, we look almost as gross with our clothes off as we did with them on. We have lost a lot of weight. Any fat that we started with, which wasn't much, is long gone, and all of our muscles have shrunk noticeably. I wonder how much weight we've lost? Who would have thought?

THIS is bliss. This IS bliss. This is BLISS. All three are true. Pure bliss. It is the best shower I've ever had. Second is so distant, I can't even remember what it might be. The hot water tank belongs to Mother Nature, and she looks as though she's not going to shut off the tap any time soon. We wash, and soak, and do it again and again. The temperature couldn't be more ideal, and the pressure of the thick stream provides a magnificent massage. I can't leave. I want to stay here forever.

301

Hunger. Apparently, there are some forces stronger than bliss. We settle in to the restaurant by our guesthouse feeling incredibly clean and refreshed, and learn that the only thing on offer this evening is the Nepalese staple called Dahl Baht. We order three portions from the cheery boy who is waiting our table. His English is excellent, and he is in the mood to practice it, chatting with us throughout the meal. The Dahl Baht is spicy, or maybe it just feels that way after a month of bland oatmeal and noodle soup. Regardless, it is a change, and change, in this case, is good. We accompany our meal with a thermos of chai, which is an upgrade on the Tibetan version, and which eases some of the burn in the mouth and feels so nice on the tummy. The increased degree of comfort of everything here is so welcome. Even the cots, which we plop onto after another long day, are firm and comfortable. It will be a good sleep.

FRESH

Time. Day? Date? Does it matter? It hasn't mattered for the whole trip, except for that visa thing, which is why we tried to figure it out once in a while. I think it's thirty... thirty days since we started cycling... maybe... but things like time have been very hazy since Tingri... since that cold Yak Butter Tea in the tent, in the windstorm before Tingri. I think some of the oil is still on the inside of my mouth, or maybe it just seeped into my brain. Never mind, we can eat FRESH veggies again. Fresh. Mmmm.

Paved roads. Paved roads are probably a good invention. Right now, it feels like the best invention in the world. The wheels like it, the bikes like it, the pack strapping likes it, the innards like it and the lungs like it too. Or, is that just the increased oxygen down here? We are cruising, and it feels orgasmic, with the lush green surroundings and the moist air. There is no wind, no dust and very little pedalling. This is cycling at its finest. The air rushes through our hair, and even the sun down here feels as though you are being licked by a puppy rather than stung by wasps. The Nepali people are wonderful to be around. They are much more used to us aliens. Almost all are friendly, but not overly curious. They don't come in droves to stare at us, they don't fiddle with our bikes and packs, and the kids don't throw rocks at us.

Down, down we go, with one short steep up, during which we get rained on. We don't care, it's nice to be wet. The further we descend the valley, the more farmed land begins to materialize, and with it comes more people, more cars, and more pollution.

Suddenly, it strikes me vividly. A night early in the journey where we camped in the huge dry river bed. We were surrounded by immense space, nothingness, silence. There were no people, and there was no noise and no stink of burned fossil fuel. This was the beauty of Tibet. Raw earth. It was an energy all encompassing, and yet unsettling. It evoked strong feelings of peace, helplessness, love and insignificance. There were moments of beauty, and of communion with your surroundings, which you'd want to hang onto forever, until those same surroundings let you know that you are alive. You can't just float along in the currents of the wind like a particle of dust. You must participate, you must contribute, you must play along and the game can be as nasty as it can be fun. This is why you need teammates, companions, fellow human beings. To make the game of life easier. And they do, though, for reasons competitive and selfish, other people hinder and destroy as much as help. This is the human condition. When it has its basis in survival, it is more easily understood why there might be fighting and war, but we live in a world that could be beyond these things. In terms of available energy, the potential for material well being for all people is there. With the right distribution of energy, all could live in reasonable shelter and consume decent food.

Food which is fresh. As we ride through another small village, we come upon a little roadside conglomeration of shops. The buzz of activity is a joy to soak in as we stare at the possibilities. Nostrils flare to take in the sweet smells, and lips must be pinched to hold back the drool. We greedily consume all the goodies, including FRESH bananas, FRESH cucumbers and FRESH corn. FRESH. What a joyous sensation. The cucumbers are a particular joy. Forget slicing them, we just take big bites, inviting the explosion of flavour to swoosh around the mouth. It is a sensation easily taken for granted, like many things, until you do without it for an extended period of time. It is one of the many things that makes life in Tibet such an immense challenge. There is so little fresh food. Slowly, however, it is coming. It is being brought by the Chinese. As much destruction as they have wrought, they will bring things into the land that are welcome, like electricity and fresh food. The question is, are those things truly welcome by the Tibetans in the context of the suppression of their beliefs and traditional ways of life? Will the Tibetans really be better off for it? Perhaps, if the Chinese had wanted to exploit the potential energy surely available in the great expanse of Tibet, they could have sought permission and offered trade. The Dalai Lama and the Tibetan government could then have been free to choose the path, going into a modern technological world, that was right for their beliefs. Now, their right to choose has been removed. They will only be able to live within the context of what the Chinese government wants in the region. Human rights? Human wrongs? These are philosophical debates that will last as long as the human race, or, at least, until the second last one of us dies.

○ ○ ○

The day of cycling goes by quickly, and it is one that we are genuinely sad to see the end of, as it has been such a delight. Nothing went wrong today! There were no lost bags, no mean dogs giving chase, no schoolyard bully holdups, no crying, not even Leatherfoot's Lemon had any issues. It was gloriously uneventful. And, after three days, the second longest downhill in the world ends at a town by a bridge at the confluence of rivers. It is not Kathmandu. That is still one more day away in a different valley. We can see the road that leaves the other end of town. It goes up again for quite a while, but that's okay. It's paved, and we'll be fresh for it in the morning. Our final morning... we "expect."

We check into a hotel, which has a surprising amount of activity going on, and are shown the only room left that might be suitable for us, which has two single beds in it. Kat and I figure we've slept in enough uncomfortable places in the past couple of months, that sharing a single shouldn't be a big deal. As the price is agreeable, we decide to stay, rather than checking out any other accommodation options, though we do notice that this hotel has an odd air about it, yet, we can't quite put a finger on why that is. Perhaps, it just feels strange to be around so many people again.

We have quit early enough today that a gorgeous sunny afternoon is still to be spent, and we head no further than the hotel deck, that has a fine view over the river. We share a large beer between the three of us, the few sips enough to hit the spot before going back to water. The food, which includes the delicacies of chicken and vegetables, is scrumptious. I have a feeling we will be doing a lot of good eating in Kathmandu. We spend a long time lounging here watching the people come and go. They are so different from the Tibetans. There are no signs of any struggle for daily existence. Clothes are cleaner and not tattered. Cigarettes are being smoked. Food scraps are left on many plates, and sips of beer or pop are left in the bottom of glasses and bottles. There is plenty, and yet, a sense of things being taken for granted. It is so hard to discern the relationship between material, and spiritual satisfaction, if there is a connection at all.

RAINBOWS and SMOG

IT WAS AN INTERESTING NIGHT. FOR A START, IT WAS WARM ENOUGH that we could take most of our clothes off for a change, which was nice. What was not so nice, was cuddling with Kat. After a month of separate sleeping bags and cots, sharing a single bed was a lot less comfortable than we'd imagined, and we reaffirmed just how much weight we've lost, as it felt as though we were hugging a fellow skeleton. Both of us, and Leatherfoot too, are nothing but skin and bones. We have no meat left. I had no idea that you could consume so much muscle fiber in such a short time period. Everything on our bodies is sharp and pointy. As best we could, we slept on our own sides of the bed, and avoided each others elbows and knees. In the end, however, it wasn't each other that kept us awake much of the night. We were repeatedly awoken by a strange chorus of voices. There was moaning, and squeaking, and even some screaming. Finally, we understand why this place has an odd feel to it. It's a working girl's hangout!

The early morning air is pleasant. We get about twenty-five pedal strokes on the flat, leading up to, and over the bridge. From then on, it's uphill. We are following a gentle stream, with a relaxing gurgle, and at first, the grade is not too intense, though, it becomes more variable with steeper sections. There are enough easier sections, however, that it doesn't become too painful. At one point along the way, we pass an army compound guarded by a couple of young Nepali soldiers. Waving excitedly, and yelling "Hello, Hello," as we pass, we are pleased, yet a little disconcerted by the rifles hanging loosely at their sides, pointed in our general direction and waggling about. I know you need to pull the trigger to make a gun fire, but still, I always feel uneasy when one is pointed at me. We wave back, but quicken the pace.

More comfortable to be separated here, we each go at our own speed, and eventually meet up for a break at a cucumber stand. We love the fact that it's cucumber season around here! They are fresh, and juicy and there is no need to cook them. Today, we act a little more civilized, and Leatherfoot "the tool man" slices, and dices and doles out the chunks. Just watching the process has us drooling with anticipation. The first chunk is gone in no time, and we greedily await the second. As fast as we eat, however, we are careful not to waste any precious drips of goodness. Contemplating the situation, we decide to buy extra, to have later as our lunch with some leftover crackers. There probably will be more stands, but you never know for sure what's going on in other parts of the valley. Leatherfoot sticks them in here and there, under his strapping around his pack, and he sets off out in front. The cucumbers acting as a carrot for Kat and I to chase.

We're on a downhill stretch, and Leatherfoot is flying out in front. I guess he trusts that new brake cable he put in. Figuring Kat will be all right at her own pace, I make a game out of trying to keep up, but I think he's slightly heavier than me, and slowly pulls away to a point where I have lost sight of him. The road surface is reasonably clean, so the speed is comfortable, as well as exhilarating. Though I know we have to climb once more, I'm hoping this doesn't end anytime soon, and, as I round another bend...

SPLAT! There is a cucumber on the road, and it looks freshly exploded. Please, no. Not our cucumbers. Our fresh, lovely, juicy... SPLAT! No, not another... oh, and even a third! This is tragic. I consider stopping to see if I can recover any decent chunks from the carnage, but I'm moving too fast to hammer on the brakes, and there doesn't look like there's much left worth the salvation, so I ride on with a sadness in my heart. We have not passed another stand after all. Is this the end of our cucumbers? I'm not sure, but I think we bought four, and Leatherfoot is carrying them all. Well, he was carrying them all. That means... SPLAT!... never mind.

"The cucumbers!"

"I know, I know, a bunch fell out. Dogi told me."

"I tried my hardest to catch up to him after I saw the first one explode, but I just couldn't get close enough. He was riding so fast!"

"Oh, that was so sad. Are they all gone?"

"No, actually two did survive, Kat, but barely. They were both dangling."

Four lost cucumbers is a tragic event in our young day, but we are thankful that we have two more, and hopeful that there will be another stand. Leatherfoot secures them with extra care this time, and we begin the climb of our final big hill of the trip. It begins steeply, and continues relentlessly, but the fact that it is paved, and will be the last assent, takes a mental edge off of the pain. Carrots, cucumbers, Kathmandu, whatever the motivation, we press on, but it is many kilometers long, and though we dip in and out of the sun, the air temperature is hot, and with the moisture in the air, we are sweating profusely. I begin to feel dizzy and nauseated. Obviously, I have not recovered my full strength yet, but I want to keep up with the two riding in front of me. At this point, Leatherfoot is only viewed in glimpses around the next corner, and then, he finally disappears. Kat I hold in my vision a little longer, but I eventually lose contact with her too. The mental battle to continue sets in one more time. I take a short break, but I know that if I stop too long, my body won't want to go anymore. The cucumbers are in front of me. I have to go. I empty all but the last sip of my small water bottle, and hit the road one more time. I can do this.

"Come on, Dogi, just a little further."

I am so happy as I round a corner, hearing Leatherfoot's voice of encouragement, and looking ahead to see them finally stopped for a break. They are hanging out in the driveway of a fancy-looking roadside eatery.

"Who's hungry?"

"Who hasn't been hungry for the last month?"

"Shall we check this place out? We don't have much left to eat anyway. It could be a little celebration on the final day of the journey."

"Did you consult with your Lemon before making such a bold prediction?"

"I want to look at the menu."

"Okay, Kat, let's go."

We do peruse the menu, and find that it is expensive in Nepali terms, though it does have a huge selection. As we wander further out into the seating area, we find that the view back down the valley is wonderful, and we are the only ones here. The menu is actually overwhelming. There are so many choices on the four pages, that making a decision is confusing. It all sounds so good.

"I'll have this please."

"No have."

"You don't have it?

"No. No have."

"Hmm. How about this?"

"No have."

"What do you have?"

It's a classic case, not uncommon in a country like Nepal. An extensive menu, with eighty percent of it not available. I can understand not having a lot of selection. Food is seasonal, as perhaps is the business in such a location, but why hand out a menu with so many choices that are not available? Oh well, we'll take what we can get.

"That is one long hill."

"Yep, do you think we're near the top yet?"

"I should hope so. We've been climbing for a long time."

"I was happy to see the cucumbers alive and well."

The cool breeze and the lush backdrop of hills are energizing. There are birds in the area playing on the wind drafts. It is a superb location, but in the end, a terrible meal. Okay, the food was better than thugpa, but it was still awful. The portions were pathetically meager, the attitude and service of the man waiting on us was uninspired considering we were the only customers, and the food quality itself, came nowhere close to being worthy of the prices being charged. On top of that, there is an overcharge on the bill. It's a tough situation, but the three of us agree to pay what we think is fair, and on our way out have a "polite" conversation with the owner, who is not sure whether to be mad at us, or his employee. In the end, however, he is still nice enough to inform us that it is four more kilometers to the top.

"See you up there!"

"Do you have those cucumbers adequately reefed down Leatherfoot?"

"Who wants to race?"

"Yea right!"

We can smell it now. We dig deep and go for it. I use my favorite old method of counting pedal strokes. I figure five thousand should get me there... Pedal... Breathe... Pedal... Breathe... Rain! A fat black cloud moves in, and starts dumping and I don't even care. I get soaked through in minutes, but it is not cold, in fact, it feels wonderful. It makes me smile and laugh.

Five thousand one hundred and sixty-three to the very summit, and the center of the small town, which is built around the hill. I stop, get off my bike, stretch my hands and face to the rain, and let out a long loud hoot. This gives me a huge head rush, to which I stumble and almost pass out, but I'm getting used to that feeling. Leatherfoot and Kat show up shortly after me, and we have another group hug. There are mixed emotions once again. We can sense Kathmandu now. The end of the road, the end of the journey. The beginning of the heavy smog and pollution. It is one of those things that you almost get used to, that you almost forget about, when you live in a large urban environment. Yet, when you come from somewhere where there is so very little of it, it is nauseating to the first degree. It stinks. It's funny, a few days ago, as I was being pummeled by wind before Nyelam, I was longing to just be back in Kathmandu. Now, as I inhale this smog, I wonder that I wouldn't rather have a strong fresh wind in my face. But this is where we are now, and what suddenly materializes in front of us, is a fully arced and gorgeous rainbow. It tells us that we are in the right place. It says "Welcome to the beginning of the end of the journey."

The remainder of the ride into Kathmandu becomes a grind and blur. The road goes down a lot, up sometimes, and eventually flat. The traffic fumes, horns, towns, noise and humanity increase with each kilometer. It's further than we anticipated, and it's not fun, but we just keep going. As we get further into the urban sprawl, it starts to get dark and confusing. Having a central Kathmandu map, but not one of the greater area, we're just going by feel. We think we know where we are, but we're not really sure. We take a break to discuss the situation, when, suddenly, most of the light around us disappears. The city appears to have had a power outage, and other than the twilight, the only illumination comes from the cars and trucks. Great. Can we find our way back? Did Leatherfoot curse us? Why can't it just end smoothly?

"Well, Dogi. Are you in the mood for one last Randomland adventure? Which way do you think we should go?"

"Oh Leatherfoot. You are simply the best Randomland adventurer. I think we should just stay on this main road for a while. I feel like it's going in the right direction."

"Sure, but I do think we need to turn left at some point."

We continue searching for any signs of familiarity, when Kat sees a temple she thinks she's seen before. Leatherfoot agrees, and we change our course accordingly. Slowly, more sights that we are familiar with begin to materialize. We have walked this neighborhood before. Durbar square is not far. One more turn, and there's Freak Street, and there, still in his office, is…

"HARI!!! HARI, it's us!"

"I don't think he recognizes us."

"It is dark out here."

"HARI, it's Kat, and Dogi and Leatherfoot!"

Hari is sitting at his office desk with candles burning. He peers out at us incredulously for a few moments before figuring out who in the heck we are. I guess we do look pretty different. Once he clues in, however, the most beautiful smile sweeps across his face, and he jumps up and comes out to greet us. He gives us all huge hugs and pats on the back. We feel euphoric. A grand blend of pride, exhaustion, and relief.

"HARI, WE DID IT! WE DID IT!"

In no time, he has us in his office and has sent one of his helpers who brings back a bottle of coke for each of us. We down them so fast that he immediately sends the boy for a second round. Ah Hari, what a guy. We sit for quite some time, randomly spitting out one story after another, which he eats up with enthusiasm, all the while shaking his head and grinning from ear to ear. He stares a lot at Kat, in particular, with a sense of admiration. That Leatherfoot and I did this crazy trip does not shock him, but that Kat rode along blows him away!

"You guys are crazy. Why you make this poor girl do this crazy trip? Look at you, all dirty. You need a shower."

"Ahh Hari. It's so good to see you again!"

By the time our stories start to dwindle, and the buzz of being back gives way to tiredness, we realize that it is quite late, and we don't even have a hotel room yet. Also, Hari still has some of our other belongings stored somewhere. No problem. He sends his helper back out to gather our things, and since he knows everyone in the community, he finds us a reasonably priced place down the street. On top of this, being the gentleman he is, he even pushes Kat's bike down the road for her, and then helps us store our bikes and carry our stuff up to our third floor room.

END OF THE CYCLE?

I AM SITTING IN A CAFÉ IN KATHMANDU. THE FRESHLY BREWED coffee is divine, and the baked goods are delicious. Food really is good. We've come to this place every day since getting back a few days ago. It's a mini Western world in here. Before Tibet, I would have described it as comfortable and normal, but now it feels decadent and spoilt, and I appreciate all that it is with a kind of depth I have never known before. The days since returning have been a wonderful blend of eating, sleeping and taking hot showers, with the emphasis on eating. The restaurant options in Kathmandu are limitless in number and ethnic variety. We have been consuming three big meals a day plus snacks in between each and before bed. Finally, today, I am feeling somewhat normal again. The canker sores are all gone, and my energy level is reasonable, though I am still disgustingly skinny. We all weighed ourselves the day after we got back and it was frightening:

Leatherfoot: 187cm (6' 1 ½") from 80 kgs (175 lbs) down to 67 kgs (147lbs)

Kat: 161 cm (5'3 ½") from 53 kgs (115 lbs) down to 47 kgs (103 lbs)

Dogi: 187 cm (6'1 ½") from 70kgs (155lbs) down to 60 kgs (132lbs)

Those are pretty significant drops for people who started with no excess fat in the first place. That's about fifteen percent of weight loss in a month, mostly in the form of consumed muscle. It kind of tells you what our bodies have been through. I'm skinnier than I was at fifteen years of age and can't stand to look at myself in the mirror. Leatherfoot says he never remembers being able to count all of his ribs before. And Kat, though her pants are falling down, says she's happy with her skinny legs.

I thought the whole trip that we were just constipated, as we only pooed every three or four days on average, and even then it was a struggle, but now I understand that there simply wasn't anything to be defecated. Whatever food went in was absorbed as wholly and completely as possible by our deprived bodies. It will be some time before I eat anymore oatmeal, noodle soup, crackers, or peanuts. Give me fruit, vegetables, meat, and dairy. And coffee! Or "regular" tea. Though I am grateful to have had it for its hydration, fat, and salt content, I can wholeheartedly say that I'd never like to drink Yak Butter Tea again. Not even ten years from now to reminisce. I'll pass on thugpa too, though good momos would still be welcome.

Other than weight, we lost very little. One face cloth, one ring, and our only roll of duct tape, which was the most tragic loss. There were several points later in the journey when we could have used it, but it wasn't there, so we made do. That was the beauty of the trip. We made do. We worked it out. We survived. Others who have done crazier journeys than this have survived because they made do with whatever they had available, including their strong spirit.

The Tibetans survive. They have so little materially, but such strong spirit. Their current philosophy is a form of Buddhism, but I don't think the details of the religion or thought are the key. Whatever the philosophy, it is just a tool or a form of maintenance to help keep the mind and the spirit strong. The doctrines of most religions, philosophies, or beliefs remind, teach, and exercise the brain, and in many cases also the body. For the Tibetans, it was things such as standing to laying flat and up again over and over (called prostrations) like at the temple in Lhasa, or walking around and around the stupas, as we saw so often. Even their daily work, or simply sitting on the ground keeps them fit and humble. The world is full of wonderful ways to exercise the mind, the body and the spirit, the choice of how to do it, or whether to do it at all, remains with the culture and the individual.

With the exception of the stone chucking rascals, the Tibetan people were wonderful. It was both a fascinating experience and a privilege to be able to spend time at a deeper level in the culture, and there are several things that stand out. Most notably, is their ability to use everything, waste nothing, and willingly share what little they had so freely. Whether it was the Sera temple monks, the numerous roadside lunch hosts, the man who pushed Kat's bike, the pony cart drivers, the nomads, Baba, or the man from Nyelam, they were incredibly generous.

Undoubtedly, they live in a harsh and challenging environment, and I marvel at their ability not only to survive, but accept and seemingly enjoy their basic and simple lives, managing it in self sufficient and traditional ways. Beyond the significant stress of coping with daily survival, I noticed few complexities in their world. I saw little in the way of pride, embarrassment, fear, or anxiety, though that is beginning to change. The influence of continued Chinese encroachment, as well as tourism, will become more significant over time. New seeds of thought will be planted, and desires will grow, and when these wants cannot be continually satiated, they have the potential to flower into mental anguish. It brings me always to wondering about happiness and whether this isn't the true measure of rich and poor. I'm sure there are cases of more extreme poverty in Tibet, but we didn't really see it. What we saw mostly was contentment and joy.

The appeal to the outside world is having little effect on slowing down the external influence into Tibet, yet as a by-product of trying to communicate their cause, new seeds of the Tibetan spiritual ways are being planted in other regions. Some are growing into their own little communities, while others blend with local thoughts and ways. I know I will always carry a little bit of Tibet with me until it is my time to return to the earth, feed new life, and perpetuate the cycle.

If there is one thing that came into focus more clearly for me in Tibet, it was the cyclical nature of the world. I can't see things in a linear manner anymore. There is no beginning and end. I see only energy in its limitless forms going around and around. Whether physical and tangible, or spiritual, I find they are not so separate. It is all intertwined. The cone falls, the tree sprouts, it is fed energy by sunshine and water, and strengthened by wind. It grows over time giving back to plants below and creatures of the forest. Perhaps it is cut by humans, its stored energy converted with the help of electricity generated from flowing water, to timber used in the construction of a home helping people stay warm and dry. Meanwhile, the stump and root, with the help of sun and wind and water, will decompose and create a bed of nutrients into which the cone from the next tree will fall and thus continue the cycle. There is no life without death. One feeds the other. It is often thought that birth implies beginning and destruction or death ending, yet they are just times of significant change in the form of energy, and the energy itself does not die.

Many cultures have gained the capacity to radically alter these micro-environments of energy to the great benefit of many humans, though we are only beginning to understand the repercussions. Being all intertwined, one change will lead to another. This is the universal truth. How much alteration is acceptable? Are we changing things to degrees that we are on the path of poisoning ourselves and the rest of the living things on the earth? Maybe. These are the great new questions of the modern generation. Can we find ways to harness and redistribute energy in a manner that is less harmful to the earth and sky? Can we use the power in flowing water, beating sun, moving wind, and growing organisms in such ways that the effects will be less damaging? Can we live in such a way that we may drink clean water, breath clean air, and be able to walk around outside in the sunshine? Can we live in a sustainable manner, in a balanced way over time? I think we can, but we are in the early stages of understanding and awareness. There is much to do, and not do, and it is how we choose to participate in the greater flow of things that makes it so interesting to be human. And though there will be pessimists, warnings, fear, negativity, and thousands of other obstacles, we can put that vision out there and just go that direction. The Tibetans believe that it's possible to live this way. Faith and spirit are powerful tools. People can accomplish just about anything we set our minds to. I once believed that I would ride a bicycle across Tibet, and though there was a lot of dust in my face along the way, with spirit, faith and help from friends, I made it.

Our bikes rested unmoving for the first couple of days after our return. None of us had the desire to even look at them, much less ride them. Kat is so deeply scarred that she says she never wants to ride a bike again, but I'm sure that will fade over enough time. Finally, we decided to give them to Hari. We let him know that they are not the most well put together vehicles on the planet, and that a few minor repairs would help, but they still function well enough. Our suggestion to him is that he uses them in a not for profit way. For himself, his helpers, or his customers that may want to borrow them for an hour or a day. We hope they will bring people some happiness.

This morning, with a big grin on his face, we saw one of Hari's helpers bouncing along the bumpy road on either mine or Leatherfoot's. It was hard to tell. We joked that he'd be better off if it was mine, as there would be less chance of it breaking down. If there was such thing as a Lemon Bike Award, the hands down winner would be Leatherfoot. After the two flat tires on the first day, I was sure I was the bearer of the curse, but with the broken wheel on the second day, it was never in doubt. It was probably good that it was him. His superior patience handled it well, though I guess we all handled it well. Looking back with a mind that has regained some clarity, I can see that the broken wheel was the beginning of the domino effect that beat us down more and more. Not that it would have been an easy trip without such significant bike damage, but this incident threw us off balance enough that we spent the rest of the trip trying to recover. High Altitude Gravel Road Bike Towing. I don't recommend that to even the most adventurous of souls. May "The Rig" rest in peace forever.

Leatherfoot has my sincerest gratitude. I don't think we'd have made it without him. No, I'm quite sure we wouldn't have made it without him. He was positive, strong, patient and funny! I cannot think of a better person to take along on any Randomland adventure.

How about Kat? That girl is one tough cookie. From a rough start and through weeks of ill health, she persevered. She has a stoic fortitude and huge curiosity about the world. And though she must have hated me more than once along the ride, somehow she's still with me.

Me. That's Dogi. What am I? Foolish for attempting such a journey so ill prepared? Yep! Stubborn for plodding all the way through it? Yep! Was it worth it Dogi? Absolutely. Strangely, the hardest things endured seem to be the best memories secured. Would I ride a bike across Tibet again? Oh no. No, no, no! Though I have already had some epic adventures in my young life, this was by far and away the most physically challenging of all, and mentally, it comes only second to dealing with the sudden death of my father. Third is distant. Would I recommend this journey to anyone else? Certainly. I think it is a trip that could be accomplished without massive hardship, assuming better preparation, more reliable equipment, and a good dose of training. Though even with these, a lot will depend on which way the wind blows.

Recuperating happily!
I hope you enjoyed the ride.
Love to all.

The end.

P.S. For your own personal home version mini adventure, put a dollop of butter and a few sprinkles of salt into your tea, give it a shake or a stir, and drink it after you put a handful of raw flour in your mouth...

(Amendment: Regrettably there has been a printing error on this final page. Eric the Author thanks you for your understanding.)

wassuming better preparation, more reliable equipment, and a good dose of training. Though even with these, a lot will depend on which way the wind blows.

Recuperating happily!

I hope you enjoyed the ride.

Love to all.

The end.

P.S. For your own personal home version mini adventure, put a dollop of butter and a few sprinkles of salt into your tea, give it a shake or a stir, and drink it after you put a handful of raw flour in your mouth...

Tu-Jay-Chay
Thanks

Dear Mom,

Thanks for all the feedback from the mini-journal that I wrote to you from Tibet. That Nepali rice paper is lovely material, but horrible to write on. I'm glad you were able to read most of it. I heard Tante Nancy transcribed it into a type written form and you shared it with all your friends. Send her my love and give my appreciation to those who enjoyed it. Whoever it was that said I should write a book from the story, tell them I will – one day.

I sent a mini-journal to our wonderful friends Jason and Haruka in Japan as well. It was in even worse condition than the one I sent to you. It was totally different than your version; less factual, but more emotional and philosophical. I heard Jason read it out loud to Haruka, and the story made her cry. They also managed to type it out and share it with some of our old friends. It makes me so happy to have a copy of each.

Love, Eric

Dear RCQFatty,

The book is finished, and its journey from ONE DAY to TODAY became its own long and undulatory ride, facing as many obstacles and trying moments as the trip itself, but just like the locals along the way, it was the people who helped that made it a special trip.

There is this girl Elizabeth the artist. She's been like the sunsets were along the ride. In their own right, a pleasant chaos of multi-coloured light, but to me, they provided a calm and an inspiration to get up the next day and keep on dealing with it.

Arden. He was like the guy who pushed Kat's bike up the hill, or the chang drinking truckers who brought her to Tingri. There when needed, and willing to help freely.

Kelly is sometimes like the Yak Butter Tea, and sometimes like the chai. Reading the manuscript, she told me her favorite part was when I got sick. She tries her hardest to leave a bad taste in my mouth, but truthfully she's sweet.

Anna is like the people who invited us for picnic lunches. She fed me enough encouragement to keep on writing.

Then there's this guy Darcy. He's like the downhill rides. Hang on! Ideas are flying by, and it's a little out of control, but it sure is fun. Then, when you get to the bottom, the landscape is mapped out in front a little more clearly.

The line between brown and blue. How you paint and interpret the picture is up to you, but when there is the right amount of definition and good overall balance, the whole image becomes that much more beautiful. That's Maggie.

Kayoko, known also as Kat. She rode her bicycle to the pool to go for a swim yesterday, and she enjoyed it. Most of the scars have healed, though she still crinkles her nose at the smell of the sun cream. Kat is the shade. She provides that place to feel calm and cool. The place where I can relax and smile.

The cucumbers taste good.

Love, Dogi

Author's Bio

Eric Heide

Born in 1969 in Ontario, Canada, Eric grew up an enthusiast of adventure and the outdoors. After graduating from University with a Business Degree, he traded his briefcase for a backpack and a journal, and a few months of exploring Europe turned into more than two years of travel around the globe. His love of writing would grow into a large stack of whimsical, and philosophical journals. After a return to Canada, two more years were spent in Japan, touring on a motorbike and teaching English, and his appreciation for the diversity of culture and language grew. The travel continued in the years to come, including the memorable account bicycling across Tibet. He currently lives in Victoria, B.C. Canada with his wife, and his beaten and battered backpack still travels with him at every opportunity.

If you never cross it,
You'll never know where the line is

ISBN 142512688-X

9 781425 126889